THE
RISE

THE RISE

‹BLACK COOKS› and the Soul of American Food

MARCUS SAMUELSSON

WITH **OSAYI ENDOLYN**
RECIPES WITH **YEWANDE KOMOLAFE** AND **TAMIE COOK**
PHOTOGRAPHS BY **ANGIE MOSIER**

VORACIOUS
LITTLE, BROWN

New York Boston London

Voracious / Little, Brown and Company
Hachette Book Group
1290 Avenue of the Americas, New York, NY 10104
littlebrown.com

First Edition: October 2020

Voracious is an imprint of Little, Brown and Company, a division of Hachette Book Group, Inc. The Voracious name and logo are trademarks of Hachette Book Group, Inc.

The publisher is not responsible for websites (or their content) that are not owned by the publisher.

The Hachette Speakers Bureau provides a wide range of authors for speaking events. To find out more, go to hachettespeakersbureau.com or call (866) 376-6591.

Photographs by Angie Mosier
Page 6: Photograph by David Zilber
Origin chapter photographic background: Bridgeman Images
(Gee's Bend Quilt, "Housetop" Variation with "Postage Stamp"
Centre Row, c. 1965 by Irene Williams)

Book design by Shubhani Sarkar, sarkardesignstudio.com

ISBN 978-0-316-48068-0
Library of Congress Control Number: 2020941777

10 9 8 7 6 5 4 3 2 1

WOR

Printed in the United States of America

This book is dedicated to my birth mother, Annu. Thank you for everything you did, and for all the love you gave us in your short life. I love you and miss you dearly. And thank you also to the many other Black women who have remained anonymous but were often the most impactful engineers of the kitchen and true leaders in the culinary arts. Those like Edith Fossett, Fanny Hern, Pig Foot Mary, and some who eventually became household names like Leah Chase, Edna Lewis, Sylvia Woods, Alberta Wright, and B. Smith. I am who I am because of all of you. I'm forever grateful.

CONTENTS

Ch 1. NEXT

Where Black food is headed:
Chefs and recipes on the cutting edge, and who's got next.

Ch 2. REMIX

Black cooking integrates many cultures and adapts to
different ingredients, methods, and geographies.

Ch 3. MIGRATION

The influence of the American South—the Great Migration and beyond.

Ch 4. LEGACY

Old and new journeys from Africa to the Americas
and stories of Black figures in food reclaiming their history.

Ch 5. ORIGIN

A pantry of ingredients, techniques, and recipes
relating to the African diaspora.

RECIPE GUIDE

THE RISE: BREAKDOWN

Black is not a taste. Or is it?

Black food is not monolithic. It's complex, diverse, and delicious—
stemming from shared experiences as well as incredible individual creativity.

Black food is American food, and it's long past time that the artistry and ingenuity of
Black cooks were properly recognized. *The Rise* is part of that conversation,
and this book is my perspective on what's so exciting about the culture we share.

The Rise *stands on three pillars:*

AUTHORSHIP
of our food and rituals.

Black Americans have contributed
so much to this country's food
and culture without proper
acknowledgment—a pattern of
erasure that continues today.

We have to name it,
so we can claim it.

MEMORY
*of history, where we started,
and where we've gone.*

Black people have a different
starting point in this country, linked
through history to enslavement
and racism. Yet Black cooks have
created an engine of culture and
creativity that inspires the world.

Let's document that.

ASPIRATION
for the future.

By celebrating the incredible
chefs, writers, and activists at
work today, we can encourage
the next generation to join
the creative space, culture,
and industry of American food,
and create a new kind of value
proposition in the food world.

This is a cookbook about race, class, and the equity of the American food landscape.

This is also an opportunity to eat deliciously. To learn and inspire yourself and others.

To come together at one table to raise each other up.

Let's cook, let's eat, let's Rise.

AUTHOR'S NOTE

It's the last week of February, and I'm in Miami setting up my new restaurant, Red Rooster Overtown. I'm talking to chefs, cooks, dishwashers, investors, all part of the frantic setup before we open.

Fast forward to a week later and this coronavirus is real.

Twenty-five years of work, from coming to the US as an immigrant in the mid-90s to growing up as a chef at Aquavit to opening Red Rooster in Harlem and expanding to Overtown, is falling apart.

It only took ten days.

My phone rings. I speak with my business partner in Miami. The opening is not going to happen. We let go of the staff we've been training for weeks. Marcus B&P in Newark, New Jersey, follows, and then Red Rooster in Harlem. I don't want to shut down. I want to hold on.

The next day, everything is still. The first time in years.

I gather with my team and we pivot. Who can help us out of this—knowing that Covid-19 will live very differently in Harlem, Newark, and Overtown compared to the rest of America? One thing about being Black and an immigrant is that I never really trust the system—you learn to go through a lot of adversity on your own. I think about my father, a leader in a small Ethiopian village. How he led his people to build a well out of nothing. How every night they prayed and held themselves with dignity. Now is the time to pull from that side of me.

The first call is to José Andrés and World Central Kitchen. In two weeks, José's team helps transform Red Rooster Harlem into a community kitchen to feed hundreds of people a day. The next question is who will stay in Harlem to help? Robert, our greeter, is in. Jamie, our server, says, "I can." Nicolette, our hostess, says to count her in as well.

I don't know what to expect from our first days of service. Would there be nurses on the line? Firemen? Teachers? Or the folks who most of the time we ignore? The homeless. Folks from the nearby methadone center. They become our new regulars. The daily number rises to five hundred, and more.

Chicken one day, gumbo the next. Then rice and beans. Chile con carne after that.

We start a new routine I never learned in cooking school. Instead of yelling "Behind you! Hot pan!" we yell "Six feet apart! Please stay in line." Robert coaches the line on social distancing. But how do you instruct someone who is high or mentally ill and appears unstable, next to a mother trying to get food for her family?

At the beginning of April, the folks who make up the food line shift again—the working class is now joining in. People start to arrive early. Jamie and Robert hold back portions for the elderly who can't make the line, do an extra run to Ms. Johnson in 4B, to aunties and uncles who cannot stand for hours to receive a nourishing meal.

The worst calls have begun to come in. The virus is more than just numbers in the news. We lost my friend Chef Floyd Cardoz. Samuel Hargess Jr., from the iconic Paris Blues, is dead—a veteran of an incredible juke joint where the best musicians in the world have performed. Gary Samuels, who played in our band for nine years every single Sunday, is now gone. Kerby, another door greeter, and Reggie, a manager, have each lost a parent. Customers are also dying.

We reach twenty thousand meals served, with kitchens firing away in Harlem, Newark, and Overtown. I never thought of cooks and servers as first responders. In this moment in America, once again, the immigrants are helping. The guy at the deli. The lady delivering your package. These people are the first to not get health insurance. The first to be looked down upon or pushed aside. They are my heroes.

Through this, we are survivors. Our heritage has long shown how we continue to prevail even when the light seems dim and fades to black. A cultural experience of healing that we must all go through now.

But Covid-19 is not the only disease infecting America. The pandemic will eventually be overcome, though its effects will stay in the Black community for longer than elsewhere.

The bigger disease we must fight is the virus of systemic racism.

Alongside the rise of the coronavirus this year, we saw the killings of Ahmaud Arbery, Breonna Taylor, and George Floyd by police. David McAtee, who ran YaYa's BBQ Shack in Louisville, often served food at no cost to struggling members of his neighborhood and police officers, yet he was killed by the Kentucky National Guard in the aftermath of Black Lives Matter protests. In these and too many other violent tragedies we have seen the ugliest and worst of America.

We have also seen the bravest and best in response. Some of the most important work in fighting back against racism has happened during this pandemic. Although John Lewis passed during this time, his legacy has never been stronger. The changes we are a part of now are having a ripple effect—not only in America's Black communities and communities of people of color, but in marginalized and Black communities throughout the world.

It will also have a tremendous impact on the food industry.

Food has always been part of the movement for racial justice. Change has often come from ordinary people doing extraordinary things through food, and changing our table. Take Georgia Gilmore, a mother of six in Alabama who fed and funded the Montgomery bus boycott for more than a year in the 1950s. Her cooking and efforts to organize the "Club from Nowhere" raised hundreds of dollars a week for the civil rights movement. Or Zephyr Wright, the chef for Lyndon B. Johnson, who was constantly in the President's ear about injustice and how America needed to change, and who later was invited by the President to personally witness the signing of the Civil Rights Act of 1964.

Sometimes leaders are famous and widely documented. Sometimes they are not as well-known. The contributions of Black people in this country have always been underdocumented and undervalued. We can change that narrative. And we must.

We have to get rid of our biggest wound in America: racism. I hope that feeding each other, learning about our food and who makes it, is part of what will help us heal.

The Rise was created to highlight the incredible talent and journey of Black chefs, culinarians, and writers at work today, and to show how the stories we tell can help make a more equitable, just industry. I hope this work, and this moment, leads to us raising up Black winemakers, authors, and farmers. I hope it leads to us supporting the next generation of Black chefs and hospitality workers who will change our industry forever. And I hope that this movement becomes a part of a permanent and much broader social change.

So much beauty and achievement has come out of tough times throughout history, and it is inspiring to see communities across the globe coming together to care for one another. We also know that the road "back" from the current crisis will be harder for Black people because of the systemic challenges that disproportionately affect Black restaurateurs and creators of all kinds. That's why it's so important for *everyone* to help bring more equity to this industry. See the Resources section on page 301 for a few starting points to take this message and turn it into action in your own life.

We are the Black Food Community: Black chefs, Black servers, Black bartenders, Black food writers, Black culinary historians, Black recipe developers. Our food stems from challenged communities and challenged times. It comprises enslavement, poverty, and war, yet our food has soul, and has inspired and fed many. We will rise, we will shine, we are survivors.

Black Food Matters.

Marcus Samuelsson
July 2020

INTRODUCTION

Black Food Is American Food

Black food is not just one thing. It's not a rigidly defined geography or a static set of tastes. It is an energy. A force. An engine.

In fact, Black cooking is *the* engine of what we commonly understand to be American food. And if you want to understand the culture and history of the United States, you need to understand Black cooks and Black food. This book is an invitation to that conversation—an invitation to open doors to history, highlight Black excellence today, and imagine a future where everyone has a seat at the table and a spot in the kitchen.

Today, Black creators in literature, music, sports, fashion, film, and the arts are finally being properly recognized. It's time we understood the contributions of Black cooks on the same level, as powerful and multidimensional forces shaping our culture.

Yet many readers may still think that Black food starts and stops with dishes like fried chicken and grits—a certain idea of "soul food" stuck in time. There's much to learn by studying these dishes, but they reflect just one of the many facets of Black cooking. Just as our country is now familiar with recognizing and exploring the regional differences in Italian or French or Chinese food, this book asserts that the food of Black cooks has its own unique richness to explore.

Think about music. What if we stopped studying Black music after the rise of bebop? We'd miss out on hip hop, Afrobeat, reggae, funk, and many other unique sounds and statements about our world. When we think Black food is just one thing, we hear one song and think it represents the entire record library. Black food is constantly engaging with its roots, adapting to new circumstances, and integrating other ideas. It is anything but monolithic.

This book is an invitation to a listening party that everyone is welcome to join—a celebration to discover the breadth, depth, and diversity of Black cooks.

You'll learn about ingredients and recipes that acknowledge this cuisine's journey from its origins in Africa to the Americas and beyond. That's because Black cooking—like all food—is local and personal, with ingredients, techniques, and traditions evolving across geography and time. And you'll meet extraordinary Black cooks and other experts whose stories reveal their personal histories and individual tastes, suggesting the wide range of family stories, cultures, and creative dimensions reflected in Black cooking today.

This work is particularly relevant right now, at a moment when we have rarely needed to learn about and understand each other more urgently. This is a historic time in which we have the power to make meaningful change. We have the opportunity to wake up to the brilliance and beauty around us, as well as to the systemic problems that create issues of justice, access, and representation around race.

What Does It Mean to Be a Black Cook?

I remember teaching a cooking class after I had moved to New York twenty years ago. I was going off about how I was inspired by Swedish food, Japanese food, and so on. A student asked me: "What about African food?"

That question made me look inward and question the assumptions I had made about what was valuable in my professional life. The energy and creative force of Black creators is why I had been drawn to the United States. But I had to ask myself: What does it mean for me to be a Black cook? I realized I had so much more to learn on the way to answering that question for myself.

After that, my work turned in a new direction. I did not have to chase French food and Michelin stars. I could also learn about cacao beans and benne seeds.

I was born in a hut in Ethiopia, adopted by parents in Sweden, trained as a chef in Europe, and chose to work in Harlem. Being an immigrant and being adopted means being uprooted. For me it also gave me a different perspective on the United States. I saw the hope that many immigrants have: that whatever is missing or broken where you are, that you can come here to find or fix it.

As a Black kid growing up in Scandinavia, Black culture coming out of the US was a lifeline. Music was the first way for me to do that—Marvin Gaye, Prince, Miles Davis, Jimi Hendrix. I learned about Harlem from James Baldwin books, movies, the writings of Malcolm X, and Amateur Night at the Apollo.

I was in search of my home, and ultimately, I found it here, Uptown. Once I started to live and cook in New York, I was shocked at how little the story of Black cooking was being told. I lived in Harlem and studied for ten years before I opened my restaurant Red Rooster. I realized that many great Black stories were rarely written down and printed; they were told to me by community elders in conversation. And while there is an oeuvre of Black-authored cookbooks spanning more than two centuries, so much great Black food was not written down and documented in that way; it was orally shared, or you had to be there. Unless you were practically a specialist in digging up these gems, Black foodways had been scrubbed from history.

I wanted to acknowledge the authorship of those who came before and the contributions of the next generations of Black chefs.

I always return to the stories behind our food. It's not a straight line, because the influences are truly global. We can't separate West Africans and their descendants from their foundational contributions to this country and we can't separate their influence on cooking from Southern food, though many have tried. We can't separate the Great Migration from the way it changed how the US developed, and so we must understand that where Black people went, their food cultures followed.

As a naturalized American citizen, this is my country, too. Black history is part of my story. I've been the beneficiary of all that Black America has accomplished. The opportunities I've enjoyed, the access I've received, are thanks to so many who came before me. In some ways, my experiences make me an outlier. I must acknowledge I can only do this work in this country. Even as an immigrant, I benefit from the work and sacrifices of the Black American generations who preceded me. I wouldn't be here without the efforts of the courageous young folks who led the Civil Rights Movement. My parents didn't slog through the indignities of Jim Crow. Unlike many in my generation, I didn't have to watch my father come back from Vietnam scarred, or live through him not coming back at all. It's important for me to acknowledge that while I share Blackness with my fellow coworkers, we experience our identities in different ways.

So: What *does* it mean to be a Black cook in this country? Every person in this book might answer that question differently. There is no one answer, nor should there be. But until we engage with that question, and recognize the roots and range of Black foodways, we won't understand who we are as a nation.

This Is Your Food, Too

Given that contributions by American people from the African diaspora have had such indelible influence on American culture, it is shocking to me at times, even as a Black man, to note how easily those contributions are dismissed. Black culture has long been taken for granted. When I've looked for contemporary cookbooks that document this constantly evolving food culture, I've been puzzled to not find the dishes I've come to know reflected in the offerings available. Online searches didn't yield much either.

Eventually it dawned on me that these stories were not being told. There are a lot of reasons for that. Black chefs and creators face a host of challenges to telling their stories, which range from being discriminated against when trying to acquire capital to launch restaurants to being historically limited by a book publishing industry that has not valued Black people's food and stories.

While many cookbooks showcase the different aspects of African American foodways, its full range is stunningly underrepresented in bookstores and home kitchens. In America, Italian food became popular in part because people who weren't Italian made it at home. Same with French recipes. We constantly reference these legacies and for good reason. But European cooking histories are not the only ones that have historic value. We know more about ricotta than we know about ayib (page 294).

I'm not so naïve to think that if someone eats tacos, they'll immediately appreciate Mexican people more. As popular as kimchi has become in so-called New American dining, I still don't know many people who ferment their own batches. Yet embracing a people's food in your home is one aspect of recognizing the value of that culture.

We have a pretty steep learning curve to overcome. The United States was never really set up for us to learn about one another's food or to honor the Black people who did the agricultural, culinary, and domestic work that shaped this nation. Our country was organized to create lasting divisions between us. Those fissures still exist.

Here's an example of how we can see the same piece of this country through two completely different lenses.

A few years ago, I visited a plantation outside of Richmond, Virginia. The nicest family took me around. During the tour, they explained to me, "We do these great weddings here, it's so beautiful. The weddings are amazing." My host, a white woman, told me that the land had been in her family for 300 years. She said, "It's a little bit smaller now—we can only afford to have eight acres. But it was a small plantation, about twenty-five acres." Then she said, "I want to show you where the workers lived." *Workers*. As though the people who were held there had the option of clocking in and clocking out. As if those Black people had the luxury of visiting friends or going away for the weekend.

I was grateful that she was doing this, taking me around her historic land. But her disposition was incomprehensible to me. Modern-day weddings on the plantation—weddings at an enslaved persons' labor camp? The woman talked about the main house from an architectural point of view, commenting on the woodwork and the ongoing maintenance. But I walked around thinking, "How can people even *live* here? How do they survive it?"

I hope this book can be a journey that helps bridge the understanding between those two perspectives.

I'm not interested in claiming who did what first. I'm not in a race to say that Black people are the only ones who eat the foods in this book. And I'm not making an argument that Black people are alone in being underrepresented and deserving of more credit. I'm saying, *We are here, too*. We have been here, as creators and innovators, since the very beginning.

No matter your background, my hope for your experience with this book is that you learn something new about the breadth and depth of Black cooking in the United States. I hope you'll enjoy the range of how Black people eat, and reflect on the challenges that many chefs and storytellers have faced. Perhaps more than anything, I hope you find yourself in these recipes, just as I'm sure you'll hear your experiences in these stories.

You might realize, this is your food, too, even if you are not Black, American, or Southern.

How The Rise Works

This isn't an encyclopedia. It's a feast. And everyone's invited. This book aims to become a platform for Black food professionals to showcase the range of their culture and imagination.

No one person could command full knowledge of every tributary of the great river that is Black food. I'm a chef and student, not a historian or ethnographer. *The Rise* is not a definitive chronicle, but rather an opening to learn more. This is also not the first book to shine a light on Black foodways. There's an appendix of many other books and resources in the back (page 301).

This book is organized in chapters that each offer some insight into Black foodways and contemporary Black chefs and experts whom I greatly admire and respect. This too is only a start; thankfully, there are far too many extraordinary cooks and other culinary experts to be collected in just one book. I am grateful to these friends, colleagues, and mentors for sharing their time and trusting us with their stories.

I am also grateful to the team who helped bring this book to light, especially Osayi Endolyn, whose essays on each person in the book offer heart and insight, and Yewande Komolafe, who developed many of the recipes here.

Each recipe in the book was created in honor of someone who is illuminating the space we share. I wanted to throw some light back on each of them. Some of the recipes, you'll see, have a direct or immediate connection to that person's story. Others don't have an obvious or direct connection. They're just a riff from me on a dish that I simply think is delicious and want to share. Check out the recipe guide on page ix for a listing of recipes by course and main ingredient; the way they are organized inside each chapter is in support of the broader story this book tells.

The roots of these recipes are born of major global shifts—from hundreds of African cultures, forcibly mixed during centuries of enslavement, whose regional culinary practices evolved on this land with cooking techniques and ingredients, both old and new. American culinary schools that train our future chefs don't yet offer a curriculum that prizes Black food culture the way they should. When that day finally comes, it will be well overdue.

We're here. And so is our food. Let's celebrate it *and* the people who make it.

Black chefs' names need to be sung. Let this book be the chorus.

Chapter 1

NEXT

Where Black food is headed:
chefs and recipes on the cutting edge, and who's got next.

IN HONOR OF:

DAVID ZILBER, chef, Copenhagen, Denmark

Baked Sweet Potatoes
with Garlic-Fermented Shrimp Butter

Chorizo Hash
with Cured Egg and Horseradish on Toast

EDOUARDO JORDAN, chef, Seattle, WA

Lagos Plantains with Yaji (Suya Spice) Dip

Oyster Cucumber Shooters

Spiced Catfish with Pumpkin Leche de Tigre

ERIC GESTEL, chef, New York, NY

Chicken Liver Mousse with Croissants

Seared Scallops
with White Soy Butter and Bok Choy

Steak Frites with Plantain Chips and Green
Vinaigrette

GREGORY GOURDET, chef, Portland, OR

Pork Griot with Roasted Pineapple and Pikliz

Haitian Black Rice and Mushrooms

Independence Soup

NINA COMPTON, chef, New Orleans, LA

Cassava Dumplings with Callaloo Puree

Roasted Cauliflower Steaks
with NOLA East Mayo

SHAKIRAH SIMLEY, food justice advocate,
San Francisco, CA

Tomato and Peach Salad
with Okra, Radishes, and Benne Seed Dressing

STEPHEN SATTERFIELD, publisher, Atlanta, GA

Spice-Roasted Black Cod and Carrots
with Benne Seed Dressing

TAVEL BRISTOL-JOSEPH, chef, Austin, TX

Coconut Fried Chicken
with Sweet Hot Sauce and Platanos

Oxtail Pepperpot with Dumplings

Smoked Venison with Roti and Pine Nut Chutney

ADRIENNE CHEATHAM, chef, New York, NY

Quick Salted Salmon
with Carrot Broth and Mushrooms

Crispy Carolina Millet Salad with Cow Peas

JJ JOHNSON, chef, New York, NY

Shellfish Stew with Black Rice

Gold Coconut Broken Rice
with Tamarind-Glazed Halibut

JONNY RHODES, chef, Houston, TX

Brussels and Dry Shrimp

Shrimp Fritters with Bitter Greens and Grapefruit

ERIC ADJEPONG, chef, Washington, DC

Island Jollof Rice

Steak Afrique with Sauce Yassa

MARIYA RUSSELL, chef, Chicago, IL

Citrus-Cured Shrimp
with Injera Handrolls and Awaze

ANONYMOUS CHEF, chef, San Diego, CA

Banana Leaf Snapper
with Chickpeas and Coconut Rice

Tuna and Scallop Aguachile

TIANA GEE, chef, New York, NY

Chicken and Shrimp Tamarind Broth
with Rice Noodles

PATRICIA GONZALEZ, chef, New York, NY

Big Ole Pork Chops with D.R. Mangú

ALMIRA SESSION, chef, New York, NY

Salmon Rillettes with Injera

e start by looking at the future. This chapter is about the way Black food is being expressed today—how a vanguard of chefs, creators, and activists are pushing the cutting edge forward. They are doing things that weren't widely acceptable or possible before. Not every person here is of a generation younger than mine—and this is far from an exhaustive compilation of the creative minds making moves. But many of these opportunities are new, and these professionals are creating an exciting, more equitable future.

What's next in Black cooking is delicious. But what excites me is not just what the food looks like on the plate. I'm excited by a change in visibility, what the food industry looks like at all levels. Representation matters—in the test kitchen or food lab like David Zilber, in the fine-dining kitchen like Gregory Gourdet, running businesses like Edouardo Jordan and Nina Compton, at the helm of a media company like Stephen Satterfield, or in City Hall like Shakirah Simley.

Even if our work isn't driven by identity, just being where we are is powerful. Representation shows a future generation what's possible.

Take Stephen's Whetstone Media—a successful, independent, Black-owned platform that publishes a magazine and podcast diving deep into the origins of food around the globe at a time when legacy media is struggling. Or Gregory, who started his professional career cooking in French traditions, but discovered new energy by sharing his own Haitian heritage at the table. Edouardo trained at the French Laundry and wanted to prove himself as a chef with his Italian restaurant Salare before he blew the doors off with JuneBaby, which focuses on African American foodways. And Shakirah, with over a decade in food and social justice, shows how food is political.

In my work, I'm constantly thinking about creating opportunities for others. At Harlem EatUp!, the festival I host that celebrates the neighborhood's food, arts, and culture, it's not at all hard to find Black talent—folks like Charles Gabriel of Charles Pan Fried Chicken, Lexis Gonzalez of Lady Lexis Sweets Shop, and Raymond Mohan and Leticia Skai Young of Lolo's Seafood Shack. There are chefs, caterers, bloggers, folks with retail businesses. You don't have to work in a traditional restaurant to be part of today's food conversation—nor should you have to. The traditional barriers to entry have maintained a system that perpetuates inequality and bias. It's past time for them to be dismantled.

It used to be that the Black culinary professionals had to work hard to seek each other out because the representation was so sparse. There's still not parity, but today, Black chefs thinking about Black food are not alone. There's a growing community. What's new is a level of visibility and the potential for equity that wasn't available before. We belong here.

What's next has been here all along. The techniques, the creativity, the ideas, the emotions. The rest of the world is just waking up to this—people are seeking out a new understanding of Black food. No matter their background, people are looking a little closer at their surroundings and seeing what's actually there.

Because of my work with *No Passport Required*, the show where I travel around the country to explore the diversity of immigrant traditions and immigrant culture that's woven through the American landscape, I will never look at a strip mall the same. What's behind that Nigerian or Senegalese or Guyanese store? Inside, there could be an African tribe leader who happens to make a particular smoked fish or another dish specific to their culture. Americans have learned to celebrate that experience in a Jewish deli or an Italian pasta store. If we've done that, we can do the same with a peanut sauce or beef suya. It's crazy to me that there are people who have lived in New York City for twenty years but haven't had fufu.

In another sense, what's next is a reclamation. A return to our own rituals—whether they're Saint Lucian–inspired like Nina Compton's at Compère Lapin, or playful twists on Guyanese roti like at Tavel Bristol-Joseph's restaurant Emmer & Rye.

"We got this" is what I imagine these folks are saying with their work. They're already running point.

"We explore food."

DAVID ZILBER

Former director of fermentation at Noma in Copenhagen, Denmark

Born in Toronto, Ontario

Known for: Immense expertise in fermented foods

The restaurant Noma in Copenhagen is at the forefront of innovations in dining, and its fermentation lab, headed by David Zilber until mid-2020, is the creative force that fuels the trailblazing and constantly changing menus that define the restaurant.

Zilber worked at Noma from 2014, and in 2018 he cowrote the definitive tome based on the lab's work, *The Noma Guide to Fermentation*. The lab seeks to celebrate and subvert the way most people eat; after all, bread, coffee, vinegar, pickled vegetables, and fish sauces are all fermented foods and can be found in pantries around the globe. The process of fermentation—using bacteria to break down edible goods—is the oldest way to prepare food, and Zilber brings this ancient practice into the future.

"We have machines from the perfume industry to extract aromas, centrifuges to separate food. We break things down and build them back up," Zilber says. "If soy sauce is made from x, y, and z, what else can we do to it? How can we create something new?"

Zilber grew up in a multicultural Toronto neighborhood. School was no fun because he was uninterested; he failed twelfth grade twice. But when his high school counselor encouraged him to focus less on grades and instead reflect on how he wanted to spend his time, cooking emerged as a possibility.

At home, Zilber's father, an Ashkenazi Jew by way of Polish heritage, was "just OK" in the kitchen. But his mother, Afro Caribbean via Curaçao and Dominica, had skills that inspired. "My mother had the cooking smarts that come from growing up in a tiny little country. There wasn't convenience. I grew up eating food from her side like pilau, codfish and bakes, sorrel stew. We were raised Jewish, that was a decision on my parents' part. There was no pork in the house. But every now and then around Christmas, she'd get a hankering and make roast pork ham." His mother also made latkes, matzo ball soup with gefilte fish, and sweet hamantaschen. "She'd *try* to make challah. It was Shabbat dinner on Friday with traditional Jewish food and mix-up things like Shake 'n Bake chicken—what my dad could pull off well. On Sunday morning for brunch she'd be making Caribbean food."

While in high school, Zilber began a restaurant apprenticeship to learn basic cooking skills. He followed that with ten years of cooking in Montreal, then moved to Vancouver where he was sous chef at Hawksworth. At 27, he realized he needed a new challenge. Soon, he was heading to Copenhagen to work on a trial basis at Noma.

Zilber describes the Noma lab as a place that floods the restaurant's kitchen with ideas. He counted himself lucky to work in a space where he could take time to uncover what works about a recipe. It might take a year to sort out whether an item is best served after fermenting for two months or three months. He had that space to discover and explore.

At home, though, he just cooks the food he likes to eat. Swedish breakfast of fish roe and boiled eggs. Pilau. "Cooking for me at home is like riffing. Pasta, stir-fried rice. It ends up being everything. One of the questions I hate: 'What's your specialty?' That's like asking a writer, 'What's your favorite letter?' You need them all."

SELLERS

BAKED SWEET POTATOES
≪with≫ GARLIC-FERMENTED SHRIMP BUTTER

This recipe is a nod to a brother who understands the B-side of cooking—David is a fermenting expert in one of the world's best restaurants in Denmark. When I think about fermentation, I think about funk: sweet, sour, bitter and salty, musty and funky. Fermentation is a process that is very structured, but it's also deep and groovy. David is like a funk band leader and he's focused his life on this craft. He deserves to be called "the future of fermentation."

The fermented notes in this dish tie together the sweetness of the potato and the plump savory profile of the shrimp. Take a bite and remember that great Prince song, "Black Sweat." I do.

ACTIVE TIME: *15 minutes*
START TO FINISH: *1 hour*
SERVES 4

4 medium sweet potatoes

1 tablespoon vegetable oil

1 teaspoon kosher salt

4 tablespoons unsalted butter

4 cloves garlic, peeled

1 teaspoon fermented shrimp paste

1 soft, ripe avocado, pitted and peeled

Juice of 1 lemon

1 tablespoon sweet soy sauce (kecap manis)

4 sprigs fresh thyme, leaves removed

Preheat the oven to 375°F.

Rub the potatoes with the vegetable oil and salt, and wrap each individually in aluminum foil. Bake until tender, 45 to 60 minutes. Let cool.

Meanwhile, place the butter, garlic, and shrimp paste into a small saucepan set over low heat and bring to a simmer. Cook, stirring continually, for 2 to 3 minutes. Reduce the heat to maintain a simmer and cook for 5 minutes, stirring occasionally, until the garlic has softened slightly. Set aside to cool to room temperature.

Once the potatoes are cooked and the butter is cooled, place the butter mixture, avocado, lemon juice, sweet soy sauce, and thyme leaves in the bowl of a small food processor and process until smooth.

Serve the sweet potatoes with the butter.

CHORIZO HASH
≪with≫ CURED EGG AND HORSERADISH ON TOAST

With this recipe, we're using a fermented paste with a cured egg in honor of David, the fermentation genius. We start with a simple hash, something everybody has had at breakfast, but what will really blow your hair back is the addition of fermented soybean paste. The flavors of this dish are like a good vintage wine that never goes out of style. That's the power of fermentation. The sauce, inspired by ssäm, gives umami, the egg yolks break open to add a level of silky richness, and then combine with the horseradish to make this hash a unique dish.

ACTIVE TIME: *30 minutes*
START TO FINISH: *50 minutes, plus 6 hours to cure the egg yolks*
SERVES 4

5 ounces fresh chorizo sausage

1 medium red onion, finely chopped

2 creamer potatoes, about 12 ounces, cut into ¼-inch dice

½ teaspoon kosher salt, plus more to taste

2 tablespoons unsalted butter

4 (½-inch-thick) pieces sourdough bread

10-ounce piece beef tenderloin, cut in ¼-inch cubes

3 tablespoons Ssäm Sauce (recipe follows)

2 teaspoons prepared hot mustard

4 Cured Egg Yolks (recipe follows)

1 (2-inch) piece horseradish, grated, for garnish

Place the chorizo, onion, potatoes, and salt in a medium skillet. Cook over medium heat, stirring occasionally, until the potatoes are just tender, 12 to 15 minutes. Remove the potato mixture from the pan, cover, and keep warm.

Melt the butter in the pan and add the sourdough bread, in batches if necessary. Coat each piece on both sides with butter and toast until golden, 3 to 4 minutes. Remove from the pan, cover, and keep warm.

Season the beef tenderloin lightly with salt, add to the pan, and cook over medium heat for 2 to 3 minutes, until browned. Add the potato mixture to the pan along with the ssäm sauce and mustard and cook until heated through, 1 to 2 minutes.

To serve, place a piece of toast on each of four plates or shallow bowls. Top with hash and cured egg yolk and garnish with freshly grated horseradish.

SSÄM SAUCE

ACTIVE TIME: 5 minutes
START TO FINISH: 5 minutes
MAKES 7 TABLESPOONS

2 tablespoons Korean fermented soybean paste (doenjang)

2 tablespoons minced scallions

1 tablespoon rice wine vinegar

1 tablespoon olive oil

1 tablespoon Korean chile sauce (gochujang)

1 teaspoon sesame seeds

¼ teaspoon sesame oil

Combine all the ingredients in a small bowl and whisk to combine and emulsify.

CURED EGG YOLKS

ACTIVE TIME: 10 minutes
START TO FINISH: 6 hours
MAKES 4 CURED YOLKS

3 tablespoons soy sauce

3 tablespoons Ssäm Sauce

2 tablespoons extra virgin olive oil

4 large egg yolks

Whisk the soy sauce, ssäm sauce, and olive oil together in a small bowl and gently add the egg yolks. Refrigerate to cure for 6 hours, gently spooning the sauce over the eggs every hour.

> *"Being a great chef, for me,*
> *means being true to myself, being true to my roots."*

EDOUARDO JORDAN

*Executive chef and owner at Salare, JuneBaby,
and Lucinda Grain Bar in Seattle, Washington*

Born in St. Petersburg, Florida

*Annotated the JuneBaby menu with an
encyclopedia of African American foodways*

Edouardo Jordan opened his Seattle restaurant Salare in 2015 to a warm welcome. Then, in 2017, his second restaurant, JuneBaby, was named *Eater*'s Best New Restaurant, followed by a shimmering three-star review from *The New York Times*. Jordan cleaned up at the 2018 James Beard Awards, earning Best New Restaurant and Best Chef in the Northwest.

JuneBaby struck a chord. The fine dining restaurant offers dishes that emerged from the South as a result of the forced migration and labor of African people, and the menu connects diners to the food of this country's roots: wheat buns and cast-iron cornbread, charred okra dressed in sorghum chili, chicken livers and fried pig ears, stewed oxtails, chitlins, and a range of rice dishes. This is food that sustained the lineage from which Jordan comes.

A St. Petersburg native, he grew up with most of his family within a four-minute walk. Jordan says the neighborhood wasn't bad but wasn't great either. "My parents made the best of what they had," he says. His father had an independent construction company; his mother was in elementary education. She in particular kept Jordan's academic momentum going, even as he was expelled from three schools and transferred to three others before junior high.

"I was a troublemaker," Jordan says now, laughing. But being removed from class wasn't funny back then. He remembers how his fourth-grade teacher cautioned that the world is tough "for a little Black boy acting up." On a hunch, she also had his aptitude tested, which revealed that he had a learning disability *and* was gifted. These results shifted the narrative for a young Jordan and the opportunities that were presented to him. Suddenly, the gifted classes he was placed in intrigued and challenged him. He became a student-athlete, which motivated him to maintain a good grade average up to and through high school. He later graduated from the University of Florida with dual degrees in sports management and business administration. But while he pursued a career as a sports agent, another interest brewed.

"I hosted some of the best parties," Jordan says of gatherings where he cooked. "Epic parties. Good people, good entertainment. But also, good food." After graduation he nabbed an externship with the Tampa Bay Devil Rays, but when they offered him a job, he didn't accept it.

He had launched a blog, *Tamburg* (for Tampa and St. Petersburg), where he wrote about the dining scene. "Being a Black, young kid, no one expected that I was critiquing or reviewing them. I had the full effect of what it was to eat as a 'minority' in some of the cooler restaurants. And I was getting more and more pissed because the food that I was cooking at home was better." The service staff often dismissed him. "It felt like a broken system. This is not what a restaurant is supposed to be like. You don't feel restored or happy." He kept seeing commercials for the Cordon Bleu. "That was the a-ha moment."

Jordan is frank about the hefty $30,000 investment in culinary school: He wouldn't recommend aspiring chefs take that route if they can find mentors on the job. But that education might have helped him land an entry role at Thomas Keller's legendary California restaurant, the French Laundry. "I will never know, but without having a culinary degree, I probably would not have been accepted there, which was the jumpstart to my career." He spent months trying to get a response to calls and letters, until he made a trip to San Francisco, drove to Napa Valley, and knocked on the door in person. He was invited to come back and work within a few weeks.

After the French Laundry, Jordan moved to Washington State, briefly returned to Florida, moved to New York to work at Keller's restaurant Per Se, and traveled to Italy. He returned to Seattle to open his own restaurant: a place that would have excited his younger food-blogger self.

Salare is driven by an Italian approach to preserving, curing, and seasoning food. Lucinda Grain Bar celebrates grain in all its forms, from legumes to distilled spirits. And JuneBaby expresses Jordan's heritage, spurred by a tour of the South that encouraged him to bring his family's food to his version of the fine dining table. His paternal grandmother was the family's go-to cook and he thinks of her dishes often, her neck bones, liver and onions, and hoecakes recipes dotting the mind.

Jordan remembers when he was in elementary school and once mentioned how much he loved chitlins. The shocked and judgmental response from his classmates shut him down. "I kinda stopped talking about it. It was a food that we ate. I enjoyed it. But I turned my back on chitlins and never brought it up to anyone again." Things are different now. "I have the ability to educate people, to embrace this food, and to re-experience it in my own manner. Being able to cook dishes that my mom and my grandmother cooked is pretty damn cool."

LAGOS PLANTAINS
≪with≫ YAJI (SUYA SPICE) DIP

Edouardo won two James Beard awards a couple of years ago, and at the time I think I was more excited than he was. He had just come back from Nigeria and I know his time there had a huge impact on him, and it continues to shape how he creates his dishes. Black chefs are traveling to Africa to learn, and young African chefs are coming to the United States to ask questions. They are connecting to their past and incorporating the flavors of the diaspora into their world. Yaji, also known as suya spice, can be found across Nigeria, and is a flavor that I'm sure Edouardo came across in his travels.

ACTIVE TIME: 25 minutes
START TO FINISH: 40 minutes
SERVES 4 AS AN APPETIZER

SPICE MIX

2 teaspoons kosher salt

1½ teaspoons five-spice powder

1 teaspoon chili powder

1 teaspoon garlic powder

½ teaspoon ground cumin

YAJI DIP

1 tablespoon vegetable oil

½ habanero chile, stemmed, seeded, and coarsely chopped

2 cloves garlic, sliced

½ cup crushed peanuts

1 tablespoon creamy peanut butter

½ cup unsweetened coconut milk

Juice of 1 lime

PLANTAINS

Vegetable oil, for frying

1 tablespoon grated Parmesan cheese

1 tablespoon chopped fresh parsley

2 teaspoons chopped fresh cilantro

2 yellow ripe plantains, cut ¼ inch thick on the bias

For the spice mix: Combine the salt, five-spice, chili powder, garlic powder, and cumin in a small bowl.

For the yaji dip: Heat the oil in a small saucepan set over medium heat. Once the oil shimmers, add 2 teaspoons of the spice mixture, the habanero, garlic, and peanuts. Cook, stirring continually, until the pepper and garlic are tender and the peanuts begin to brown slightly, 2 to 3 minutes. Add the peanut butter and coconut milk, bring to a boil, and remove from the heat. Transfer to a blender, add the lime juice, and process until pureed. Set aside until ready to use.

For the plantains: Heat 1 inch oil in a heavy pot over high heat and bring to 325°F.

Place the remaining 4 teaspoons of the spice mixture in a large bowl and add the Parmesan cheese, parsley, and cilantro. Toss to combine.

Gently add half of the plantains to the oil and fry until golden brown, 4 to 5 minutes. Transfer to the bowl with the seasoning mix and toss to coat. Transfer from the bowl to a serving platter, leaving behind the remaining seasoning. Repeat with the remaining plantains and seasoning mix. Serve with the yaji dip.

OYSTER CUCUMBER SHOOTERS

Oysters and cucumbers remind me of the Prince song, "Diamonds and Pearls": The oysters are elegant; the cucumbers bring an extra layer of cool. This dish is inspired by the Pacific Northwest, where Edouardo has made his home.

ACTIVE TIME: *45 minutes*
START TO FINISH: *45 minutes*
MAKES 24 OYSTERS

1 medium cucumber, halved and seeded

1 medium Granny Smith apple, halved and cored

24 oysters on the half shell, oyster liquid reserved

Juice of 1 lemon

2 tablespoons rice wine vinegar

1 tablespoon soy sauce

½ teaspoon fish sauce

1 shallot, minced

1 small, hot finger chile pepper, stemmed and minced

Peel one cucumber half and chop into pieces. Peel one apple half and chop into pieces. Place the reserved oyster liquid in a blender and add the chopped cucumber, chopped apple, lemon juice, vinegar, soy sauce, and fish sauce. Puree until smooth. Pass through a fine mesh strainer and discard the pulp. You should have about 1 cup liquid.

Finely chop the remaining unpeeled cucumber and apple and transfer to a small bowl. Add the shallot and chile pepper and stir to combine.

Place the oysters on a platter filled with crushed ice. Top each oyster with ½ teaspoon of chopped cucumber mixture and 1 teaspoon of liquid and serve immediately.

SPICED CATFISH
《with》 PUMPKIN LECHE DE TIGRE

The best cooking blends our personal influences with local ingredients. One thing I admire about Edouardo is how he sheds new light on the foods commonly associated with the South. Catfish is often blackened or fried; here's a way to enjoy it with leche de tigre, a citrusy, traditional Peruvian sauce and marinade. The dashi and ginger bring umami and spice.

ACTIVE TIME: *35 minutes*
START TO FINISH: *35 minutes*
SERVES 4 AS AN APPETIZER

PUMPKIN LECHE DE TIGRE

3½ tablespoons vegetable oil

6 cloves garlic, minced

3 tablespoons peeled and chopped fresh ginger

1 cup dashi

1 tablespoon ají amarillo paste

½ cup unsweetened coconut milk

½ cup freshly squeezed lime juice

¼ cup pumpkin puree

1 tablespoon chopped clams

Kosher salt

SPICED CATFISH

1 tablespoon ground Aleppo pepper

½ tablespoon kosher salt

1 teaspoon ground coriander

1 teaspoon smoked paprika

1 teaspoon garlic powder

½ teaspoon ground cumin

2 tablespoons unsalted butter

1 tablespoon adobo paste

4 (6-ounce) catfish fillets, cut into 2-inch strips

2 tablespoons extra virgin olive oil

¼ cup toasted pumpkin seeds, for serving

1 lime, cut into 4 wedges, for serving

For the pumpkin leche de tigre: Heat 1 tablespoon of the vegetable oil in a small sauté pan over medium heat until it shimmers. Add the garlic and ginger and cook for 2 to 3 minutes, until the garlic is aromatic. Set aside to cool.

Transfer the garlic and ginger to a blender and add the dashi, ají paste, coconut milk, lime juice, and pumpkin puree. With the blender running, add the remaining 2½ tablespoons vegetable oil in a stream and blend until smooth. Add the clams and pulse three or four times to incorporate. Season with salt to taste. Set aside until ready to serve.

For the spiced catfish: Combine the pepper, salt, coriander, paprika, garlic powder, and cumin in a small bowl and set aside.

Combine the butter and adobo paste in small saucepan set over low heat and whisk until butter is just melted and ingredients are combined. Brush the butter mixture on all sides of the fish and sprinkle evenly with the spice mix.

Heat the olive oil in a large skillet over medium heat. Once it shimmers, add the fish and cook for 5 minutes. Turn the fish over and continue to cook for 3 minutes while continually basting with the oil and butter in the pan, until just cooked through.

To serve: Transfer the fish to four shallow bowls. Divide the leche de tigre among the bowls and sprinkle with the pumpkin seeds. Serve with lime wedges.

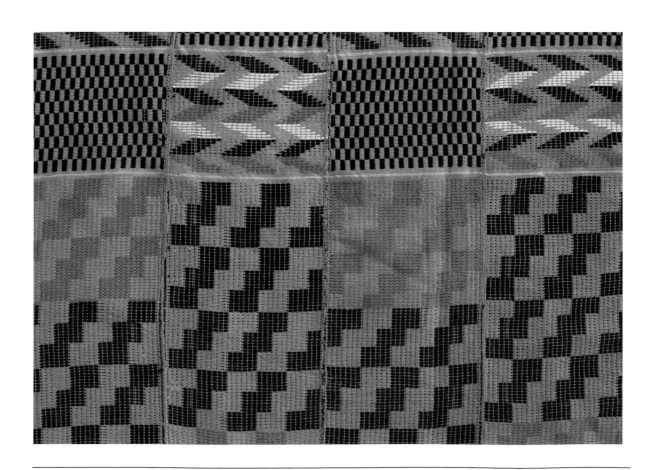

> *"At Le Bernardin, we use different products from different cultures. Asian, South American—I relate to all of it. There's always a connection in food."*

ERIC GESTEL

Executive chef at Le Bernardin in New York, New York

Cooked on The Martha Stewart Show, Late Night with David Letterman, *and* Good Morning America

Born in Le Lamentin, Outre-Mer, Martinique

Food memory: Whole beef head—tongue and everything—that his father cooked in a big hot pot

Eric Gestel spent the first eleven years of his life in Martinique, an island in the Lesser Antilles where his family has lived for generations, descendants of African people brought to the Caribbean during the slave trade. That childhood in the countryside near Le Lamentin and along the coast in Le Robert, where tropical produce and fresh seafood were plentiful, still influences his approach to food and cooking.

Since 1996, Gestel has cooked at Le Bernardin in Midtown Manhattan, the top-rated restaurant renowned for exquisite seafood tastings framed by luxurious and attentive service. He worked every station and became executive chef in 2015. For many of Le Bernardin's most impressive accolades—the World's Best 50 Restaurants, three Michelin stars, four-star reviews from *The New York Times*—Gestel has been a quiet legend and leader in the kitchen. "We keep moving. We keep changing. The dining room, the kitchen, the food," Gestel says. "It's not the same old place. If you don't change, you get behind."

Consider the snapper. Le Bernardin style, the fish is cooked separately from other components, but is served with a sauce on the side with garnish. Gestel's interpretation might include a baked sweet potato with a sauce made of peppers, garlic, shallots, and chicken jus mixed with mirepoix. "You finish your sauce with lime," Gestel says. "When you've got these four products, a spicy Jamaican pepper, garlic, onion, and lime, that will tell you everything about food in the Caribbean."

In Le Robert, he doesn't remember the family shopping for groceries much. The terrain offered plenty: from bananas, pineapple, and grapes, to melon, sweet potatoes, and christophine—the Martiniquais name for chayote. He loves accra, a cod fritter like a dry bacalou. Banana beignet. Conch. "It smells so good, the flavor that comes out of all those dishes. That's what makes me feel good. Like, 'man I'm in the Caribbean.'"

When he was nearly twelve years old, Gestel's parents sent him to France to study and live with an uncle who'd moved there. France was "a shock." He lived in Combs-la-Ville, in the north central region. His uncle's wife was a white Frenchwoman who did the cooking. "In the Caribbean I was used to eating everything basically well done. Rice, pasta, the vegetables, the meat, the fish. When I went to France, the first time I ate rice I said 'wow.' I told my aunt it was not cooked!"

At fourteen, Gestel was directed to *active* school in lieu of more traditional academic pursuits. Active school taught a trade, and he found a rhythm in cooking—one week in classes, the next week in a restaurant or hotel *apprentissage*.

After graduating, Gestel worked at the noted Joel Robuchon in Paris, where he met Eric Ripert, Le Bernardin's founding chef. Years later, Gestel would rejoin his friend in Manhattan, but not before cooking at Jamin, also in Paris, on staff for the French Army's minister of defense, and in four-star restaurants in Montreal and Chicago. Of Ripert, he says, "We relate well because we know where we're coming from," referring to the dues they paid coming up in Paris. "I have a trust for him. He trusts me. I'm happy to stay at Le Bernardin."

Brownstones in Harlem

CHICKEN LIVER MOUSSE
≪with≫ CROISSANTS

There have always been two Erics at the acclaimed French restaurant Le Bernardin in New York City. Everybody knows my friend Eric Ripert, but fewer are aware of Eric Gestel, one of the most accomplished Black chefs in the world. He's worked there for more than twenty-five years. If you get the chance to go to Le Bernardin, ask for the other Eric.

I love this recipe because it combines technical and simple cooking. Making a croissant is very technical, but the simplicity of chicken liver is what makes it one of the world's most beloved home-cooked dishes. Together, the result is delectable.

The mousse will keep for 3 days. I love it on fresh-baked croissants, but it's also fantastic on purchased croissants or spread on crusty bread. You can also use it to thicken a sauce.

ACTIVE TIME: *10 minutes*
START TO FINISH: *45 minutes*
MAKES ABOUT 2 CUPS

1 pound chicken livers, cleaned

¼ teaspoon pink curing salt

¾ pound (3 sticks) unsalted butter, room temperature

¼ cup cognac

2 tablespoons saba (or balsamic vinegar)

½ teaspoon kosher salt

Place the livers in a small bowl, sprinkle with the pink curing salt, toss to combine, and set aside for 30 minutes.

Rinse the livers under cold water and pat dry.

Heat 2 tablespoons of the butter in a medium sauté pan set over medium-high heat. As soon as the butter melts, add the livers and cook until they are slightly browned but still pink on the inside, 5 to 6 minutes. Transfer the livers to the bowl of a food processor.

Return the pan to the heat and carefully add the cognac. Deglaze the pan, being careful not to flame the cognac. Scrape the cognac and browned bits into the food processor and add the saba and salt. Allow the mixture to cool to room temperature.

Process for 4 minutes, adding the remaining butter a little at a time, until smooth, occasionally stopping to scrape down the side of the bowl.

Pass the mixture through a chinois or other fine mesh strainer. Transfer to a container and press plastic wrap against the surface of the mousse. Cover and refrigerate until completely chilled.

(Continued)

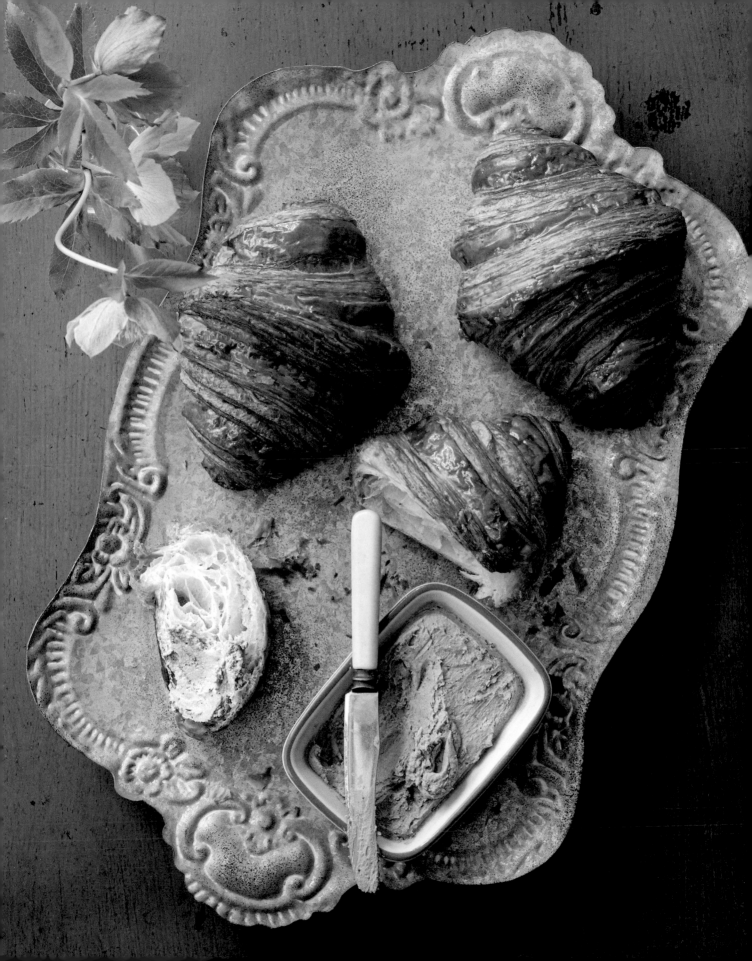

CLASSIC CROISSANTS

ACTIVE TIME: *15 minutes*
START TO FINISH: *2 to 3 days*
MAKES 16 CROISSANTS

3¼ cups all-purpose flour, plus extra for rolling

½ cup plus 2 tablespoons water

½ cup plus 2 tablespoons cold milk

¼ cup sugar

3 tablespoons unsalted butter, melted and cooled

3½ teaspoons instant dry yeast

4 teaspoons kosher salt

10 ounces (2½ sticks) unsalted butter, chilled

1 large egg plus 1 teaspoon water, lightly beaten

Combine the flour, water, milk, sugar, melted butter, yeast, and salt in the bowl of a stand mixer fitted with the dough attachment. Mix for 3 minutes on low speed, until the dough comes together. Transfer the dough to the counter and knead until smooth, 2 to 3 minutes. Shape the dough into a flat disk, cover or wrap in plastic, and refrigerate overnight.

Meanwhile, cut the cold butter into ½-inch pieces and lay on a large piece of parchment paper. Arrange the pieces to form a 6-inch square. Cover with plastic wrap and pound until the butter creates a 7-inch square. Cover and also refrigerate overnight.

The next day, dust a working surface with flour and roll out the dough to a 10-inch square.

Place the butter square on the rolled-out dough at a 45-degree angle, with its corners pointing to the straight edges of the dough. Fold a corner of dough over the butter so the point of the dough reaches the center of the butter slab. Repeat with the remaining corners of the dough, creating an envelope. Press down on the dough with your hand to seal the edges together.

Dust the counter with more flour and roll the dough and butter to an 8- by 24-inch rectangle.

Fold the dough in thirds letter-style, one end to the center and the other end over this. Cover and refrigerate for 30 minutes. Repeat this two times, turning the dough 90 degrees before rolling and resting 30 minutes after each new fold. Wrap the dough in plastic and refrigerate overnight.

The following day, dust a working surface with flour and roll the dough to an 8- by 45-inch rectangle.

Once the dough has reached the intended length, lift up the edges and allow it to shrink back to its natural size. Using a pizza wheel, trim the edges to create a uniform piece of dough.

Mark the dough on the long side at 5-inch intervals, and cut into eight 5- by 8-inch pieces. Cut each piece on the diagonal into triangles. You should have 16 triangles.

Line a rimmed baking sheet with parchment paper.

Very gently stretch each triangle to 9½ inches in length. Starting with the wide end of one triangle, roll the dough into a croissant shape. Lay the croissant on the parchment-lined baking sheet and brush with egg wash. Repeat with each triangle. When done, refrigerate the egg wash.

Bring 2 cups of water to the boil. Pour into a 9- by 13-inch metal baking pan and set on the bottom rack of the oven. Place the croissants in the oven on the rack above, close the door, and proof for 1½ to 2 hours, until the dough has puffed and wiggles slightly when you shake the tray. Remove the croissants from the oven.

Preheat the oven to 400°F.

Remove the egg wash from the refrigerator and brush the croissants a second time. Bake for 15 to 20 minutes, until golden brown.

Serve the hot croissants with the chicken liver mousse.

SEARED SCALLOPS
«with» WHITE SOY BUTTER AND BOK CHOY

This dish blends influences from Eric's culture, French Caribbean, and that of his wife, who is Japanese. Be careful not to overcook the bok choy; it should be slightly undercooked, which makes the dish juicier. The soy butter, a cross between a beurre blanc (the famous butter sauce of French cooking) and soy ponzu (simply a combination of soy sauce and citrus fruit, often yuzu), blends Japanese and French cultures as well. Ackee is a popular fruit in Jamaica. It looks, tastes, and feels like scrambled eggs crossed with sea urchin, with a soft texture and an amazing, unique taste. You can buy it canned in any Caribbean store. Just rinse it before using.

ACTIVE TIME: 35 minutes
START TO FINISH: 1 hour 10 minutes
SERVES 4

¼ cup white wine

Sprig fresh thyme

2 tablespoons white soy sauce (or 1 tablespoon regular soy sauce)

2 tablespoons freshly squeezed lime juice

2 tablespoons heavy cream

½ cup (1 stick) butter, cold and cubed

¼ teaspoon fish sauce

2 tablespoons extra virgin olive oil

1 tablespoon Island XO Sauce (page 228)

2 small heads bok choy, blanched and cut in half lengthwise

Salt

Freshly ground black pepper

3 slices bacon, finely chopped

16 dry-packed sea scallops, patted dry, tough muscles removed

½ cup chopped ackee, drained and rinsed

Preheat the oven to 200°F.

Combine the wine, thyme, soy sauce, and lime juice in a small oven-safe saucepan, set over medium-high heat, and reduce to about 3 tablespoons, or until the liquid is almost syrupy.

Reduce the heat to low and whisk in the cream. Cook, whisking continually, for 1 minute. Add the butter, a few pieces at a time, adding additional butter before the last piece completely melts. Continue whisking until all of the butter has been added and the sauce has thickened enough to coat the back of a spoon, 6 to 7 minutes. Add the fish sauce and stir to combine. Place the soy butter in oven to keep warm.

Heat 1 tablespoon of the olive oil in a medium sauté pan set over medium-high heat. Once it shimmers, add the XO sauce and bok choy and sauté until the bok choy is heated through, 4 to 5 minutes. Season with salt and black pepper. Transfer the bok choy to an oven-safe dish and place in the oven to keep warm.

Wipe out the pan, add the bacon, and cook over medium-high heat until crispy. Remove the bacon to a paper towel–lined oven-safe plate, leaving the bacon fat in the pan. Set the bacon in the oven to keep warm.

Season the scallops on both sides with salt and pepper.

Return the pan to medium-high heat and add the remaining 1 tablespoon olive oil. When the oil shimmers, add the scallops and sear for 2 minutes. Flip and sear on the other side, just until cooked through, about 1 minute. Remove the scallops to an oven-safe plate and place in the oven to keep warm.

Add the ackee to the pan and gently toss just until heated through.

To serve, place 4 scallops in each of four shallow bowls along with one piece of bok choy. Spoon the soy butter over the top and garnish with the bacon and ackee.

STEAK FRITES
⟪with⟫ PLANTAIN CHIPS AND GREEN VINAIGRETTE

Imagine you are on the French Caribbean island of Martinique, an island that has produced a large portion of the French national soccer team. It's the afternoon, you're watching a local game. Your favorite team won and now you're out there celebrating. Soca, reggaeton, and French Afro beats fill the air. A food truck is there, the rum truck is there. Life is good, and steak and plantains is the dish you want to eat. It's casual, it's French, it's Caribbean, and it's delicious. (Note that you'll need to season the steak and let it sit at room temperature for 1 hour before cooking.)

ACTIVE TIME: *45 minutes*
START TO FINISH: *1 hour 15 minutes*
SERVES 2

GREEN VINAIGRETTE

1½ cups fresh parsley

½ cup blanched spinach

½ cup fresh cilantro

4 cloves garlic, smashed

1½ tablespoons red wine vinegar

½ Thai red chile, stemmed

½ teaspoon kosher salt

½ cup olive oil

Water, as needed

AIOLI

½ cup mayonnaise

1 tablespoon capers, drained

½ teaspoon freshly grated lemon zest

2 tablespoons chopped fresh dill

Kosher salt

PLANTAIN CHIPS

1 green plantain

Vegetable oil, for frying

Kosher salt

STEAK

2 (12-ounce) center-cut New York strip steaks

½ teaspoon salt

Freshly ground black pepper

2 tablespoons vegetable oil

For the green vinaigrette: Place the parsley, spinach, cilantro, garlic, vinegar, chile, and salt in a blender and blend until smooth. With the blender running, slowly add the oil and continue to blend until incorporated. If the sauce is too thick, add 1 tablespoon water until desire consistency. Transfer to an airtight container and set aside until ready to use.

For the aioli: Combine the mayonnaise, capers, zest, and dill in a small food processor and process until well combined. Taste and add salt as desired.

For the chips: Peel the plantain. Thinly slice, lengthwise, using a mandoline or vegetable peeler. Heat 1 inch of oil to 375°F in a large Dutch oven or other heavy pot set over medium-high heat. Place a paper towel–lined cooling rack in a baking sheet and set aside.

Gently place the "chips," a few at a time, into the hot oil and fry until golden and crispy, 3 to 4 minutes. Transfer to the prepared rack and season with salt.

For the steak: Season the steak on both sides with the salt and pepper to taste and set aside at room temperature for 1 hour.

Preheat the oven to 375°F.

Heat the oil in a large oven-safe sauté pan over high heat. When the oil shimmers, add the steaks and cook until golden brown on both sides, about 5 minutes total. Transfer the pan to the oven and cook steaks until medium rare, about 8 minutes.

Remove the steaks to a rack, cover, and rest for 5 minutes. Serve the steaks with the chimichurri sauce, along with the plantain chips and aioli.

> *"I remembered every single dish and every single bite that I'd ever had."*

GREGORY GOURDET

*Director of culinary operations
at Departure in Portland, Oregon*

*Developing a restaurant inspired
by Haitian cuisine*

Born in Brooklyn, New York

*Known for: Celebrating pan-Asian and
Haitian cooking*

At Departure in Portland, where Gregory Gourdet has been executive chef since 2010, the menus influenced largely by South Asian cuisines have hordes of fans. Peking duck dinners are sell-out events, while dishes like spicy wok-fried Brussels sprouts with mint and whole-roasted fish brightened with fresh citrus keep diners coming back.

When Gourdet hosted his first dinner service at the James Beard House—a bucket-list honor for many chefs—he cooked the food that made his name in the national press and on *Top Chef*. The late-summer menu featured tiger prawns with fermented pineapple, rib eye steak with ssämjang paste, and grilled squab with green mango dressed in rice vinegar.

A year later, when the James Beard House asked Gourdet to return, he was interested in serving the food he grew up eating but hadn't focused on professionally: Haitian cuisine. Dishes common to the big island's culinary table were in constant rotation at the spacious home in Queens.

"Rice and beans for sure," Gourdet name checks. "Kidney bean soup or julien sauce pois. Stew chicken—chicken that's been marinated with lime juice and Scotch bonnet chiles, garlic, thyme, cooked and braised with tomato paste. Griot— twice-cooked pork. You take a pork shoulder and marinate it with Scotch bonnets, onions, garlic, and scallions. Simmer until it's tender, then roast in the oven to get it crispy on the outside." They ate Haitian-style macaroni and cheese, which includes "a little bit of mayonnaise and it was the '80s so, Kraft cheese out of the box." Of course there were fried and boiled plantains, boiled yams, sweet potatoes, cassava, and taro root. Mornings were meant for hot chocolate spiced with star anise, cinnamon, and vanilla. The liquid comfort washed down polenta cooked with evaporated milk, Haitian vanilla, and warming spices.

Gourdet was born in Brooklyn, but his parents sent him to live with family on the island for a few years, while they got life in the States underfoot. Both his parents would go on to manage chemistry labs at a hospital and a college in New York City. At their house in Queens, the family had a pear tree and a garden that grew corn and tomatoes. Relatives from Haiti rotated in and out, many at the start of their own American journeys. Haitian Creole bounced off the walls and against the backdrop of a Catholic school education, and elders repeated adages about how to work hard and make sacrifices.

Attending a boarding school for high school in Middletown, Delaware, marked his first foray into non-Haitian cooking. "It was a beautiful, super quiet town, and if you have seen *Dead Poets Society*, then you know my school," he says. "I was so absorbed in everything else—being away, discovering my homosexuality. It wasn't until much later that I wanted to dive into my Haitian cuisine heritage." Almost twenty years later, in fact: It was following a pre-med stint at NYU, during an encounter with wildlife biology at the University of Montana where he ultimately graduated with a French degree. It was in Missoula that he started cooking for himself for the first time.

After college, he went to culinary school, then spent seven years in French-focused restaurants that increasingly looked to countries like China and Thailand to expand their repertoire. Gourdet's first chef position was at a Chinese-style restaurant. By the time he opened Departure he'd racked up thousands of airline miles and months abroad, traveling, eating, and cooking dishes from or inspired by Asia. So when a Beard House staffer asked Gourdet about cooking Haitian food for his next dinner, Gourdet realized he hadn't engaged with Haitian cooking the way he had with other cuisines. "I couldn't just go off memory."

Gourdet visited Haiti twice in one year where he spent time with family. He was pleased to realize he understood the Kreyòl. He recognized that the acid and heat that he loved in Southeast Asian dishes were present in the food of his childhood, too. "These were all the things I grew up eating: the chiles, the citrus, the coconut.

"Everything came back to me. I felt like I remembered every single dish and every single bite that I'd ever had. There's a dish, it's cornmeal that you cook into porridge with smoked herring, onions, and Scotch bonnet. You have it for breakfast. I hadn't had that dish in probably thirty years and you know, within the first bite, I was transported back to our kitchen in Queens."

A mural at the National Black Theater in New York

PORK GRIOT
«with» ROASTED PINEAPPLE AND PIKLIZ

Gregory is a Haitian chef—this is going back to his roots here. Griot—pork shoulder marinated with citrus and spices and then roasted and fried until fragrant and crispy—is a big food for the Haitian community. Pikliz are Haitian pickles that are used on so many things in their cuisine. I love to use pikliz on everything, not just Haitian dishes.

To make this dish come together, start by roasting the pork. Make the pikliz while the pork is in the oven, and then roast the pineapple and prepare the vegetables when the pork is set aside to cool. Assemble everything together after the pork crisps on the stovetop.

ACTIVE TIME: *35 minutes*
START TO FINISH: *About 11 hours,*
plus 3 days for pickling
SERVES 6 TO 8

PIKLIZ

3 cups julienned red cabbage

1½ cups shredded carrots

1½ cups thinly sliced cauliflower florets

1 Scotch bonnet (or habanero) chile, stemmed and julienned

1 tablespoon minced fresh ginger

3 sprigs fresh thyme

1 bay leaf

2 cups distilled white vinegar

1½ cups cider vinegar

1½ cups sugar

2 tablespoons honey

8 teaspoons kosher salt

PORK

1 cup orange juice

3 allspice berries

6 sprigs fresh thyme

½ tablespoon whole black peppercorns

4 cloves garlic, peeled

3 pounds boneless pork shoulder, cut into ½-inch cubes

Vegetable oil, for frying

VEGETABLES

1 tablespoon vegetable oil

2 red bell peppers, stemmed, seeded, and chopped

2 Scotch bonnet (or habanero) chiles, stemmed, seeded, and chopped

4 cloves garlic, minced

1 (2-inch) piece fresh ginger, peeled and minced

1 cup orange juice

2 tablespoons Worcestershire sauce

2 tablespoons blonde miso paste

1 teaspoon fresh thyme leaves

PINEAPPLE

1 teaspoon brown sugar

1 teaspoon chili powder

1 teaspoon ground cumin

1 teaspoon kosher salt

1 small pineapple

1 tablespoon unsalted butter, melted

Chopped fresh parsley, for garnish

For the pikliz: Place the cabbage, carrots, cauliflower, chile, ginger, thyme, and bay leaf in a 2-quart glass jar with a lid.

Combine both vinegars, the sugar, honey, and salt in a medium pot set over high heat and bring to a boil. Pour the mixture over the vegetables, seal with the lid, and refrigerate for at least 3 days. The quick-pickled vegetables will keep for up to 3 weeks in the refrigerator.

For the pork: Place the orange juice, allspice, thyme, peppercorns, and garlic in a blender and pulse four or five times to combine. Transfer to a large zip-top bag, add the cubed pork, and seal. Marinate in the refrigerator for 4 to 6 hours.

Preheat the oven to 250°F.

Remove the pork from the marinade and pat dry. Spread on a foil-lined baking sheet, cover, and roast for 2 hours, until tender. Set aside to cool.

Heat 1½ inches of vegetable oil in a large Dutch oven or other heavy, deep pot set over high heat and bring to 350°F. Carefully add the pork, 1 cup at a time, and fry until crispy, 2 to 3 minutes. Remove to a paper towel–lined dish to drain. Keep warm. Repeat until all pork is cooked.

For the vegetables: Cook the oil, bell peppers, chiles, garlic, and ginger in a medium sauté pan set over medium heat until the peppers are tender, 4 to 5 minutes. Add the orange juice, Worcestershire, miso, and thyme leaves and simmer for 10 minutes, or until the liquid reduces slightly.

For the pineapple: Preheat the oven to 375°F.

Combine the brown sugar, chili powder, cumin, and salt in a small bowl and set aside.

Peel the pineapple, then cut it in half lengthwise and remove the core. Brush the pineapple with the melted butter and sprinkle with the spice blend. Transfer to a baking sheet and roast for 30 minutes, or until the pineapple is just tender. Cool slightly and cut into ¼-inch cubes.

To serve: Toss the pork with the pineapple and pepper mixture and serve topped with chopped parsley and pikliz.

NEXT

HAITIAN BLACK RICE AND MUSHROOMS

The elegance of Haiti's cuisine often gets over-looked. And since the US doesn't trade with Haiti, and we often only hear about the country in the context of international aid, we miss out on all the incredible things this island country has to offer. It's unfortunate that we miss the deeper stories of this cuisine due to an American media focus on aid and hurricanes, which is why it's so important that we celebrate this food culture in its own right.

Americans don't eat Haitian food as much as we could, but that will change, I promise you. There's so much of Haitian food that brings you to a higher level, and this dish is an example. A rare black mushroom found in Haiti called djon djon darkens rice in the traditional preparation—here, we sub-stitute shiitakes and use squid ink for color. Eat up and revel in the complexity of Haitian cuisine. Every bite tells a story of both survival and culinary sophistication.

ACTIVE TIME: *30 minutes*
START TO FINISH: *1 hour*
SERVES 4 TO 6

3 tablespoons extra virgin olive oil

1 medium onion, diced

1 poblano chile, stemmed and diced

2 tablespoons minced garlic

1 tablespoon dried shrimp

2 teaspoons powdered sumac

2 teaspoons celery salt

1 teaspoon fermented shrimp paste

2 tablespoons squid ink

1 cup long-grain rice

2 cups lobster (or any seafood) stock, warmed

1 pound chopped shitake mushrooms

Preheat the oven to 375°F.

Heat 1 tablespoon of the oil in a 4-quart Dutch oven set over medium-high heat. When the oil shim-mers, add the onion and chiles and cook until the onion is translucent, 4 to 5 minutes. Add the garlic and cook an additional minute. Add the dried shrimp, sumac, celery salt, shrimp paste, squid ink, and rice and stir to combine. Add the stock and cover. Transfer to the oven and bake until the liquid has been absorbed and rice is tender, 25 to 30 minutes.

While the rice is cooking, heat the remaining 2 table-spoons oil in a medium sauté pan set over medium-high heat. When the oil shimmers, add the mushrooms and cook until they release their liquid and are golden brown, 4 to 5 minutes. Transfer the mushrooms to a food processor or blender and puree.

Add the mushroom puree to the rice, stir to com-bine, and serve.

INDEPENDENCE SOUP

Haitians often commemorate Independence Day on January 1 by eating Soup Joumou. While rebellion was ongoing throughout slavery, the Revolution began in 1791 and by 1804, Haitians had wrested control from the French. Black people in Haiti had been forbidden from eating Soup Joumou during enslavement, as the dish was a delicacy. Upon Independence, the dish became a symbol for Black Haitians' freedom. This is my take on it.

ACTIVE TIME: 45 minutes
START TO FINISH: 1 hour 15 minutes
SERVES 6

2 sticks cinnamon, toasted

1 tablespoon whole allspice, toasted

1 teaspoon whole cloves, toasted

2 tablespoons extra virgin olive oil

1 medium onion, coarsely chopped

1 teaspoon kosher salt

2 pounds fresh pumpkin, cubed

½ cup garlic puree

¼ bunch fresh thyme

1 teaspoon freshly grated nutmeg

3 cups vegetable stock

3 cups unsweetened coconut milk

Toasted Chestnuts (recipe follows), for serving

Chili-Nutmeg Oil (recipe follows), for serving

Place the cinnamon sticks, allspice, and cloves in a small muslin bag, tie, and set aside.

Heat the olive oil in a 6-quart Dutch oven or other heavy pot set over medium-high heat. When the oil shimmers, add the onion and salt and cook until the onion is translucent, about 5 minutes. Add the pumpkin and continue to cook for 3 to 5 minutes, until the pumpkin begins to brown slightly. Add the garlic puree, thyme, and nutmeg, stir to combine, and cook for 1 to 2 minutes.

Add the vegetable stock, deglazing the bottom of the pot. Add the sachet of spices and bring the stock to a simmer. Decrease the heat to maintain a simmer, cover, and cook, stirring occasionally, until the pumpkin is tender, about 1 hour.

Remove the sachet and add the coconut milk. Simmer for 5 minutes. Puree the soup, using an immersion blender or food processor, until smooth. Serve topped with toasted chestnuts and a drizzle of chili-nutmeg oil.

TOASTED CHESTNUTS

8 ounces chestnuts

2 tablespoons sugar

1½ teaspoons berbere seasoning

1½ teaspoons vegetable oil

½ teaspoon kosher salt

Preheat the oven to 400°F. Combine the chestnuts, sugar, berbere, oil, and salt in a small mixing bowl and toss to combine. Spread the chestnuts on a baking sheet lined with parchment paper and bake for 10 to 15 minutes, until the nuts are browned and the sugar has created a syrup. Cool the nuts and then coarsely chop. Set aside until ready to use.

CHILI-NUTMEG OIL

1 tablespoon red pepper flakes, toasted

1 teaspoon freshly grated nutmeg

½ cup vegetable oil

Place pepper flakes and nutmeg in a heat-proof glass jar with a lid. Heat the oil in a small saucepan over high heat and bring just to a simmer. Gently pour the oil over the chile flakes and nutmeg, then let steep for 1 hour. Cover and store at room temperature until ready to use.

"You can never stop learning. That's the beauty of being a chef."

NINA COMPTON

Chef and owner of Compère Lapin and Bywater American Bistro in New Orleans, Louisiana

Took second place in Top Chef: New Orleans

Born in Gros Islet, St. Lucia

Major influences: Her granny, her father, Sir John George Melvin Compton, a former prime minister of St. Lucia, and a collection of old Caribbean cookbooks

When Nina Compton opened Compère Lapin in 2015, a New Orleans fine dining restaurant inspired by her native St. Lucia, she was deferential to the restaurants that preceded her. "There were so many heavyweights that have been open for 100 years," Compton says. "I didn't want to cause too many ripples in the water." She'd fallen hard for the city while competing on *Top Chef* two years earlier, recognizing its mixed cultural aesthetic as reflective of home.

Named for the Creole title of a Caribbean folktale rooted in West African oral history, Compère Lapin merges Compton's French and Italian culinary training with flavors from her island country. The result is dishes like curry goat with sweet potato gnocchi, dumplings mixed with tender hunks of meat in a spicy stew. She pairs escovitch snapper, a standard of countless Caribbean restaurants, with carrot beurre blanc. Her cow heel soup, tied to another folktale, is among her more personal dishes, rich with the flavor of the roasted, gelatinous beef. "Compère Lapin was me digging deep on things that I grew up with," she says.

As a young girl, Compton was her grandmother's kitchen companion. A white English woman who met and married Compton's Black St. Lucian grandfather during World War II, she adapted to staples like dasheen, a root vegetable in the yam family, and salt fish. "I'd watch her cook British classics, but then she'd cook island foods like flying fish," Compton says. Her grandmother served it pan-fried with parsley sauce and lemon juice; the next meal might shift course to accra, a fritter often made with salted cod, or black-eyed peas.

Compton attended a boarding high school in Kent, England, and made the reverse cultural adjustment of her grandmother's, trading tropical ingredients for mushy peas and fish and chips. As she got older, she noticed she marked home visits to St. Lucia with food, sharing small bites and afternoon beverages with her family.

"I could make something and people actually enjoyed it. I was sixteen. That stuck with me." Compton told her mother she wanted to become a chef. "She was like, 'Why do you want to be a chef?' It's too stressful! You're gonna work long hours, you're gonna be in the heat, you're gonna burn yourself,

NEXT

you're gonna cut yourself.'" Compton cooked in Jamaica, Miami, and New York in prestigious kitchens. Her time with chef Norman Van Aken showed her that fine dining could include the foods of her childhood, like conch and yuca, presented in new ways.

She also saw that shaping her path as a professional demanded a better understanding of her past. She dove into old Caribbean and African cookbooks and talked extensively with chefs in the American South to learn how they cooked their grits and treated their okra. The South was full of geographic, cultural, and culinary diversity she could learn from, just as cooking in Jamaica taught her things she couldn't learn in St. Lucia.

Research was important "because it stems from not where we are right now, but where we came from, and tracing it back to Africa. Rice and grains and okra—treating those things with respect is very important. That's where the conversation should begin." At Bywater American Bistro, the cozy sister restaurant to Compère, Compton and her team add to this history. Tucked in a former rice mill, one signature dish adapts jerk chicken as a brothy bowl of shredded meat with rice and butter beans with a hit of spicy heat. "You go to Jamaica and the jerk chicken is completely charred and they give you a piece of a white bread. That's it. And I love that," Compton says. "But I can't put a jerk pit outside the restaurant. So we give people something similar where they know the flavor, but it's a little different."

Casks of housemade hot sauce inside Compère Lapin on Tchoupitoulas Street in New Orleans

CASSAVA DUMPLINGS
《with》 CALLALOO PUREE

We all know Black women have been the backbone of American food. We also know about the queens Sylvia Woods and Leah Chase, whose restaurants in Harlem and New Orleans paved the way for all of us cooking Black food in America today. Let me introduce you to the next generation of royalty: Nina Compton is everything. She really is. Young and ambitious, she works her butt off. Her moment is now and she's crushing it. When I see her in action, I see the fruits of Leah's efforts. Nina is living in New Orleans and people just know she's going to carry Leah's culinary torch forward. This dumpling dish is inspired by Nina living in Nola and being an island girl.

Callaloo greens are extremely flavorful with the yucca dumplings. It's incredible comfort food from the West Indies. And if you're not West Indian, it's just plain good.

ACTIVE TIME: *25 minutes*
START TO FINISH: *About 2 hours*
SERVES 4

CALLALOO PUREE

1 tablespoon olive oil

1 tablespoon unsalted butter

1 shallot, sliced

2 cloves garlic, minced

½ habanero chile, seeded and diced

¼ teaspoon kosher salt

1 (19-ounce) can callaloo greens, drained and rinsed

½ cup unsweetened coconut milk

DUMPLINGS

8 ounces yucca, peeled and cut into uniform 2-inch pieces

1 tablespoon olive oil

1 teaspoon kosher salt

1 large egg, beaten

¾ cup all-purpose flour, plus extra for rolling

2 tablespoons unsalted butter

Grated Parmesan cheese, for serving

For the callaloo puree: Heat the olive oil and butter in a medium sauté pan set over medium-high heat. When the butter melts, add the shallot, garlic, habanero, and salt and cook until the shallot is translucent, 2 to 3 minutes. Add the greens and cook until they are heated through, 3 to 4 minutes.

Transfer the greens to a blender, add the coconut milk, and puree. Keep warm until ready to serve.

For the dumplings: Place the yucca in a medium saucepan, cover with water by 1 inch, and bring to a boil over medium-high heat. Cook until the yucca is tender, about 30 minutes. Transfer the yucca to a paper towel–lined dish and set aside to dry for 10 minutes.

Place the yucca in the bowl of a food processor, add the olive oil, salt, and egg, and puree until smooth.

Transfer the yucca to a medium mixing bowl, add the flour, and knead with your hands until the dough is smooth. If the dough sticks to your fingers, add more, a little at a time, until the dough no longer sticks.

Turn the dough onto a lightly floured surface and knead until slightly stretchy, about 5 minutes. Cover and set aside to rest for 45 minutes.

Divide the dough into four pieces and roll each piece into a snake-like rope about ½ inch wide. Cut into ½-inch pieces.

Bring a large pot of water to a boil over high heat. Add the dumplings in batches and cook until they float to the surface, about 3 minutes. Transfer the dumplings to a parchment-lined baking sheet and keep warm.

Melt the butter in a large sauté pan set over medium-high heat. Add the dumplings and cook until golden brown, 2 to 3 minutes.

To serve: Toss the dumplings with the callaloo puree and serve with Parmesan cheese.

ROASTED CAULIFLOWER STEAKS
≪with≫ NOLA EAST MAYO

This dish was inspired by Nina's home of New Orleans, where the ingredients in this tasty mayo sauce reflect the city's diverse African, Haitian, and French populations. And now the east side has a growing Vietnamese community as well. When I eat a dish like this, it makes me happy. I imagine a brass band, a second line, the Neville Brothers, and Lil Wayne. My stomach is nodding along with the music. This dish pairs perfectly with Jollof Rice (page 65).

ACTIVE TIME: *20 minutes*
START TO FINISH: *55 minutes*
SERVES 4

1 cup mayonnaise

¼ cup minced dill pickle

2 tablespoons minced onion

1 tablespoon sambal oelek

1 teaspoon fish sauce

¼ teaspoon celery salt

¼ teaspoon paprika

1 large head cauliflower, tough outer leaves removed

2 tablespoons olive oil

1 tablespoon ras el hanout

½ teaspoon kosher salt

Place the mayonnaise, pickle, onion, sambal, fish sauce, celery salt, and paprika in a small bowl and whisk to combine. Cover and set aside.

Preheat the oven to 375° F.

Do not remove the stem of the cauliflower. Set the cauliflower on the counter and slice from top to bottom into four 1-inch-thick steaks. Reserve any florets that remain or have fallen apart for another use.

Lay the four steaks on a baking sheet. Brush all sides with olive oil and evenly sprinkle with the ras el hanout and salt. Roast 30 to 35 minutes, until golden brown and cooked through.

Serve with the mayo.

"Food is my lens, but people are my focus."

SHAKIRAH SIMLEY

Director, Office of Racial Equity, for the city and county of San Francisco, California

2017 Exchange fellow at the Stone Barns Center for Food and Agriculture and former community program manager at Bi-Rite Market

Born in New York, New York

Known for: Using food as a tool for resistance

When South Bronx–born, Harlem-raised Shakirah Simley moved to California a year after college, she was clear on one thing: "Food is political," she says.

That the Ivy League graduate would forgo law school to head west to do "organizing work" took time for her East Coast family—five generations in NYC—to absorb. But the foundation for Simley's outlook had been laid early on. "I was close to my maternal grandmother who was part of the Black Panther Party, a licensed social worker in New York who helped victims of domestic violence and substance abuse." Simley had come to see access to food as an issue of justice. "When my mom was growing up, my grandmother would make things from scratch and not buy processed foods." But Simley's childhood was different. There was a dearth of affordable fresh foods in Uptown Manhattan. At home, the focus was on quantity, convenience, and time.

"I learned very young how to stretch a dollar. We ate franks and beans, spaghetti, baked ziti, roast chicken if we were fancy . . . a lot of packaged and processed foods. Rice-A-Roni, cereal, Hamburger Helper. We did the best that we could." Her grandmother was diagnosed with cancer and passed away about six months later. "We tried to keep her to a healthy diet of fresh fruits, low-sodium foods, but [the options] in her neighborhood grocery stores

didn't allow her to maintain that diet," Simley says.

It wasn't until she moved to California that Simley realized she'd never shopped at a farmers' market. "I became more attuned to the seasons." A perfect meal for her now is marinated chicken thighs, roasted veggies, and an herb and tomato salad with olive oil and burrata.

Simley has become a nationally heard voice for social change and food justice. For nine years, she owned Slow Jams, where her small-batch locally sourced jams and preserves supported urban and organic farmers. While coordinating citizen engagement for the City of San Francisco's Public Utilities Commission, she was awarded a fellowship at New York's Stone Barns Center for Food and Agriculture. There, she blended her knowledge of farming with "agroequity," an idea that recognizes the shadow that slavery casts over agriculture, with an intent to create equity, real ownership, and investment in one's food system.

After graduating from the University of Pennsylvania, and before her move to California, she became a Fulbright Scholar at the University of Gastronomic Sciences in Pollenzo, Italy. There, she earned a master's on how food and class impact the eating habits of lower-income immigrants in northern Italy. "One of the sites of my research was

a halal butcher literally on the periphery of town where the brown and Black folks lived. There was this focus on Italian food, which was borderline xenophobic, but when I was there, people didn't have parlance around what that meant. Why is this pasta dish any more important than the couscous?"

In 2016, she formed Nourish|Resist, a women-led Bay Area organization that through food, teaches youth and people of color to organize and fully own their political power by means of protests, teach-ins, and other direct actions confronting discriminatory policies. For Simley, this is no intellectual exercise. Policy decisions affect real people. They affected her family.

"It was really interesting when Pathmark opened on 125th [Street] and then on 145th where we lived. It was like: Who is this grocery store for? It was slightly more expensive than CTown, where we'd been going." She noticed that the new store had better tended shelves and it comprised the ground floor of a condo development. "The neighborhood got a much-needed amenity only because it was an anchor for gentrification. A Starbucks opened across the street. The landscape started to change, and so did the people," Simley says. "The things that my grandmother and her colleagues fought for started to happen, but who were they for?"

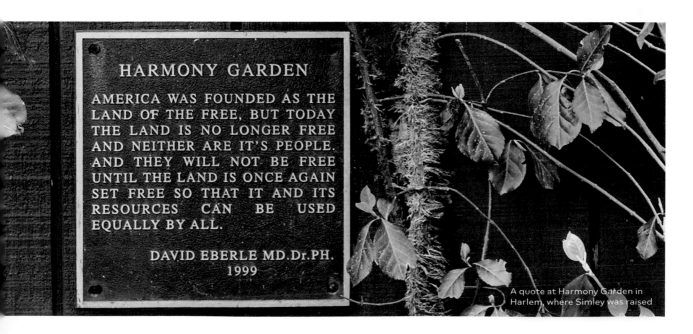

A quote at Harmony Garden in Harlem, where Simley was raised

TOMATO AND PEACH SALAD ≪with≫ OKRA, RADISHES, AND BENNE SEED DRESSING

The heirloom tomato might be the most fascinating food ever. They can be yellow, purple, pink, green, black, and white. They're ugly and have strange names like Arkansas Traveler, Cherokee Purple, Mortgage Lifter, Mexico Midget, Black Russian, and Box Car Willie, but they all have a family story. They have, in fact, been "open pollinated," meaning these old varieties were pollinated by breezes and bugs and passed down through generations of a family because of their unique and appreciated characteristics. Instead of being bred and manipulated for mass market, they are grown for their juiciness and taste. If someone had broken the chain, these cherished tomatoes would have been lost forever. Shakirah worked with Dan Barber at Stone Barns, which celebrates and preserves heirloom produce. What I love about this recipe is that the tomato, peaches, and radishes create sweet and bitter flavors.

ACTIVE TIME: 20 minutes
START TO FINISH: 25 minutes
SERVES 4 TO 6

½ pound fresh okra, stemmed and halved lengthwise

2 tablespoons extra virgin olive oil

½ teaspoon kosher salt

Freshly ground black pepper

1 ear corn

1 medium ripe heirloom tomato, cut into ½-inch wedges

3 medium peaches, plums, or any stone fruit, pitted and cut into ½-inch wedges

4 radishes, thinly sliced

1 shallot, thinly sliced

2 tablespoons fresh dill leaves

2 tablespoons fresh mint leaves

¼ cup fresh parsley leaves and tender stems

½ cup Benne Seed Dressing (page 284)

Combine the okra, oil, salt, and pepper to taste in a medium bowl and toss to coat. Heat a medium cast-iron skillet over high heat until hot. Add the okra in a single layer and cook until dark and lightly charred in spots, about 6 minutes. Remove the okra from the heat and allow to cool.

Cut the kernels off the cob into a large mixing bowl. Add the okra, tomato, peaches, radishes, shallot, dill, mint, and parsley and toss to combine. Add the dressing and gently toss. Taste and adjust seasoning as desired.

"I wish my grandmother could have seen how influential she was with her food, so much so that I committed my life to the same thing."

STEPHEN SATTERFIELD

Co-founder of Whetstone Media in San Francisco, California

Combines his experiences as a former sommelier, server, culinary student, and writer

Born in Atlanta, Georgia

Host of the podcast Point of Origin

When he's feeling poetic, which is often, Stephen Satterfield refers to himself as an "origin forager." He travels the globe to document the small, often unsung communities that grow or cultivate the food and drink that makes its way around the world. His mission is to promote empathy—to use stories about the things we eat to uncover what we often miss about one another.

His platform is Whetstone Media, an independent company led by people of color and women, created to tell stories that the mainstream outlets can't or won't see. One of Whetstone's short films takes Satterfield to an active 400-year-old vineyard not far from the Turkish border in Georgia. On his podcast, *Point of Origin,* he treats listeners to an exploration of geothermic salt in Icelandic foodways as easily as he talks with chef BJ Dennis (page 202) about Gullah Geechee culture in Charleston. In the quarterly magazine *Whetstone,* coconuts are a touchstone for Puerto Rican writer Von Diaz's family and readers learn about the annual saffron harvest in Iran.

That such a broad embrace of history comes from someone who acknowledges the gaps in his own narrative is perhaps exactly how it should be. "It's a similar story for so many Black people in this country, which is understanding our identity through this [Western] region and having little specificity for our arrival in this region," Satterfield says. He describes the suppression of memory common in many Black families, combined with the forced displacement of Black people from their origin cultures as parts of a history that can be almost "too painful to look at."

But Satterfield does look back. His grandmother and his father shared a special bond over cooking. "Every Sunday we'd go to her house after church.

The kids are all spiffy from church, I had the clip-on bow tie, heavily starched off-the-rack clothes, shiny like a penny from having Vaseline rubbed on my face." His father cooked for large church functions with 200 people, making fried fish, chicken, and cornbread. "If my mom was in charge, it would be canned tuna, a tuna salad. When my dad was cooking, he would make spaghetti and meatballs, collard greens, mac and cheese. We had hushpuppies a lot. He would smoke ribs. He would really throw down; that's his true love language."

Satterfield learned to speak the language of food, too. He attended culinary school in Portland, Oregon, then transferred to a hospitality and managerial program to learn about wine. "That's what took my love of food to a whole new level...understanding wine as a language and an accessory to eating." He became a sommelier two years later. After working at top-rated restaurants in the Northwest, he launched a nonprofit in Atlanta to support Black-owned wineries in South Africa by generating greater market access through distribution and direct-to-consumer sales. It was a meaningful way to integrate his politics into his work.

After a few years, challenging the history of apartheid through winemaking led to burnout. He moved to California, worked on a friend's farm, and took up serving for a while. Satterfield brought his restaurant colleagues to local farms and documented those experiences. He wanted to tell fuller stories about the sacrifice and resources that result in a beautifully plated dish and came up with Whetstone. It's a big idea meant to celebrate diverse food stories presented by diverse storytellers, shifting the nature of food media. And so, the man consumed with beginnings, the origins of food stories, is positioned with an eye on the future.

The John Lewis Mural in Atlanta

NEXT

SPICE-ROASTED BLACK COD AND CARROTS ⟨*with*⟩ BENNE SEED DRESSING

When I think about benne seeds, I think about Afro beats, with a base of Fela Kuti (Africa's answer to the artist Prince) and hip-hop combined. Benne seeds were brought along with other imported foods from West Africa to the Carolinas during slavery. Enslaved people planted benne in various areas of the South. Today, the seeds are still used to make stews and soups like Stephen's ancestors did hundreds of years ago. These seeds were ground to a paste to thicken the stew but also added flavor.

Today, we get to build on tradition and use a seed that was once eaten out of necessity as a base for dynamic riffs on classic dishes.

ACTIVE TIME: *15 minutes*
START TO FINISH: *45 to 50 minutes*
SERVES 4

2 tablespoons chopped fresh herbs, any combination of basil, parsley, thyme, and rosemary

1½ teaspoons kosher salt

1 teaspoon Urfa pepper flakes

½ teaspoon berbere seasoning

½ teaspoon ground cardamom

½ teaspoon ground coriander

1 pound carrots, cut into 3-inch-long batons

½ cup Benne Seed Dressing (page 284)

4 (6-ounce) black cod fillets, skin on

2 scallions, sliced thinly on the bias

Preheat the oven to 375°F.

Place the chopped herbs, salt, Urfa pepper, berbere, cardamom, and coriander in a small bowl and stir to combine.

Place the carrots and 2 tablespoons of the benne seed dressing in a medium bowl and toss to coat. Add half of the spice-herb mixture and toss to coat. Place the carrots on a baking sheet in one layer and roast for 10 minutes.

Meanwhile, brush the fish with 2 tablespoons of the dressing and sprinkle evenly with the remaining spice-herb mixture. Set aside at room temperature.

Toss the carrots and move them to the edges of the pan. Place the fish, skin side down, in the center of the pan. Return the pan to the oven to bake for another 20 to 25 minutes, until the fish is just cooked through and the carrots are tender. Drizzle the remaining ¼ cup dressing over the fish and carrots, garnish with the scallions, and serve immediately.

> *"When I make food, people are happy.*
> *This is what I can do to contribute, to be accepted."*

TAVEL BRISTOL-JOSEPH

Pastry chef and partner at Emmer & Rye in Austin, Texas

Voted a Rising Star Pastry Chef in 2017

Born in Georgetown, Guyana

Known for: Artful, sophisticated desserts, and a love for mass-produced candy

Tavel Bristol-Joseph's cooking effortlessly glides from comforting and simple to whimsical and imaginative: At his restaurant Emmer & Rye, diners find Guyanese-style roti made with fresh-milled wheat, or koji egg cream with coriander or bay leaf. Growing up in Georgetown, in a community where folks struggled to make ends meet, food wasn't a source of creativity or a pathway to find oneself, Bristol-Joseph says. Dinner, in a place where meals could be spotty, was survival. "It would be rice, sugar, milk powder from the government, mixed up in a bowl. Or—we don't have any food—so I gotta climb the coconut tree. Or go to my neighbor, probably steal a guava, and that's dinner. We ate a lot of rice because that's cheap."

For many in 1980s Guyana, perched on the northern tip of South America, the quest for economic flexibility meant moving abroad, often to the United States. Bristol-Joseph's mother emigrated to the US without him when he was about ten months old; years later his father followed, leaving a six-year-old Bristol-Joseph with relatives. Within a year, his father had been killed in New York, a victim of a drug encounter gone bad. Before his sudden death, his father had filed paperwork to request a visa for his son, but this change in circumstances meant Bristol-Joseph would stay put in the two-bedroom house with his grandparents, six of their children, and his cousin.

As a teenager, he moved in with a family friend who was like an aunt—her mother and Bristol-Joseph's grandmother were best friends growing up. Auntie's household was different. The kids went to the best schools in Guyana. His aunt made what the Guyanese call cook-up rice for dinner with coconut milk, scallions, and meaty bits, from beef to chicken feet. "Throw it in there, cook the rice, bring everything up in a boil, then season with chiles. Add peas, spinach, anything you want. It's like a Guyanese version of a jambalaya," he says.

Other nights, there'd be pepper pot, an India-influenced dish with different meats and hints of cinnamon. His aunt baked cookies, pine tarts (triangular pie dough filled with pineapple jam in the center), and cheese rolls. She always had a sweet fruit drink in the refrigerator, and she'd place a pound cake on the dining table just in case someone came over. Cake made from scratch, available all the time—*just in case.*

"It was a bittersweet situation," Bristol-Joseph remembers. The contrast between his early childhood and his new circumstances made him resentful. He was incredulous at what he missed out on, and what so many others took for granted. He'd had to fight kids for money so he could eat; it surpassed his teenage understanding that others never had to consider such limited choices. He began to perform poorly in school and when he missed curfew, his aunt would make him assist her baking the next day as punishment. In Guyana, toward the end of high school, students choose a trade-focused course of study. Bristol-Joseph opted for home economics: "I know that I know how to bake," he says laughing.

When Bristol-Joseph's mother came back to Guyana for his high school graduation, they stopped at the US Embassy. His paperwork to move to America was approved and within two weeks, they headed to Brooklyn. He graduated culinary school with a pastry arts degree, then worked at New York's River Café and the W Hotel's Blue Fin. While working in Tucson as an executive pastry chef, he met his future business partner, Kevin Fink. Bristol-Joseph moved to Austin to launch Emmer & Rye in 2016, where they mill the heritage grains used there. Now he gets to think creatively about food and be playful—black garlic ice cream, roti with curry, a dark and dense black rum cake, white Sonoran wheat chocolate chip cookies with Texas pecans. Food, for Bristol-Joseph, is still a means to survive. But these days it's a path to explore and celebrate, too.

COCONUT FRIED CHICKEN
«with» SWEET HOT SAUCE AND PLATANOS

Guyana is in South America; the language is English; the culture is Caribbean; and it's a cultural mix of Chinese, indigenous Guyanese, African, and European. Tavel is a product of all of that. Coconut was a recurring motif in his early life, when he sometimes climbed coconut trees for breakfast. In this recipe, coconut milk is key to making delicious fried chicken, and the hot sauce packs a ton of flavor in the sweetness of the honey layered with the mole. The platanos and hot sauce also make a great snack on their own.

ACTIVE TIME: *50 minutes*
START TO FINISH: *3 hours*
SERVES 4 TO 6

1 cup mole verde

2 (14-ounce) cans unsweetened coconut milk

8 boneless, skinless chicken thighs

2 tablespoons soy sauce

1 cup plus 1 tablespoon unsweetened coconut flakes

½ teaspoon garlic powder

2 teaspoons white pepper

1 teaspoon ground cumin

1 teaspoon ground cinnamon

1 teaspoon ground coriander

1 teaspoon kosher salt

1 cup panko breadcrumbs

1 cup rice flour (or all-purpose flour)

2 tablespoons honey

Vegetable oil, for frying

2 ripe plantains, black with some yellow

Place ¾ cup of the mole verde and 1 can of the coconut milk in a large mixing bowl and whisk to combine. Add the chicken and toss to coat. Cover and refrigerate for at least 2 hours, or up to 4 hours.

Remove the chicken from the marinade and transfer to a large saucepan. Add 2 tablespoons of the remaining mole verde, the remaining 1 can coconut milk, the soy sauce, 1 tablespoon of the coconut flakes, and the garlic powder. Bring to a simmer over medium-high heat. Decrease the heat to maintain a low simmer and cook for 15 minutes, or until chicken is partially cooked through. Remove the chicken from the pot, shaking off excess sauce, and set aside.

Continue to cook the coconut milk mixture until it has reduced by half. Set aside and keep warm.

Combine the white pepper, cumin, cinnamon, coriander, and salt in a small bowl.

Place the remaining 1 cup coconut flakes, the panko, and rice flour in a large zip-top bag. Add two-thirds of the seasoning mix and shake to combine. Add the chicken, a few pieces at a time and shake to coat. Remove the chicken to a baking sheet and cover until ready to fry.

Combine the honey and remaining 2 tablespoons mole verde in a small bowl and set aside.

Heat 1 inch of oil in a large Dutch oven or other heavy pot to 350°F.

Cut the plantains into 1-inch pieces on the bias and toss with the remaining seasoning mix. Add four or five plantain pieces at a time to the oil and fry for 4 to 5 minutes, until golden brown. Transfer to a paper towel–lined plate and keep warm. Repeat until all plantains have been fried.

Add the chicken to the oil, a few pieces at a time, and cook until golden brown and cooked through, 5 to 6 minutes, turning halfway through cooking.

Drizzle the chicken and plantains with the honey sauce and serve with the reduced coconut sauce alongside.

OXTAIL PEPPERPOT
≪*with*≫ DUMPLINGS

Oxtail is one of my favorite meats and I like it best when it has been slow-cooked for hours, so I recommend cooking it the day before and letting it sit overnight. What makes this dish so homey and delicious is the mix of the oxtail and the dumplings, which everyone can relate to as being an example of comfort food at its finest.

This traditional Caribbean dish—mostly from Guyana—is made by stewing meat in a dark, rich gravy flavored with cinnamon, brown sugar, hot chiles, and *cassareep*, a special brown sauce made from cassava root. African Americans adapted the recipe using oxtail instead of offal, which are the internal organs of butchered animals. Regardless, this is a dish that only gets better with time in the pot.

ACTIVE TIME: *1 hour*
START TO FINISH: *3½ hours, plus time for rice and peas*
SERVES 4 TO 6

OXTAIL

1 (4-pound) piece oxtail

1½ teaspoons kosher salt

1 teaspoon freshly ground black pepper

½ cup vegetable oil

2 carrots, peeled and diced

1 onion, diced

21 cloves garlic, minced

7 tablespoons minced ginger (3-inch piece)

2 plum tomatoes, diced

2 scallions, sliced

1 Scotch bonnet (or habanero) chile, stemmed and chopped

3 sprigs fresh thyme

7 tablespoons brown sugar

2 tablespoons soy sauce

2 tablespoons ketchup

1 tablespoon whole allspice berries

6 cups chicken stock

DUMPLINGS

2 cups all-purpose flour

2½ tablespoons cornmeal

1 teaspoon kosher salt

½ cup plus 2 tablespoons water

Rice and Peas (recipe follows), for serving

(Continued)

For the oxtail: Season the oxtail on all sides with the salt and pepper. Heat ¼ cup of the oil in a large (8-quart) Dutch oven set over medium-high heat. When the oil shimmers, add the oxtail and brown on both sides, about 15 minutes.

Remove the oxtail to a paper towel–lined dish. Heat the remaining ¼ cup oil in the Dutch oven and add the carrots, onion, garlic, ginger, tomatoes, scallions, chile, thyme, brown sugar, soy sauce, ketchup, and allspice and stir to combine. Return the oxtail to the pot, add the chicken stock, and bring to a simmer. Reduce the heat to maintain a simmer and cook, covered, for 2½ hours, or until the oxtail is tender and the meat is falling away from the bone.

For the dumplings: Place the flour, cornmeal, and salt in a medium bowl and stir to combine. Add the water and use your hands to work the mixture into a dough ball. Knead the dough in the bowl for 2 to 3 minutes. Divide the dough in half and cover one half with a damp towel.

Continue to knead one dough ball for 5 minutes, or until smooth. Roll the piece of dough into a 21- to 24-inch snake-like piece. Cut the dough into 1-inch pieces, set on a baking sheet, and cover with a damp towel.

Repeat with remaining dough ball.

Stir the dumplings into the oxtail stew for the last 30 minutes of cooking time and cook until dumplings are tender and cooked through.

Serve the stew with the rice and peas.

RICE AND PEAS

ACTIVE TIME: *25 minutes*
START TO FINISH: *2 hours (plus soaking beans overnight)*
SERVES 6 TO 8

8 ounces (1 cup) dried red beans	1 tablespoon finely chopped fresh ginger
2 tablespoons extra virgin olive oil	1 Scotch bonnet (or habanero) chile, stemmed and seeded
1 small onion, cut into medium dice	3 sprigs fresh thyme
1 cup diced green bell pepper	1 bay leaf
½ cup diced red bell pepper	2 quarts chicken stock
1 stalk celery, diced	1 (14-ounce) can unsweetened coconut milk
1 teaspoon kosher salt	2¼ cups long-grain rice
2 tablespoons minced garlic	

Place the beans in a pot, cover with water by 2 inches, cover, and let sit overnight.

Drain the beans and rinse under cool water.

Heat the oil in a large Dutch oven set over medium-high heat. When the oil shimmers, add the onion, green and red bell pepper, celery, and salt. Cook, stirring frequently, until the onion is translucent, 4 to 5 minutes. Add the garlic and ginger and continue cooking for 1 to 2 minutes, until the garlic is fragrant.

Add the beans, chile, thyme, bay leaf, stock, and coconut milk. Stir to combine and bring to a simmer. Decrease the heat to maintain a simmer, cover, and cook until beans are just tender, 1½ to 2 hours.

Add the rice and stir to combine. If necessary, increase the heat to bring to a simmer. Decrease the heat to maintain a simmer, cover, and cook until the rice is tender, about 25 minutes.

Taste and adjust the seasoning as desired. Serve with the oxtail.

SMOKED VENISON
≪with≫ ROTI AND PINE NUT CHUTNEY

I have a lot of experience with venison because I grew up eating it. People don't always associate game meat with Black people, but it has always been a part of Black cooking heritage, especially since we have been farming and living in rural areas forever. Tavel, who started his career as a pastry chef, has lived a life steeped in Caribbean culture. He now lives in Texas, where hunting game and smoking meat is part of the culture. When you step back and take in the total artistry of Tavel's cuisine, it feels like hip-hop—a little bit from here, a little bit from there, everything moving to an incredible beat. That's what makes this such a fitting dish.

Beef is an easy swap for the venison, but look for that game meat flavor if you can find it.

ACTIVE TIME: 35 minutes
START TO FINISH: 3 hours
SERVES 4

12 ounces venison fillet, cleaned (or beef rib eye)

4 tablespoons extra virgin olive oil

1 tablespoon jerk sauce

4 juniper berries, crushed

1 cup applewood chips

1 bay leaf

1 tablespoon water

2 tablespoons unsalted butter

¼ fresh pineapple, peeled, cored, and finely diced

1 clove garlic, minced

1 finger chile, stemmed and finely diced

¼-inch piece fresh ginger, peeled and finely diced

1 teaspoon jerk seasoning

2 large egg yolks, lightly beaten

1 teaspoon Dijon mustard

Pine Nut Chutney (recipe follows), for serving

Freshly grated horseradish, for serving

Roti (recipe follows), for serving

Place the venison, 2 tablespoons of the olive oil, the jerk sauce, and 2 juniper berries in a zip-top bag and seal. Massage the bag to distribute the marinade. Marinate in the refrigerator for 2 hours. Remove from refrigerator and allow to sit at room temperature while preparing the smoker.

Preheat a grill to high.

Place the remaining 2 juniper berries, the wood chips, bay leaf, and water in a metal box or metal pie pan large enough to hold the chips and the venison. Place a small cooling rack to the side of the chips, so when you add the venison it is not directly on the bottom of the pan. Cover with foil and place on the grill and smoke for 10 minutes.

Remove the venison from the marinade and pat dry. Lift the foil on the smoker, move the chips to one side, and lay the venison on the rack beside the chips. Cover with foil, decrease the heat to low, and smoke for 10 minutes. Turn off the heat and let sit on the covered grill for 30 minutes.

Finely dice the venison and set aside.

Heat the remaining 2 tablespoons olive oil and the butter in a medium sauté pan set over medium-high heat until the butter melts. Add the pineapple, garlic, chile, and ginger and sauté until the garlic is tender, 2 to 3 minutes. Remove from the heat and stir in the jerk seasoning. Set aside to cool to room temperature.

Combine the smoked venison, pineapple chile mixture, egg yolks, and mustard and mix until well combined.

For each serving, pack about ½ cup of the mixture into a small, 2- to 3-inch ring mold and unmold in the middle of a plate. Gently top with chutney and a grating of fresh horseradish and serve immediately with roti.

ROTI

ACTIVE TIME: *5 minutes*

START TO FINISH: *45 minutes*

MAKES ABOUT 20 ROTI

⅔ cup water

1 tablespoon vegetable oil, plus extra for cooking

2 tablespoons unsalted butter

1 tablespoon finely chopped fresh cilantro

½ teaspoon ground turmeric

½ teaspoon ground cumin

1 teaspoon kosher salt

2 cups all-purpose flour, plus extra for rolling

Bring the water to a boil in a small saucepan. Remove from the heat and add the oil, butter, cilantro, turmeric, cumin, and salt and stir to combine and cool slightly.

Place the flour in a medium bowl, add the butter mixture, and stir with a spatula until the dough just comes together. Using your hands, knead the dough 4 to 5 minutes, until it becomes smooth and pliable. Divide the dough into 20 to 25 golf ball–size pieces and roll into rounds.

On a lightly floured surface, roll out each ball to a 4- to 5-inch round. In the meantime, heat a sauté pan or griddle to medium-high and lightly brush the surface with oil. Cook each roti for 1 minute on each side, or until golden brown and puffed in spots. Adjust heat to maintain 1-minute cooking time for each side. Transfer to a towel-lined plate or dish and cover to keep warm.

PINE NUT CHUTNEY ≪with≫ HONEY

ACTIVE TIME: *40 minutes*

START TO FINISH: *About 1½ hours*

MAKES 2½ CUPS

2 tablespoons extra virgin olive oil

¼ cup pine nuts

¼ cup sesame seeds

1 teaspoon garam masala

1 teaspoon turmeric

½ teaspoon kosher salt

4 slices bacon, finely chopped

2 poblano chiles, seeded and finely chopped

2 cloves garlic, minced

1-inch piece fresh ginger, finely chopped

6 dates, pitted and finely chopped

6 dried apricots, finely chopped

2 tablespoons raisins

Freshly grated zest and juice of 1 orange

½ cup red wine

¼ cup balsamic vinegar

2 tablespoons honey

1 tablespoon brown sugar

1 tablespoon adobo paste

1 tablespoon chopped fresh cilantro

Heat the oil in a medium, high-sided sauté pan set over medium heat. When the oil shimmers, add the pine nuts, sesame seeds, garam masala, turmeric, and salt. Cook, stirring continually, until the seeds and nuts turn golden and are aromatic, 3 to 4 minutes. Transfer to small bowl and set aside.

To the pan on the heat, add the bacon, chiles, garlic, and ginger and sauté until golden brown, 5 to 7 minutes.

Add the dates, apricots, raisins, orange zest and juice, wine, vinegar, honey, brown sugar, and adobo paste. Return the nut and seed mixture to the pan and stir to combine well. Decrease the heat to low and simmer for 45 minutes, or until the fruit is soft and plumped and the liquid has been absorbed.

Remove from the heat and stir in the cilantro. Taste and season with salt as desired.

QUICK SALTED SALMON
≪with≫ CARROT BROTH AND MUSHROOMS

Let's talk about Adrienne for a second: She's got grit and a hard-core work ethic. You can't mess with her. She was brought up on the South Side of Chicago, where she studied ballet. She's full of elegance and grace. She lives in Harlem and worked at Le Bernardin. She was on *Top Chef* and founded the Sunday Best series of dinner parties. But I knew her best when she was my executive chef at Red Rooster. Adrienne's what's next.

This dish is light, crisp, and delicious, and works best with sushi-quality, grade-A salmon.

ACTIVE TIME: *45 minutes*
START TO FINISH: *1 hour*
SERVES 4

SALMON

1 (12-ounce) fillet sushi-grade salmon, sliced into ¼-inch-thick slices

1 teaspoon kosher salt

CARROT BROTH

1 cup carrot juice

Juice of 1 lemon

2 tablespoons rice wine vinegar

1 tablespoon soy sauce

1 tablespoon olive oil

1 teaspoon ají amarillo paste

AVOCADO CREMA

1 avocado, pitted and peeled

1½ tablespoons yuzu juice

½ teaspoon yuzu kosho

½ cup extra virgin olive oil

1½ tablespoons crème fraîche

Kosher salt

MUSHROOMS

1 tablespoon olive oil

2 cups sliced shiitake mushrooms

½ medium cucumber, peeled, halved, and sliced into ¼-inch-thick half-moons

4 radishes, quartered

1 tablespoon soy sauce

Chopped cilantro, for garnish

Tortilla chips, for serving

For the salmon: Lay out the salmon on a plate and sprinkle with the salt. Set aside for 10 minutes.

For the carrot broth: Combine the carrot juice, lemon juice, vinegar, soy sauce, olive oil, and ají amarillo in a blender and blend to combine. Set aside.

For the avocado crema: Place the avocado, yuzu juice, kosho, and salt in a small food processor and process to combine, stopping to scrape down the sides of the bowl as needed. With the processor running, slowly add the olive oil and then the crème fraîche. Taste and add salt as needed.

For mushrooms: Heat the oil in a medium sauté pan over medium-high heat. When the oil shimmers, add the mushrooms and cook, stirring frequently, until they give up their liquid and begin to brown slightly, 7 to 8 minutes. Add the cucumbers, radishes, and soy sauce and toss to combine. Remove from the heat.

To serve: Divide the avocado crema evenly and spread on the bottom of each of four shallow bowls. Top the crema with half of the mushroom mixture. Place the salmon on top, then the remaining mushrooms. Gently pour the carrot broth around the salmon. Garnish with chopped cilantro and serve with tortilla chips.

CRISPY CAROLINA MILLET SALAD
≪with≫ COW PEAS

Millet is an ancient grain that has been a staple in Asia and Africa since forever. If you go to West Africa, it's part of everyday life, as common as white flour, but many people in the United States gave millet no nevermind, seeing it as merely birdseed. But stay woke on millet. It's gluten free, delicious, comforting, and versatile—smooth like oatmeal, crunchy like granola, and fluffy like rice. Millet can be used in place of grains like bulgur and quinoa, or couscous. Recently, scientists found a 4,000-year-old bowl of noodles made out of millet, which bolsters previous claims that millet was more important to the development of farming than rice.

ACTIVE TIME: *35 minutes*
START TO FINISH: *4 hours to overnight*
SERVES 6 TO 8

1 cup cooked Carolina Gold rice

½ cup dried cowpeas, soaked overnight

1 teaspoon kosher salt

½ cup water

½ cup apple cider vinegar

1 tablespoon sugar

1 teaspoon kosher salt

1 yellow beet, trimmed, peeled, and shredded

3 tablespoons vegetable oil

4 cups thinly sliced (¼-inch-wide) collard greens, tough stems removed

1 cup cooked millet

4 scallions, sliced

Benne Seed Dressing (page 284)

1 tablespoon toasted benne seeds

Spread the cooked rice on a parchment-lined baking sheet and allow to dry out for 4 hours, or up to overnight.

Combine the cowpeas and salt in a small saucepan and cover with water by 3 inches. Set over high heat and bring to a boil. Decrease the heat to maintain a simmer and cook until the cowpeas are tender, about 45 minutes. Set aside until ready to use, leaving the peas in their cooking liquid to prevent drying out.

Combine the ½ cup water, vinegar, sugar, and salt in a small bowl and stir until the sugar dissolves. Add the shredded beet and set aside at room temperature for at least 30 minutes, or up to 1 hour. Drain the beets and refrigerate until ready to use.

Heat the oil in a large, nonstick sauté pan set over medium-high heat. Once the oil shimmers, add the rice and spread evenly in the pan. Cook until the rice is crispy on one side and can be flipped, in sections, like a pancake, 4 to 5 minutes. Flip the rice and continue to cook until crispy on the other side, 2 to 3 minutes. Transfer the rice to a paper towel–lined baking sheet and spread out to cool.

Transfer the cowpeas with a slotted spoon from the cooking liquid to a large mixing bowl. Add the rice, beets, collard greens, and scallions and toss to combine. Add ¼ cup of the benne seed dressing and toss to combine. Taste and adjust seasoning as desired. Add more dressing as desired. Sprinkle with toasted benne seeds and serve.

SHELLFISH STEW ‹with› BLACK RICE

JJ is like my cuz. Not only is he my neighbor, but he's also brought so much to Harlem by creating jobs and opportunities as chef and owner of the brilliant Fieldtrip. We've done so much cooking together—from the South Beach Wine and Food Festival in Miami Beach to Harlem EatUp!. Right now, Uptown is doing such cool things on the food scene. Sometimes, I step back and check out what's going on around me. I look to the left and look to the right. I've got Melba on one side and JJ on the other. All of us are pushing and looking at the young chefs coming to Harlem. Aunt Sylvia and Roberta would be proud.

JJ's always looking beyond the culinary horizon. I know going back to Africa had a huge impact on him. When he studied there, he became deeply passionate about rice. This dish highlights his passion for rice and works as a side dish or main course. It works for a family reunion or a large gathering—perfect for JJ's life in Harlem with his young family. More than anything, he's an amazing dad to twins.

ACTIVE TIME: *55 minutes*
START TO FINISH: *2 hours*
SERVES 4 TO 6

GARLIC MAYONNAISE

1 tablespoon vegetable oil

3 cloves garlic, peeled

1 cup mayonnaise

1 tablespoon chopped fresh parsley

¼ teaspoon kosher salt

RICE AND SEAFOOD

1 medium delicata squash

7 tablespoons extra virgin olive oil

1¾ teaspoons kosher salt

1 cup black rice, soaked in water overnight

1¾ cups chicken stock

1 small sheet kombu

6 dried shiitake mushrooms

1 medium tomato, quartered

1 small onion, quartered

1 small green bell pepper, stemmed, seeded, and coarsely chopped

3 cloves garlic, peeled

16 littleneck clams, cleaned and rinsed

1 pound mussels, beards trimmed and cleaned

1 pound large shrimp, peeled and deveined

Juice of 1 lemon

¼ cup fresh parsley leaves

For the mayonnaise: Heat the oil and garlic in a small sauté pan set over low heat. Stirring frequently, cook until the garlic is soft, but not browned, about 10 minutes. Remove the garlic from the pan and smash to form a paste. Place the garlic, mayonnaise, parsley, and salt in a small bowl and whisk to combine. Refrigerate until ready to use.

For the rice and seafood: Preheat the oven to 375°F.

Cut the squash in half lengthwise and remove the seeds. Brush the flesh with 1 tablespoon of the oil and sprinkle with ½ teaspoon of the salt. Lay each half, cut side down, on a parchment-lined baking sheet. Roast for 35 to 40 minutes, until the squash is tender. Scrape out the flesh and set aside until ready to use.

NEXT

Bring the rice, stock, kombu, mushrooms and ½ teaspoon of the salt to a boil in a medium saucepan set over high heat. Decrease the heat to maintain a low simmer and cook until the rice is tender and the liquid is absorbed, about 20 to 30 minutes. Remove and discard the kombu and mushrooms and set the rice aside until ready to use.

Combine the tomato, onion, bell pepper, and garlic in a food processor and process until finely chopped.

Heat the remaining 6 tablespoons olive oil in a large skillet or 6- to 8-quart Dutch oven set over medium heat. When the oil shimmers, add the chopped vegetables and remaining ¾ teaspoon salt and cook for 7 to 8 minutes, until the onions are translucent and the liquid has reduced slightly. Add the rice and toss to combine and heat through. Add the squash, clams, mussels, and shrimp and toss to combine. Cover and transfer to the oven to bake for 10 to 15 minutes, until the clams open.

Squeeze lemon juice over the dish, garnish with parsley, and serve with the garlic mayonnaise.

The Women's Health Community Mural Project in Harlem

GOLD COCONUT BROKEN RICE
《with》 TAMARIND-GLAZED HALIBUT

I had the honor to cook with Maya Angelou in her house in the Carolinas, where there was always a rice pot on the stove. Listening to her talk about her life while swaddled in the smell of rice was one of the most moving experiences I've had. I didn't say a lot; I just listened, spellbound. I think about her when I cook with broken rice (aka rice grits; see page 292). Its risotto-like texture makes it a delicious matchup with a rich sauce. Here we pair it with halibut broiled with a tamarind glaze. For me, this recipe showcases both comfort and finesse, which is JJ's background. He's thrived in fast-casual and fine-dining kitchens.

ACTIVE TIME: *25 minutes*
START TO FINISH: *35 minutes*
SERVES 4

2 teaspoons kosher salt	1 cup unsweetened coconut milk
2 cups Carolina Gold rice grits	Nonstick spray
4 tablespoons unsalted butter	4 (4-ounce) center-cut skin-on halibut fillets
1 small onion, finely diced	Tamarind-Ginger Glaze (recipe follows)
2 cloves garlic, grated	4 scallions, sliced on the bias

Bring 4 cups water and the salt to a boil in a large saucepan. Stir the grits into the boiling water, reduce the heat to maintain a simmer, and cook until the rice is almost tender, about 20 minutes.

Heat 1 tablespoon of the butter in a small sauté pan set over medium heat. When the butter melts, add the onion and garlic and cook until the onion is translucent, about 5 minutes. Remove from the heat and set aside.

Once the rice is almost tender, add the onion mixture and coconut milk and heat through. Add the remaining 3 tablespoons butter and stir to melt. Cover and set aside until ready to serve.

Preheat the oven to the high broil function. Spray a small baking dish with nonstick spray. Add the halibut fillets to the dish and brush generously with the tamarind glaze. Place in the oven 5 inches from the broiler and broil for 5 to 6 minutes, until the fish is just cooked through.

Serve the grits topped with halibut, drizzled with remaining glaze, and garnished with scallions.

TAMARIND-GINGER GLAZE

ACTIVE TIME: *10 minutes*
START TO FINISH: *15 minutes*
MAKES ABOUT ½ CUP

2 tablespoons tamarind paste, seeds removed	2 tablespoons grated fresh ginger
2 tablespoons hot water	2 tablespoons rice wine vinegar
2 tablespoons fish sauce	2 tablespoons light brown sugar
2 tablespoons soy sauce	

Place the tamarind paste in a small bowl, add the hot water, and stir to combine. Set aside for 5 minutes.

Combine the tamarind mixture, fish sauce, soy sauce, ginger, vinegar, and brown sugar in a small saucepan and bring to a boil over medium heat. Cook until reduced to ½ cup, about 10 minutes.

BRUSSELS AND DRY SHRIMP

At Jonny Rhodes's Indigo in the Northside of Houston, his food interprets African and Black American history. From explaining to his customers the significance of yam and sweet potato to our culture's food, to his ideas of Afrofuturism, Jonny takes storytelling seriously. When I met him at Indigo to film *No Passport Required*, folks asked us if we were shooting a rap video. But I was there for Jonny. The shrimp paste in this dish pays homage to his adoptive Igbo parents who hail from Nigeria, where dried shrimp is a key ingredient in cooking.

ACTIVE TIME: *30 minutes*
START TO FINISH: *50 minutes*
SERVES 4

4 tablespoons extra virgin olive oil

2 tablespoons chopped dry roasted peanuts

2 tablespoons chopped egusi seeds

1 pound Brussels sprouts, trimmed and halved, or quartered if large

2 cups chopped broccolini

2 cloves garlic, sliced

1 tablespoon fermented shrimp paste

1 tablespoon soy sauce

1 tablespoon rice wine vinegar

2 teaspoons honey

1 teaspoon fish sauce

1 teaspoon Urfa pepper flakes

Heat 2 tablespoons of the olive oil in a large sauté pan set over medium heat. When the oil shimmers, add the peanuts and egusi and cook, stirring continually, until aromatic and slightly browned, about 5 minutes. Remove the peanuts and seeds to a paper towel–lined plate and set aside to drain.

Pour the remaining 2 tablespoons oil into the pan and add the Brussels sprouts, broccolini, and garlic. Sauté for 8 to 10 minutes, until some Brussels sprouts begin to brown slightly.

Add the shrimp paste, soy sauce, vinegar, honey, fish sauce, and Urfa pepper and simmer for 3 to 5 minutes, until the liquid reduces to a glaze and the Brussels sprouts are just tender.

Remove from the heat and stir in the peanuts and egusi. Serve immediately.

SHRIMP FRITTERS
≪with≫ BITTER GREENS AND GRAPEFRUIT

This West African–inspired dish features a perfect sour note of grapefruit, which celebrates the bitter in the greens. Try pink grapefruit, which will allow you to get both sweet and bitter tastes. The fritters provide texture and moisture. When all these flavors come together, the result is a very refreshing meal, perfect for hot weather.

ACTIVE TIME: *1 hour*
START TO FINISH: *1 hour*
SERVES 4

SHRIMP FRITTERS

Vegetable oil, for frying

2 tablespoons chopped fresh chives

2 cloves garlic, minced

2 teaspoons berbere seasoning

1 teaspoon miso

1 teaspoon fermented shrimp paste

¼ teaspoon kosher salt

1 large egg, beaten

½ pound chopped shrimp

¼ pound ground pork

¾ cup panko breadcrumbs

BITTER GREENS

2 teaspoons sambal oelek

1 teaspoon sugar

1 teaspoon fish sauce

1 teaspoon fermented shrimp paste

2 tablespoons peanut oil

1 tablespoon sesame oil

2 tablespoons chopped peanuts

2 cloves garlic, thinly sliced

1½ cups coarsely chopped mustard greens

1 cup diced green asparagus

½ cup fresh corn kernels

1 grapefruit, segmented over a bowl, juice and segments reserved

½ cup cubed (¼-inch) extra firm tofu

1 tablespoon chopped fresh mint, for garnish

1 tablespoon chopped fresh cilantro, for garnish

(Continued)

For the fritters: Heat 1 inch of vegetable oil to 325°F in a 4- to 6-quart Dutch oven set over medium-high heat. Place a cooling rack in a baking sheet and top with paper towels. Set aside.

Place the chives, garlic, berbere, miso, shrimp paste, and salt in a medium bowl. Use a fork to combine, mashing the shrimp paste so it is evenly distributed. Add the egg, shrimp, pork, and ¼ cup of the panko and mix with your hands.

Place the remaining ½ cup panko in a small bowl. Form the shrimp mixture into 12 golf ball–size pieces and roll in the panko to coat.

Gently place six of the fritters in the hot oil and fry for 4 to 5 minutes, until they are golden brown and cooked through. Transfer to the prepared cooling rack. Allow the oil to return to temperature and repeat with remaining fritters.

For the greens: Place the sambal, sugar, fish sauce, and shrimp paste in a small bowl and use a fork to mash and combine. Set aside.

Heat the peanut and sesame oil in a medium sauté pan set over medium-high heat. When the oil shimmers, add the peanuts and garlic and cook, stirring continually, for 1 minute. Add the sambal mixture, mustard greens, asparagus, and corn. Cook, stirring frequently, for 3 to 4 minutes, until the greens have wilted. Remove from the heat and add the grapefruit and its juice and the tofu and toss to combine and heat through.

To serve: Divide the greens mixture among four plates and top each with three fritters. Garnish with mint and cilantro and serve immediately.

ISLAND JOLLOF RICE

When I think of Eric's food, I think of the West African dance called the highlife, full of Afro beats and guitars and brass instruments. The syncopation of the music moves you. Eric and his wife have a catering company in DC, but most of America knows him from *Top Chef*. He represents the new African chef who gives a nod to the past, but also to the future. When you eat his food, you can taste that blend and complexity. He brings the African food tradition he grew up with into everything he does, and he does it in the most modern and beautiful way.

This rice dish is inspired by Eric and his Ghanaian roots. I eat it and hear the trap beats of "Pour Me Water," a big Afro beat song. It's layered and deliciously complicated in your mouth. Jollof rice is such a beloved dish that every West African takes ownership of it. Nigerians and Ghanaians especially squabble over who makes it better and where it was first created. Historians believe it was actually created in Senegal, but that doesn't stop the competition.

ACTIVE TIME: *1 hour 15 minutes*
START TO FINISH: *About 2 hours*
SERVES 6 TO 8

JOLLOF RICE

2 cups jasmine rice

3 tablespoons extra virgin olive oil

3 tablespoons chopped peanuts

3 slices turkey bacon, chopped

1 large red onion, diced

3 cloves garlic, minced

1 (1-inch) piece fresh ginger, peeled and finely chopped

1 Scotch bonnet (or habanero) chile, stemmed and minced

1 tablespoon tomato paste

1 teaspoon kosher salt

1 cup canned crushed tomatoes

1 cup shredded white cabbage

4 ounces smoked fish, such as mackerel or trout

1 carrot, diced

1 cup water

1 cup unsweetened coconut milk

1 bay leaf

2 sprigs fresh thyme

2 teaspoons curry powder

½ teaspoon cayenne pepper

1 teaspoon ground cumin

Juice of 1 lime

2 scallions, chopped

2 small tomatoes, chopped

1 tablespoon chopped fresh mint

1 tablespoon chopped fresh parsley

SPINACH

3 tablespoons red palm oil

1 red onion, chopped

2 cloves garlic, minced

1 (1-inch) piece fresh ginger, peeled and finely chopped

1 teaspoon kosher salt

1 boneless, skinless chicken thigh, chopped

1 red bell pepper, stemmed, seeded, and chopped

1 Scotch bonnet (or habanero) chile, stemmed and minced

1 teaspoon five-spice powder

1 cup canned crushed tomatoes

1 cup unsweetened coconut milk

1 teaspoon dried crayfish powder

4 ounces smoked fish, skin removed and coarsely chopped

2 cups packed spinach, chopped

2 cups packed mustard greens, chopped

(Continued)

For the rice: Place the rice in a colander or fine mesh strainer and rinse under cool water for 5 minutes, or until the water is clear.

Heat the olive oil in a large saucepan set over medium-high heat. When the oil shimmers, add the peanuts, bacon, onion, garlic, ginger, scotch bonnet chile, tomato paste, and salt. Cook, stirring frequently, for 3 to 4 minutes, until the onion is translucent.

Add the rinsed rice, crushed tomatoes, cabbage, smoked fish, carrot, water, coconut milk, bay leaf, thyme sprig, curry powder, cayenne pepper, and cumin. Stir to combine and bring to a simmer. Cover and decrease the heat to maintain a low simmer. Cook for 10 minutes, or until the rice is just tender. Remove from the heat and allow to sit for 20 minutes.

Remove the bay leaf, thyme sprig, and fish and discard. Stir in the lime juice, scallions, chopped tomatoes, mint, and parsley.

For the spinach: Heat the palm oil in a large saucepan set over medium-high heat. When the oil shimmers, add the onion, garlic, ginger, and salt. Cook, stirring frequently, for 3 to 4 minutes, until the onion is translucent.

Add the chicken, bell pepper, chile, and five-spice and cook, stirring frequently, for about 5 minutes, or until the chicken is cooked through.

Add the crushed tomatoes, coconut milk, crayfish powder, chopped smoked fish, spinach, and mustard greens and stir to combine. Decrease the heat to low and simmer for about 10 minutes, or until the greens are tender.

To serve: Top the rice with spinach.

STEAK AFRIQUE ⟨*with*⟩ SAUCE YASSA

Think about how often you see steak frites on a menu, any menu, anywhere in the world. What if one day steak Afrique held that spot?

Chimichurri brought great vibes to the steak frites dish and now it's commonly found on dining menus across the US; I hope yassa, popular in Senegalese cuisine and typically served with chicken, gets its place in the American spotlight, too.

ACTIVE TIME: *40 minutes*
START TO FINISH: *1 hour*
SERVES 2 TO 3

SAUCE YASSA

¼ cup vegetable oil

2 large yellow onions, sliced (6½ cups)

½ Scotch bonnet (or habanero) chile

1 tablespoon minced peeled fresh ginger (from 1-inch piece)

2 cloves garlic, sliced

2 tablespoons sherry vinegar

2 teaspoons lime juice

Kosher salt

STEAK

4 tablespoons unsalted butter

1½ pounds bone-in rib eye, cut about 1 inch thick, room temperature

Kosher salt and freshly ground black pepper

1 whole head garlic, halved crosswise

Large flake sea salt

For the sauce yassa: Heat a dry large skillet, preferably cast iron, over medium-high heat. Add the oil and onions and stir and sauté until softened, about 10 minutes. Reduce the heat and cook until the onions begin to caramelize to a nice deep golden brown, about 20 minutes. Add the chile, ginger, and garlic and cook until fragrant, about 2 minutes. Stir in the vinegar and lime juice and season with salt to taste. Spread the yassa on the bottom of your serving platter and set aside. Rinse and wipe out the skillet.

For the steak: Heat the butter in the same skillet over medium-high heat. Add the steak and sear to a nice golden brown on both sides, about 4 minutes per side. Continue cooking, turning every 2 minutes or so and basting with the pan juices and oil, for 8 to 10 minutes longer, until a deep brown crust forms and the internal temperature is a few degrees below your preferred doneness (120°F to 125°F for medium-rare). Add the garlic head, cut sides down, the last few minutes of cooking and sear in the pan juices until the cloves are golden brown. Move the steak to a board once it's done and allow to rest for at least 10 minutes before serving.

Cut the meat from the bone and slice 1 inch thick against the grain. Arrange the slices on top of the yassa and spoon some infused pan juices over the steak. Pop out the garlic cloves over the steak, sprinkle all with sea salt, and serve.

CITRUS-CURED SHRIMP
≪with≫ INJERA HANDROLLS AND AWAZE

Mariya Russell is a woman who has arrived, and folks are taking note. Mariya, most recently chef de cuisine of both Kumiko and Kikko in Chicago, has become the first Black woman to receive a Michelin star. We are so lucky to have a super talent like her: I'm inspired by all she has accomplished. Mariya, I'm so impressed with you, here's a dish in your honor. Go and get it!

This handroll features injera, an Ethiopian staple. The citrus marinates the shrimp, using a ceviche technique in which the acid in the orange, lemon, and lime "cooks" the shrimp. This recipe is loaded with texture and flavor. Serving it when the rice is still warm will make it taste even better.

ACTIVE TIME: 25 minutes
START TO FINISH: 1 hour
SERVES 4 TO 6 AS AN APPETIZER

1 pound shrimp (21 to 25 per pound), peeled, deveined, and tail removed

Juice of 1 orange

Juice of 1 lemon

Juice of 2 limes

½ cup julienne red onion

½ cup finely diced cucumber

1 jalapeño chile, seeded and finely diced

4 radishes, thinly sliced

1 avocado, pitted, peeled, and diced

2 tablespoons fresh cilantro leaves, coarsely chopped

Kosher salt

Injera (page 79)

1 sheet nori

Awaze (page 281)

1 cup cooked broken rice (see page 292)

Cut the shrimp into ½-inch pieces and place in a bowl with the orange juice, lemon juice, and half of the lime juice. Toss to coat. Cover and refrigerate for 25 minutes.

Drain the liquid from the shrimp. Add the remaining lime juice, the red onion, cucumber, jalapeño, radishes, avocado, and cilantro. Toss to combine. Taste and adjust seasoning as desired.

Cut the injera into 2- by 3-inch pieces. Cut the nori into 2- by 2-inch pieces. To eat, take a piece of the injera bread and top with a nori sheet, a teaspoon of cooked broken rice, then a tablespoon of the shrimp. Roll and eat. Use the awaze as a dip.

BANANA LEAF SNAPPER
«with» CHICKPEAS AND COCONUT RICE

During the 16th century, the Spanish enslaved hundreds of thousands of Africans in Mexico. That lineage persists today, with increasing numbers of Mexicans who identify as Black. Now, Black pride is on the rise and self-identified Black Mexicans such as this anonymous chef have successfully fought for recognition in the census. He works for my amazing friend in San Diego and wants to stay anonymous since he is an undocumented immigrant. You can see African influence in all facets of life in Mexico, and especially in Mexican cuisine, including the use of plantains, peanuts, taro, sweet potatoes, malanga, and cassava.

From Asia to Latin America, people have invented methods (casing, plating, wrapping, and even creating boats) to use enormous banana leaves. Grilled fish and other provisions, both spicy and sweet, are wrapped, enclosed, and even roasted inside the flexible leaf.

ACTIVE TIME: *45 minutes*
START TO FINISH: *1½ hours*
SERVES 4

SNAPPER

4 (6-ounce) snapper fillets

4 banana leaves (thawed, if frozen)

½ teaspoon kosher salt

8 sprigs fresh cilantro

8 sprigs fresh mint

2 cloves garlic, minced

1 (1-inch) piece fresh ginger, peeled and sliced

1 lime, cut into 8 slices

1 cup unsweetened coconut milk

COCONUT RICE

1 cup water

½ cup unsweetened coconut milk

½ teaspoon kosher salt

½ cup jasmine rice

CHICKPEAS

2 tablespoons extra virgin olive oil

2 jalapeño chiles, seeded and diced

2 cloves garlic, minced

½ teaspoon kosher salt

1 cup canned chickpeas, drained

½ teaspoon ground coriander

½ teaspoon ground turmeric

Juice of 1 lemon

2 tablespoons rice wine vinegar

1 tablespoon chopped fresh mint

1 tablespoon chopped fresh cilantro

½ cup unsweetened coconut flakes, toasted

(Continued)

For the snapper: Lay each fish fillet on a piece of banana leaf that is four times the size of the fillet. Divide the salt among the fillets and top each with two sprigs cilantro and two sprigs mint. Then divide the garlic and ginger evenly over the fillets, top each with two slices of lime, and pour ¼ cup of coconut milk over each. Wrap each fillet with its banana leaf. Set aside for 30 minutes.

Preheat the oven to 400°F.

Place the packets on a baking sheet and roast for 15 to 20 minutes, just until the fish is cooked through and flaky.

For the rice: Combine the water, coconut milk, and salt in a small saucepan set over medium-high heat and bring to a boil. Add the rice and stir. Decrease the heat to maintain a simmer, cover, and cook until the rice is tender, 20 to 25 minutes.

For the chickpeas: Heat the oil in a medium sauté pan set over medium-high heat. When the oil shimmers, add the jalapeños, garlic, and salt. Cook, stirring frequently, until the peppers are tender, 3 to 4 minutes. Add the chickpeas, coriander, turmeric, lemon juice, and vinegar. Cook until the chickpeas are heated through and the liquid has reduced to a glaze, 8 to 10 minutes.

Remove the pan from the heat and stir in the mint and cilantro.

To serve: Spoon the rice into four shallow serving bowls. Top with half of the coconut. Lay the fish fillets on top of the coconut, top with chickpeas, and finish each with remaining coconut. Serve immediately.

TUNA AND SCALLOP AGUACHILE

This aguachile, which translates as "chile water," reminds me of a dish I ate on the roadside south of Southern California in Tijuana, Mexico, en route to coastal Ensenada. This region features an incredible seafood scene. Aguachile is often mixed with cucumbers, chiles, and herbs.

ACTIVE TIME: *45 minutes*
START TO FINISH: *2 hours*
SERVES 4

PICKLED ONIONS

1 medium onion, julienned

½ cup freshly squeezed lime juice (from about 3 limes)

2 teaspoons Mexican oregano

RED AGUACHILE SAUCE

2 dried chiles de arbol, stemmed and seeded

4 Fresno chiles, stems removed

1 cup freshly squeezed lime juice (from about 6 limes)

1 tablespoon Worcestershire sauce

2 teaspoons Tapatío hot sauce

Kosher salt

8 sushi-grade scallops, sliced ⅛ inch thick

6 ounces sushi-grade tuna, sliced ⅛ inch thick

1 English cucumber, cut in half lengthwise, seeded, and thinly sliced into half-moons

4 teaspoons fresh cilantro leaves

Saltine crackers

For the onions: Place the onion, lime juice, and oregano in a small bowl and toss to combine. Cover and refrigerate for at least 2 hours before using.

For the aguachile: Place the chiles de arbol in a small sauté pan set over medium-high heat and toast until aromatic.

Remove the seeds from all but one of the Fresno chiles.

Place the chiles de arbol, Fresno chiles, lime juice, Worcestershire, and hot sauce in a blender or small food processor and puree until smooth, 1 to 2 minutes.

To serve: Place one-fourth of the scallops and tuna in each of four shallow serving bowls. Add ½ cup aguachile sauce, 2 tablespoons pickled onions, one-fourth of the cucumber, and 1 teaspoon cilantro leaves to each bowl and serve with saltines.

CHICKEN AND SHRIMP TAMARIND BROTH ⟪with⟫ RICE NOODLES

One of the bright young stars in the kitchen at Red Rooster is Tiana, who at twenty-four years old inspires me as an ambitious chef. She's got the skills, and you can see it on her YouTube channel and in her work at the restaurant. She's pushing through and I have no doubt that she's going to do great things. This dish is a riff on a traditional Filipinx broth, inspired by Tiana's Filipinx background. Tamarind is a common ingredient that likely originated in Africa, but is used in Indian and other Asian cuisines to make sauces, stews, and even desserts.

ACTIVE TIME: *35 minutes*

START TO FINISH: *About 3 hours*

SERVES 4 TO 6

½ pound (13 to 15) shell-on raw shrimp

1 (4-pound) whole chicken, rinsed

1 red onion, coarsely chopped

2 carrots, peeled and coarsely chopped

1 (1-inch) piece fresh ginger, peeled and sliced

4 cloves garlic, smashed and peeled

1 tablespoon white miso paste

1 tablespoon kosher salt

1 bay leaf

1 whole star anise

1 cup white wine

6 cups water

2 tablespoons tamarind paste

½ teaspoon fermented shrimp paste

8 ounces rice noodles

4 cups chopped mustard greens

¼ cup sliced scallions

4-minute eggs, for serving

Peel the shrimp. Place the shells in a 5- to 6-quart pot and reserve the bodies in the refrigerator until ready to use. Add the chicken, onion, carrots, ginger, garlic, miso, salt, bay leaf, star anise, wine, and water to the pot. Bring to a simmer over medium-high heat. Decrease the heat to maintain a bare simmer, cover, and cook for 2 hours.

Place the noodles in a large bowl and cover with cold water. Set aside for 30 minutes.

Remove the chicken from the pot and allow to cool slightly. Remove the thigh and leg meat from the bones and set aside. (Save the breast meat and carcass for another use.)

Strain the solids from the broth. Return the broth to the pot, add the tamarind paste and shrimp paste, and whisk to combine. Add the raw shrimp to the broth and cook for 3 minutes.

Drain the noodles and add them to the broth and shrimp along with the mustard greens and chicken leg and thigh meat. Stir to combine and heat through over medium heat.

Garnish each serving with sliced scallions and serve with a 4-minute egg alongside.

BIG OLE PORK CHOPS ⟨*with*⟩ D.R. MANGÚ

Patricia is this young kid who started working with us as an intern when she was eighteen through Careers through Culinary Arts Program (C-CAP), an organization that helps youth with careers in the culinary arts. Not two years later, she's already a part of menu planning, coming up with things that makes my hair stand back. Patricia acts as a young mentor to me, and sometimes I have to remind myself she's not even twenty. She tells me what's happening beyond food, but we also talk about what's happening right now. She shows me modern food that comes from the Dominican Republic—this isn't what her mom and auntie used to do. Also, she's surrounded by a woman-led kitchen, so she can see her progress around her. It's a great environment for women and C-CAP alums and I love the back and forth.

This recipe takes a pork chop, a New York restaurant staple, and brings it into Patricia's kitchen, adding a twist with this take on Dominican mangú, which is essentially a mix of mashed up plantains with a little butter, salt, and coconut milk.

ACTIVE TIME: *50 minutes*
START TO FINISH: *1½ hours*
SERVES 4

MANGÚ

¼ cup extra virgin olive oil

1 tablespoon unsalted butter

2 green plantains, peeled and chopped

1 small sweet potato, peeled and cubed

2 cloves garlic, chopped

1 small jalapeño chile, diced

1 teaspoon kosher salt

½ teaspoon fresh thyme leaves

½ teaspoon ground cumin

½ teaspoon chili powder

½ teaspoon whole cloves

1 cinnamon stick

½ cup unsweetened coconut milk

½ cup water

PORK CHOPS

4 (12-ounce) boneless pork chops

1½ teaspoons kosher salt

4 slices bacon, diced

3 cloves garlic, sliced

1 teaspoon fresh thyme leaves

½ pound fresh tomatoes, chopped

1 teaspoon ground turmeric

½ teaspoon ground cumin

Juice of 2 limes

½ cup unsweetened coconut milk

¼ cup crabmeat

(Continued)

For the mangú: Heat the olive oil and butter in a large saucepan or Dutch oven set over medium heat. When the oil shimmers, add the plantains, sweet potato, garlic, jalapeño, salt, thyme, cumin, and chili powder. Cook, stirring frequently, for 5 minutes, or until aromatic. Place the cloves and cinnamon stick in a sachet and add to the pot along with the coconut milk and water. Decrease the heat to maintain a simmer, cover, and cook for 45 minutes, or until the sweet potatoes are tender. Remove from the heat and use a fork to mash.

For the pork chops: Season the chops with ½ teaspoon of the salt. Set aside at room temperature.

Cook the bacon in a large sauté pan set over medium-high heat until crispy. Remove the bacon to a paper towel–lined plate and set aside. Add the pork chops, garlic, and thyme to the pan and cook for 5 minutes on each side, or just until the chops are cooked through. Remove the chops to a plate and tent with foil. Add the tomatoes, turmeric, cumin, lime juice, and coconut milk to the pan and stir to combine. Simmer for 5 minutes. Add the bacon and crabmeat and stir to combine. Return the pork chops to the pan and cook just to heat through.

Serve the pork chops over the mangú.

SALMON RILLETTES ⟨with⟩ INJERA

Almira has two kids, lives near Yonkers, and works at the Rooster. With all that travel and family responsibility, she still never fails to show up. Not just physically, but mentally as well. She's got her head in the game. When we throw her curve balls at the restaurant, she turns around and catches them. Almira is a quick learner who's not only passionate, but who also sees a path to her success and is doing everything she can to stay on it. Of course, she has a side hustle making cakes and running a pop-up. Watching her work, I think I'm looking at the next Pig Foot Mary—the legendary Black cook and entrepreneur from the early twentieth century. I'm rooting for her.

This dish is a nod toward Almira's hustle, and it's one that MC Solaar could rap about. The technique for the rillettes is French, and there's an African twist from the injera flatbread.

This is one of those "special effort" recipes that is totally worth it when you have friends you want to impress. If you find yourself running out of time, you can easily turn this dish into a much simpler affair by skipping the confit step. Once you've cured the salmon, simply chop it into ¼-inch pieces and toss with 2 tablespoons grapeseed oil, 1 teaspoon finely chopped fresh dill, ¼ teaspoon chopped fresh thyme leaves, and a pinch of salt. Serve alongside the injera and top with chives.

ACTIVE TIME: *1 hour*
START TO FINISH: *26 hours*
**SERVES 6 TO 8 AS AN APPETIZER*

SALMON CURE

½ cup kosher salt

½ cup sugar

1 bunch fresh dill

1 (1-pound) skin-on salmon fillet, pin bones removed

SALMON RILLETTES

5 sprigs fresh thyme

1 bay leaf

2 tablespoons Maldon salt

Grated zest of 1 lemon

1 quart duck fat, melted

Injera (recipe follows)

Fresh chives, for serving

(Continued)

Cure the salmon: Combine the salt and sugar in a small bowl.

Lay out a large piece of aluminum foil on the counter and top with a large piece of plastic wrap. Sprinkle half of the salt cure on the plastic wrap covering the shape and size of the salmon. Top with half of the dill. Lay the salmon on the dill and sprinkle with the remaining salt mixture and dill. Wrap the salmon first in the plastic wrap and then the foil. Place in a baking dish (in case of leaks), top with a heavy dish to weigh down the salmon, and refrigerate for 24 hours.

For the rillettes: Preheat the oven to 200°F.

Remove the salmon from the cure, rinse well, and pat dry. Place the salmon in a medium baking dish and add the thyme, bay leaf, salt, zest, and duck fat, making sure the salmon is completely submerged in fat. Cover with foil and bake until the fish is tender, flaky, and cooked through, about 1½ hours.

Remove the salmon from the duck fat and discard the skin and fat. Set aside the salmon to cool slightly. Transfer the flesh to the bowl of a stand mixer fitted with the paddle attachment. Blend the salmon on low speed for 25 to 30 seconds. With the mixer running on low speed, gradually add 1 cup of the duck fat and continue to mix until well combined.

Transfer the rillettes to a serving bowl or glass jar, cover, and refrigerate until ready to serve or up to 1 week.

Serve the injera with the rillettes, garnished with chives.

INJERA

ACTIVE TIME: 10 to 15 minutes
START TO FINISH: Up to 2 days
MAKES 9 (6-INCH) ROUND PIECES

1¾ cups water

1¼ cups teff or whole wheat flour

Place the water and flour in a large mixing bowl and stir to combine with your fingertips. Cover the bowl loosely with plastic wrap and set aside on a countertop overnight, or up to 2 days, or until the mixture begins to bubble.

Drain off and reserve the liquid that has settled on top. Stir the mixture and add back enough of the liquid to create a batter that is thinner than pancake batter, but slightly thicker than crepe batter.

Heat a small, 8-inch nonstick skillet over medium-high heat. Pour about 3 tablespoons batter into the pan and quickly lift and tilt the pan in order to move batter evenly over the bottom of the pan. Cook for 20 to 30 seconds, until bubbles appear and pop. Cover, turn off heat, and steam for 30 to 40 seconds. Carefully remove to a parchment-lined baking sheet.

Continue making injera, stacking them with a layer of parchment paper in between each piece.

Chapter 2

REMIX

Black cooking integrates many cultures and adapts to different ingredients, methods, and geographies.

IN HONOR OF:

ADRIAN MILLER, author, Denver, CO

Flaky Andouille and Callaloo Hand Pies
with Red Pepper Sambal

Hoja Santa Cheese and Chorizo Blue
Corn Grit Cakes

Chermoula Rainbow Trout with Slab Bacon

CHRIS WILLIAMS, chef, Houston, TX

Marinated Croaker Collars
with Citrus and Green Mango Salad

Lettuce Wraps with Tamarind-Ginger Roasted
Pork and Coconut-Spiced Rice

DEVITA DAVISON, activist, Detroit, MI

Crudités with a Carrot Double Dip

Grilled Piri Piri Shrimp
with Papaya and Watermelon Salad

Couscous and Roasted Figs
with Lemon Ayib and Honey Vinaigrette

NYESHA ARRINGTON, chef, Los Angeles, CA

Country-Style Spare Ribs
with Pickled Greens Slaw

Crab Curry with Yams and Mustard Greens

THERESE NELSON, writer and chef,
New York, NY

Roasted Carrots with Ayib and Awaze Vinaigrette

Pork and Beans with Piri Piri Sauce

TONI TIPTON-MARTIN, author, Baltimore, MD

Beets with Sage Leaf and Dukkah Spice

Tigernut Custard Tart
with Cinnamon Poached Pears

DARRELL RAYMOND, chef, New York, NY

Crab and Chile Chitarra Pasta

TRISTEN EPPS, chef, New York, NY

Seafood Stew
with Cassava Dumplings

ALEXANDER SMALLS,
restaurateur, New York, NY

Ayib and Sweet Potato Ravioli
with Berbere Spice Brown Butter

EDEN FESEHAYE,
home cook, New York, NY

Lamb Wat with Fries and
Cauliflower Cheese Sauce

KINGSLEY JOHN, chef, New York, NY

Bake and Shark Island Fish Sandwiches

MAYA HAILE SAMUELSSON,
model, New York, NY

Kitfo with Berbere Spice Brown Butter

Zaza's Doro Wat Rigatoni

TIFFANY JONES, chef, New York, NY

Good Vibes Curry Goat

Portland Parish Lamb Pie

YEWANDE KOMOLAFE, cook and author,
New York, NY

Okra and Creek Seafood Stew

Smoked Duck with Sorghum-Glazed Alliums

ecipes are rituals. They're more than an ingredient list and a series of steps. They're personal meditations, small celebrations. They connect us to loved ones we remember well and those we wish we had known. Recipes introduce us to cultures that are new to us, and they reflect our own histories in the lives of others.

In cooking, I appreciate not just the end result of a recipe, but the entire ritual of making it. If I can get my cooks to follow the *ritual* of making Swedish meatballs, or pounded yams, they won't get bogged down in the mechanics. Rather than obsessing over specific measurements or how long to run the food processor or how many times the pestle should hit the mortar, they'll focus on the consistency of the yam dough. Does it pull and release the way it should? They'll consider the meatball seasoning and make adjustments to get it right. When ritual is at the heart of following a recipe, that focus reveals itself in how the food looks, tastes, and how it makes the eater feel.

I often think about how recipes link us. As someone who's lived in different countries and is now raising a son in Harlem, a place far from where I grew up, I think of how recipes change as people move. They must. No matter how much we bring with us to our destination, something gets left behind and we inevitably adopt, adapt to, and bring our own change to what's around us.

Adaptation is one of the strongest skills a cook can have. As chefs we rely on it. When you can't get a certain ingredient, at first you're worried. Then you realize the dish tastes good without it, or something else turns out to be even better! There can be beauty in the challenge of not having an ingredient from your motherland, even if there's also a sense of loss. That's when cooking can reinterpret the original, making possible something that wasn't back home. During wars people roasted peanuts instead of coffee beans. Potato bread is great, but it started as an outgrowth of poverty. Salted cod was once a requirement in the Caribbean, but now it's a staple that cooks choose not to do without.

Black cooks in the United States have always adapted, both out of necessity as well as inspiration. Sometimes, as in my life, adapting recipes and rituals can be a way to create belonging. Last fall, my wife Maya and I celebrated Thanksgiving with our son. It's a holiday neither of us had grown up with, but raising Zion in the United States made us want to create a new family ritual. We had the typical staples that included stuffing and cranberry sauce. We made a traditional turkey, but to make the day our own, we served celebratory Ethiopian food too, like kitfo. The day after, we made a killer turkey curry that was loaded with heat and spice. That beautiful dark meat picked from the bones was so delicious in its new iteration. For my family, this practice is a way for us to make this holiday our own.

This chapter is about what can happen when recipes and rituals from different families, cultures, and experiences meet. And that evolution isn't just happening on the plate. I'm excited by the different paths to success in the food world as a writer, activist, or chef.

Adrian Miller is carving a new role in food scholarship. Chris Williams, whose great-grandmother Lucille was widely known for the hot roll mix she developed in the 1940s, interprets country cooking through a haute-cuisine lens in Houston. Nyesha Arrington's cooking in Los Angeles draws from family history in Mississippi and Korea. Devita Davison is redefining what African American cuisine means for herself—and as a way to build a more equitable food system in Detroit. And, inspired by the work of Edna Lewis, Therese Nelson created the Black Culinary History website to help tell the story of Black cooking. And Toni Tipton-Martin's work documents the centuries-long canon of Black cooking.

Things change yet keep a similar beat. That kind of remix gives me energy.

"If soul food is going to survive into the future, people have to make it at home. Any cuisine is in for the long haul when people make it at home."

ADRIAN MILLER

Author, Denver, Colorado

Executive Director of the Colorado Council of Churches

James Beard Award winner for Soul Food, *author of* The President's Kitchen Cabinet

Known as the Soul Food Scholar

When Adrian Miller completed his first book, *Soul Food: The Surprising Story of an American Cuisine, One Plate at a Time,* he'd eaten at 150 restaurants in 15 states and 35 cities. And as he likes to joke, he lived to tell the story. A self-proclaimed recovering lawyer whose interest in politics landed him a role in the Clinton administration, Miller turned his skill for research and narrative toward African American celebration food—the standout dishes curated from generations of agricultural and culinary expertise that followed Black people as they migrated throughout the US during the decades-long Great Migration. Miller's text is a go-to reference for food enthusiasts seeking a conversational yet grounded approach to the African influence on American cuisine.

Born in Denver, Colorado, Miller grew up in Aurora, a suburb just outside of the city. He recalls Saturday mornings in front of the television with his siblings, transfixed by the music and dance on *Soul Train,* the 1970s definition of cool blackness. Despite the appointment viewing, choir practice at Campbell Chapel African Methodist Episcopal Church began at 11 o'clock. Miller's parents refused to be late, which meant less time watching young folks sporting Afros and the latest moves. "It was always before the *Soul Train* line," Adrian recalls. "I always hoped we could stay."

Many middle-class African American families like the Millers enjoyed the reasonable house prices, wide streets, and well-funded public schools that governmental policies like redlining excluded them from in metropolitan centers. But a move to white-dominant suburbs, a result of white flight, could unintentionally sever a Black family's main link to culturally centered community life. The Miller tradition of participating in church life throughout the week served to keep those ties intact.

Miller's mother, Johnetta, a factory employee at Wonder Bread, ran the kitchen at home and her church family benefitted, too. Her food was sought out all year, from the "y'all come" Harvest Rally fundraiser, a potluck to help pay the church's winter heating bill, to the summer picnic. She baked cakes. She handled the grill. She made dressing. For dinners, soul food was the foundation: pot roasts, fried chicken, and fish on Fridays.

The family loved her "cannoli," a misnomer for what were actually calzones. "I don't know how the name thing happened, but we never fixed it," Miller says. Another favorite was smothered burritos in green chili, one way she interpreted the area's Mexican culture.

The nightly news guided conversations around the dinner table: Social justice. Racism. Political maneuverings that unraveled civil rights progress for Black folks. Miller's introverted father, who worked in a classified job at Rockwell International after serving in the Air Force, suddenly had a lot to say—"especially during the Reagan years," Miller recalls.

In 2017, Miller followed *Soul Food* with *The President's Kitchen Cabinet: The Story of the African Americans Who Have Fed Our First Families, from the Washingtons to the Obamas.* In the NAACP Image Award–nominated book, he celebrates the Black chefs, cooks, stewards, and butlers who've kept the First Families fed since the beginning of this nation. In his forthcoming book, *Black Smoke,* Miller pays homage to the history of American barbecue, another part of American cuisine that has often left out the Black innovators.

Miller still attends Campbell Chapel AME, his family church that was established in 1886. He still attends the Harvest Rally and now it's his recipe for chorizo blue corn dressing that's sought after by fellow parishioners.

The Blair Caldwell African American Research Library in Denver

Inside Blair Caldwell African American Research Library

Campbell Chapel AME Church, where Miller attends

FLAKY ANDOUILLE AND CALLALOO HAND PIES «with» RED PEPPER SAMBAL

In the Caribbean, callaloo can refer to the leaves of particular plants like the taro or amaranth, and the dish of greens stewed with broth or coconut milk and meat or fish as seasoning in the way many eat collard, mustard, or turnip greens.

These hand pies are flexible. You can fill them with anything you have on hand—sausage, fish, ham, veggies, even ingredients like fresh crab and chopped pumpkin.

ACTIVE TIME: *45 minutes*
START TO FINISH: *About 1 hour*
MAKES ABOUT 24 PIES

1 tablespoon extra virgin olive oil

10 ounces andouille sausage, cut into ¼-inch pieces

1 medium yellow onion, finely chopped

½ teaspoon kosher salt

¼ teaspoon freshly cracked black pepper

4 cloves roasted garlic, minced

1 teaspoon ground cumin

6 cups chopped fresh callaloo leaves and tender stems (from 1 bunch, or 3 cups frozen)

¼ cup unsweetened coconut milk

2 sheets puff pastry, defrosted

1 egg plus 1 teaspoon water, lightly beaten

Roasted Red Pepper Sambal (page 288)

Line a cooling rack with paper towels, set inside a baking sheet, and set aside.

Heat the olive oil in a large sauté pan set over medium heat. Once the oil shimmers, add the andouille and cook until warmed through and golden brown, about 3 minutes. Remove the andouille to a paper towel–lined plate.

Add the onion, salt, and pepper to the pan and cook until translucent, 3 to 4 minutes. Add the garlic and cumin and cook until fragrant, about 1 minute. Add the callaloo and cook until softened and wilted, about 5 minutes.

Add the coconut milk and simmer until the greens are softened and the liquid reduces completely, about 5 minutes. Transfer the cooked greens to the prepared cooling rack and allow to drain until completely cool. Once cooled, combine the greens with the cooked andouille sausage.

Preheat the oven to 400°F. Line two baking sheets with parchment paper.

Unfold one sheet of puff pastry onto a lightly floured surface. Use a lightly floured rolling pin to roll out to a rectangle, approximately 12 by 16 inches.

Cut the rectangle into three 4- by 16-inch strips using a sharp knife, then cut each strip into 4-inch squares. Place a heaped tablespoon of the filling a little off-center on each square. Fold each square over to form a triangle and press the edges together to seal tightly. Use a fork to crimp around the edges to further seal. Place the sealed pies on the prepared baking sheet.

Repeat the process of rolling, cutting, filling, and sealing with the remaining puff pastry sheet and callaloo filling.

Brush the tops of the hand pies with the beaten egg and use the fork to poke tiny holes in the top of each. Bake the pies until a deep golden brown, 15 to 20 minutes. Serve the pies warm with the red pepper sambal for dipping.

HOJA SANTA CHEESE AND CHORIZO BLUE CORN GRIT CAKES

If I do say so myself, this dish is delicious. The leaf hoja santa is native to Meso-America. In today's Central and South America, the leaf is known as yerba santa, Veracruz pepper, and Mexican pepper leaf. It's used in savory and sweet dishes, and the big, heart-shaped leaves are usually wrapped around meat, fish, and occasionally tamales. You can burn the wrapping for aromatic purposes, similar to burning incense. Its flavor has been likened to sassafras, mint, tarragon, and even eucalyptus. Hoja santa cheese was originally wrapped in the leaf. You can substitute for your favorite cheese.

This one's for Adrian in honor of the chorizo blue corn dressing he cooks for his church.

ACTIVE TIME: *40 minutes*
START TO FINISH: *2 to 3 hours*
MAKES 12 (3-INCH-SQUARE) GRIT CAKES

2 tablespoons extra virgin olive oil, divided, plus more for brushing

8 ounces fresh chorizo

½ cup sliced scallions (about 5 stalks)

4 cups chicken or vegetable stock

1 tablespoon unsalted butter, melted

1 teaspoon kosher salt

¼ teaspoon cracked black pepper

1½ cups blue corn grits

1 cup crumbled hoja santa cheese

Poached eggs, for serving

Hot sauce or Locust Bean and Chili Oil (page 286), for serving

Rub two 9-inch baking pans with 1 tablespoon of the olive oil.

Heat the remaining 1 tablespoon of olive oil in a saucepan over medium heat, and brown the chorizo for 5 to 6 minutes, breaking it up and crumbling into pieces. Add the scallions, stir, and remove from the heat. Strain off any excess oil and set aside.

Bring the stock, butter, salt, and pepper to a boil in a medium pot over high heat. Whisk in the grits, lower to a simmer, and cook, stirring frequently, until the grits are tender, about 25 minutes. Remove from the heat and fold in the chorizo mixture.

Pour the hot grits into one prepared baking pan. Spread the crumbled hoja santa cheese over the top and press down into the grits using a spatula. Allow the grits to cool completely.

Preheat the oven on the low broil setting and position a rack in the top of the oven.

Cut the grits into 3-inch squares and place in the second prepared baking pan. Make sure to leave about 1½ inches of space between each cake to toast evenly.

Generously brush the tops of each grit cake with olive oil. Place under the broiler and broil for about 3 minutes, until evenly browned and crispy along the edges.

Serve the grit cakes topped with a soft poached egg and a dash of hot sauce or chili oil.

CHERMOULA RAINBOW TROUT
≪with≫ SLAB BACON

Bacon and fish: You know it's good. The salty pork and the delicate fish are a perfect marriage. The chermoula adds a flavorful but not too spicy yum in your mouth and that's what makes the dish taste so good. Rainbow trout and slab bacon: Check yourself.

ACTIVE TIME: *30 minutes*
START TO FINISH: *1 hour*
SERVES 4

CHERMOULA

½ preserved lemon, flesh removed, brine rinsed off skin

3 to 4 cloves garlic, peeled

¼ cup fresh oregano leaves

½ cup fresh parsley leaves and tender stems

½ cup fresh cilantro leaves and tender stems

1 tablespoon Aleppo pepper

2 teaspoons coriander seeds, toasted and crushed

1 teaspoon cumin seeds, toasted and crushed

2 tablespoons fresh lemon juice

¾ cup vegetable oil

TROUT

4 (5-ounce) fillets rainbow trout or similar lake fish, skin on

Kosher salt and freshly ground pepper

8 ounces slab bacon, cut into ½-inch pieces

Lemon wedges, for squeezing

For the chermoula: In the bowl of a food processor, pulse the preserved lemon peel and garlic cloves until roughly chopped. Add the oregano, parsley, cilantro, Aleppo, coriander, and cumin and process until coarsely blended. Add the lemon juice and oil and pulse to combine into a roughly chopped puree. (Makes about 1 cup chermoula.)

For the trout: Season the fillets with salt and pepper and rub both sides generously with about 1 tablespoon of the chermoula. Allow to sit with the marinade while you cook the bacon and preheat the oven to 400°F.

Slowly render the slab bacon in a large oven-safe skillet over medium heat until crisp, 12 to 15 minutes. Remove the pan from heat. Transfer the bacon to a paper towel to drain and set aside.

To the bacon pan, add three-fourths of the remaining chermoula. Add the marinated fillets, skin side down, in a single layer. (The fillets should be allowed to rest in the liquid almost completely submerged.) Spoon some of the chermoula from the pan over the fillets. Place the pan in the oven and cook until the fish is opaque and pulls apart gently with a fork, about 10 minutes. Transfer the fillets with a spatula to a platter or individual plates. Pour the juices from the pan over the fillets.

To serve: Garnish the fish with a piece of the rendered bacon, a lemon wedge for squeezing, and any leftover chermoula.

"They're like, 'What is this? This isn't soul food.'"

CHRIS WILLIAMS

Chef-partner at Lucille's in Houston, Texas

Born in Houston, Texas

Major influence: His great-grandmother Lucille

Chris Williams and his brother, Ben, opened Lucille's, a cozy spot featuring modern takes on Southern classics, in Houston in 2012. Known for upscale renditions of pork with beans and whole-roasted gulf fish, the brothers named the restaurant for their great-grandmother Lucille Bishop Smith. Born in 1892 in Crockett, Texas, Smith navigated an ambitious path in food, setting fire to the limitations placed on Black women in the early twentieth century.

Williams grew up on stories about her determination and wit. Smith died in 1985 when he was seven. In addition to managing the food service at a central Texas girls camp for more than forty years, Smith launched a commercial food training program at Prairie View A&M College in 1937, one of the country's first such programs (she wrote the teaching manual). In 1941 she published *Lucille's Treasure Chest of Fine Foods,* a recipe card collection formatted as a tidy file box, still sought by collectors today. But Smith's most popular culinary legacy is her all-purpose hot roll mix, a recipe she developed in the 1940s. Hers was the first of its kind to be distributed in the United States, and a version of it, along with her famous chili biscuits, can be found at Lucille's.

"They're our best sellers," Williams says. Each biscuit, made with flour, sugar, and water, is dusted with grated American cheese, then served with a dollop of beef chili. Given what Williams could glean from Smith's cookbook and family lore, his recipes are as close as he can get them to Smith's version. "All chefs, especially matriarchs, they always leave something out," Williams says with a laugh.

Even if Smith didn't spill all her baking secrets, her entrepreneurial spirit kept Williams focused on the future during the restaurant's challenging early days. As a classically trained chef attempting to interpret country cooking through his haute-cuisine skills, Williams's vision didn't always resonate with early diners.

"My food is based on a Southern style," Williams says. "The braises, the slow cooking, the ingredients. But it also has huge influences from my experience." Williams spent a year at Le Cordon Bleu in Austin, and four years cooking professionally throughout Europe and in Washington, DC. He knew that the standard for high-quality dining was perceived to be French and Italian cuisine. Like many young African American chefs coming through culinary academies, Williams was frustrated that the cooking canon was so narrow. He knew that way of thinking about food was incomplete. Homestyle, Black, Southern cooking deserved to have as many interpretations as chefs could create.

When Williams drew initial criticism for his food at Lucille's he didn't hide his exasperation. "They're like, 'What is *this*? This isn't soul food.' You're so caught up in your expectations. You can't appreciate what's going on because you want to see what's in your head. My stuff didn't even have a chance with you."

A chicken pot pie for Williams can mean a chicken roulade served with creamy velouté sauce, and picture-perfect vegetables. He does a spin on the go-to recipe of his father, himself a talented home cook known for duplicating complex restaurant dishes for dinner. The original is a lightly breaded and fried bone-in pork chop topped with raw, sliced tomato and served with black-eyed peas and white rice. Even though Williams hated tomatoes as a boy, his dad's combination was magical to him. William's homage takes a braised shank in place of the chop and nestles it in a mixed-bean ragu, then drizzles it with a sweet and sour agrodolce.

Southern food is more than memory. And Black cooking is more than the usual favorites. "In a Southern kitchen, if you really look at it, the basis of American cuisine is us. The food has always been there. It's ours and I have every right to interpret it the way I want."

Lucille's in Houston, TX, named for Williams's great-grandmother

Lucille Smith's coveted recipe card collection, originally published in 1941

MARINATED CROAKER COLLARS
⟪with⟫ CITRUS AND GREEN MANGO SALAD

I love to cook with ingredients that might otherwise be discarded, like fish collars. If you're tempted to treat them as scraps, please don't throw them away or use them merely for a stock. They're delicious as the main focus of a dish—think of them as the spareribs of the sea. Here, croaker collars are marinated in citrus, chipotle, ginger, and fish sauce, and served with a mango salad full of funk, spice, and crunch.

ACTIVE TIME: *1 hour*
START TO FINISH: *2 to 3 hours*
SERVES 4

2 limes

2 lemons

2 oranges

⅓ cup extra virgin olive oil

1 chipotle pepper in adobo sauce, finely chopped

1 (3-inch) piece peeled fresh ginger, finely chopped

1 teaspoon plus 1 tablespoon chopped fresh cilantro

1 teaspoon fish sauce

4 (6-ounce) croaker collars (or snapper or cobia fillets)

1½ teaspoons kosher salt

1 green mango, pitted, peeled, and julienned

1 ripe mango, pitted, peeled, and julienned

1 tablespoon vegetable oil

1 shallot, minced

2 cloves garlic, minced

1 tablespoon dried shrimp, minced

1 bird's-eye chile, minced

½ cup peanuts, finely chopped

½ teaspoon chili powder

2 tablespoons unsweetened coconut flakes, toasted

6 fresh mint leaves, chiffonade

Juice 1 each of the limes, lemons, and oranges into a medium mixing bowl. Add the olive oil, chipotle pepper, ginger, 1 teaspoon of the cilantro, and the fish sauce. Whisk until well combined. Divide the marinade in half.

Place half of the marinade in a large zip-top bag. Season the fish with ½ teaspoon of the salt and add to the marinade. Seal and move the fish around to evenly coat. Refrigerate for at least 30 minutes, or up to 2 hours.

Segment the remaining lemon, lime, and orange and add to the marinade in the mixing bowl. Add the mangos and stir to combine.

Heat the vegetable oil in a small sauté pan set over medium-high heat. When the oil shimmers, add the

shallot, garlic, dried shrimp, chile, peanuts, chili powder, and remaining 1 teaspoon salt. Cook, stirring occasionally, until shallot is translucent and peanuts are browned slightly, 3 to 4 minutes. Transfer the mixture to the bowl with the mango and toss the salad to combine.

Bring 1 inch of water in a large pot to a simmer over medium-high heat. Remove the fish from the marinade and set in a steamer basket. Place the basket in the pot, cover, and steam until fish is cooked through, 8 to 10 minutes.

Garnish the fish with the coconut flakes, mint, and remaining 1 tablespoon of cilantro and serve with the mango salad.

LETTUCE WRAPS 《with》 TAMARIND-GINGER ROASTED PORK AND COCONUT-SPICED RICE

This recipe makes me wish I was chilling on a beach and eating a lettuce wrap with my hands. Tamarind and ginger enliven the roasted pork, which is wrapped in lettuce leaves with coconut rice.

Pick a pork shoulder with a good amount of fat. The fat helps to constantly baste the meat as it roasts and helps to ensure the meat turns out very tender. Most of it will drain off but you can pick off any remaining fat once cooked.

ACTIVE TIME: *40 minutes*
START TO FINISH: *6 to 8 hours*
SERVES 4 TO 8

TAMARIND-GINGER PORK

4 tablespoons vegetable oil

1 shallot, diced

1 (4-inch) piece fresh ginger, peeled and chopped

4 cloves garlic, chopped

1 tablespoon powdered shrimp (or fish sauce)

½ habanero chile, stemmed and seeded

½ cup tamarind puree

2 tablespoons honey

Kosher salt

1 whole (8- to 10-pound) bone-in Boston pork butt

2 tablespoons water

COCONUT-SPICED RICE

1½ cups water

1 cup unsweetened coconut milk

1 teaspoon good-quality turmeric powder

1 cup long-grain rice

4 scallions, sliced

Kosher salt

FOR SERVING

1 shallot, sliced

½ bunch fresh cilantro, leaves and tender stems picked

½ cup fresh mint leaves

1 head Bibb lettuce, leaves separated and washed

Marinate and roast the pork: Heat 1 tablespoon of the oil in a small saucepan over low heat. Add the shallot, ginger, and garlic and sauté until softened, about 3 minutes. Add the powdered shrimp and toast until just fragrant, about 1 minute. Add the chile, tamarind, and 1 tablespoon of the honey and cook, stirring frequently, until just beginning to simmer. Remove from the heat. Puree the ingredients using a handheld immersion blender until smooth. (Alternatively, if you don't have a blender, grate the ginger and garlic using a Microplane before adding, and mince the habanero chile.) Season the tamarind marinade with salt and divide evenly between two small bowls; cover one bowl and refrigerate.

Cut a crosshatch design into the pork shoulder: Use a very sharp paring knife to cut long parallel lines into the skin of the roast, spacing about ¾ inch apart. Try to cut through the fat completely without cutting into the meat itself. Repeat going the opposite direction cutting into the skin and fat to make a crosshatch pattern.

Rub the entire pork with half of the marinade, making sure to work it into all the nooks and crannies in the meat. Wrap the shoulder in plastic and refrigerate to marinate for at least 4 hours, or up to overnight.

Remove the pork from the refrigerator and allow to sit out for at least an hour to take the chill off. Preheat the oven to 275°F. Line a baking sheet with heavy-duty aluminum foil. Place the pork on a baking rack and place the rack on the foil. Slowly roast the pork, basting occasionally with the fat that drains off, until the meat is completely tender and pulling away from the bone when prompted with a fork, about 8 hours.

While the meat is cooking, combine the remaining tamarind marinade with the remaining 3 tablespoons vegetable oil, remaining 1 tablespoon honey, and the water. Stir in the sliced scallions and set the sauce aside.

Make the rice: In a small saucepan, combine the water, coconut milk, and turmeric powder. Add the rice and a pinch of salt and bring to a simmer over medium heat. Reduce the heat to low and cook until the rice is tender and all the liquid is evaporated, 15 to 18 minutes. Remove from the heat and fluff with a fork.

When the meat is done, let it rest at room temperature for at least 30 minutes. Using two forks, pull the roast pork into chunks and toss with ¼ cup of the reserved tamarind sauce.

Divide the rice among four bowls and top with a healthy helping of the roast pork. Garnish with sliced raw shallots, cilantro, and mint leaves. Peel off whole lettuce leaves and wrap individual leaves around the rice and pork to make a roll. Serve with the sauce for dipping.

Reserve the leftover pork to serve throughout the week in sandwiches, over the fonio, sorrel, and roasted fig salad (page 102), or with rice, topped with a soft poached egg.

> *"I'm still very much rooted in African American cuisine, but I'm also redefining it for myself."*

DEVITA DAVISON

Executive director of FoodLab Detroit in Detroit, Michigan

Born in Detroit, Michigan

Known for: Using food to build local economies

When Devita Davison speaks, she talks about food. She knows what to eat and where to find it, and sees food as a beacon of opportunity for those who need it most.

In her 2017 TED Talk, "How Urban Agriculture Is Transforming Detroit," Davison described the hometown she returned to after the 2008 recession prompted widespread economic abandonment. She spoke of a city "hungry for culturally appropriate, fresh, delicious food that helps small, neighborhood, burgeoning food entrepreneurs start and scale healthy food businesses." As executive director of the nonprofit FoodLab, an incubator that supports more than 185 businesses through community-driven entrepreneurship and training, she believes in the power of food to help others gain economic mobility, political influence, and knowledge of self.

In the TED talk, while images of a blighted city flashed behind her, she countered with examples of Detroiters creating new possibilities through food: incubation, education, tech assistance, and $7 million in revenue produced the year before, thanks to Detroiters' support of local farmers, restaurateurs, and other food-based businesses.

In person and over the phone, Davison is no less engaging. "In times of dishevelment, times of uncertainty, times of upheaval when you can't control any damn thing, what is that one part of your life that you can have control over?" she asks. "For many people, it's food. 'At least I can control what I put in my mouth. At least I can have sovereignty over how my family eats.'" Perhaps it's no surprise to learn that Davison's father was a pastor.

In 1970s Detroit, Davison and her brother relied on their mother's intricate weekly cooking routine, born of her parents' upbringing in Selma, Alabama. Their families had tended their own farmland, but in Michigan, the Wayne State University graduates pursued careers in banking and marketing.

Sunday played off the Southern tradition of "meat and three": chicken, fish, or pork with sides like field peas, macaroni and cheese, or corn. Hot-water cornbread, or yeast rolls, always. Monday was leftovers. Tuesday was a quick meal, something fried or neck bones in the pressure cooker served with potato salad or carrot salad. "Mama was cooking thirty-minute meals before Rachael Ray," Davison says proudly. Wednesday was spaghetti, chili, tacos, or sloppy joes. Teenage Davison was tasked with this meal, and still boasts of her mastery of ground chuck. Thursday was one-pot: soup, beef stew, or jambalaya. Maybe a casserole of chicken, broccoli, and cheese, or a crisp lasagna. On Fridays, the family dined out. Saturdays were filled with music lessons and athletics, so her mother made sandwiches. Sometimes her father grilled hot sausage shipped from family in Alabama. Next Sunday, the process repeated.

These days, Davison doesn't cook like her mother did. A hectic work schedule makes home cooking a rare feat, and she loves to explore other cultures through food. Detroit offers a bounty of options, like Flowers of Vietnam and Detroit Vegan Soul, FoodLab member businesses she's seen leap from idea to community stalwart.

When she does get in the kitchen, she may eat steamed edamame instead of string beans, kale instead of mixed turnips and mustard greens, to her mother's dismay. "She thinks I'm stepping away from my heritage," Davison says with affectionate understanding. "My mother was all about soul food and she still is...I'm still very much rooted in African American cuisine, but I'm also redefining it for myself." In the process, she's developing a food system that's equitable, sustainable, and community driven.

Three murals adorn the buildings of downtown Detroit

CRUDITÉS ⟨with⟩ A CARROT DOUBLE DIP

This double-sauce eats like a romesco sauce, which has been called the "Spanish ketchup." I love the idea of peanuts, carrots, and dipping back and forth. Think about this as a carrot-dip crudité plate—go ahead, bring in cucumber, apple sticks, radishes, and any other favorite veggies. You have two dip sauces—go ahead, this is your crudité party. Devita comes from Detroit, where farmers are super connected to the city. The Eastern Market is one of the oldest farmers' market in the country. This dish is inspired by the farm–city connection, with benne seeds and peanuts bringing it back to Africa.

Serve with vegetables, as an accompaniment to the chicken kofta (page 152), or a dollop alongside any of the grain bowl recipes.

ACTIVE TIME: *45 minutes*
START TO FINISH: *1 hour 10 minutes*
MAKES ABOUT 3 CUPS DIP

CARROT DIP

1 pound carrots with leafy tops

4 cloves garlic, peeled

3 tablespoons extra virgin olive oil

½ teaspoon kosher salt

1 (15.5-ounce) can chickpeas, drained

¼ cup peanut or cashew butter

2 tablespoons freshly squeezed lemon juice

GROUNDNUT ROMESCO

1 tablespoon coriander seeds

1 tablespoon cumin seeds

2 tablespoons raw benne seeds

½ cup raw peanuts

1 roasted red pepper, stemmed, seeded, and roughly chopped

6 cloves garlic, peeled

1 bunch carrot tops (about 2 cups), chopped

2 tablespoons peanut oil

2 tablespoons freshly squeezed lemon juice

1 teaspoon smoked paprika

¼ teaspoon kosher salt

Seasonal vegetables such as radishes, broccoli, celery, carrots, cauliflower

Preheat the oven to 400°F.

Make the carrot dip: Scrub the carrots and rinse off any dirt. Trim the tops off and set aside to use in the romesco. Place the carrots in a large foil pouch, add the garlic and 1 tablespoon of the oil, and season with the salt. Place on a baking sheet and roast until the carrots are tender and a knife inserted goes right through, about 40 minutes.

Transfer the contents of the foil pouch to a food processor and pulse to chop. Add the remaining 2 tablespoons olive oil, the chickpeas, peanut butter, and lemon juice and puree the mixture until smooth, 2 to 3 minutes. Taste and season with additional salt as needed. Set aside.

Make the romesco: In a small skillet over low heat, toast the coriander and cumin seeds until fragrant. Remove from the pan and set aside.

In the same pan, gently toast the benne seeds until fragrant and a light golden brown, about 1 minute. Remove from the pan and set aside. Toast the peanuts in the same pan until fragrant and a light golden brown, 2 to 3 minutes. Remove from heat and once cool enough to handle, roughly chop.

Using a mortar and pestle, crush the toasted cumin and coriander seeds. Add the roasted red peppers and garlic cloves and crush by using the pestle against the side of the mortar. Add the carrot tops and peanut oil and lightly crush with the pestle. Transfer the rough-chopped paste to a bowl and stir in the lemon juice, paprika, and salt. Add the benne seeds and chopped peanuts and toss to combine.

Place the carrot dip in a bowl, spoon the romesco over the center, and swirl lightly across the surface. Serve with your crudités of choice.

GRILLED PIRI PIRI SHRIMP
≪with≫ PAPAYA AND WATERMELON SALAD

This is a dish for grilling on a hot summer day, with the watermelon there to cool everything off. I just imagine working the grill, loving the heat. I'm drinking beers with my friends while they watch me flip a fat shrimp with my tongs. So good.

ACTIVE TIME: *35 minutes*
START TO FINISH: *1 hour*
SERVES 4 TO 6

1 pound large shrimp, peeled and deveined, tails on

½ cup Piri Piri Marinade (page 287)

2 cups diced watermelon

1 small papaya, peeled, seeded, and diced

4 cups fresh watercress or purslane

1 cup Harissa Charred Tomato Vinaigrette (page 285)

Kosher salt and freshly ground black pepper

½ cup egusi seeds, toasted

Toss the shrimp with the marinade, cover, and refrigerate for at least 30 minutes.

Prepare a grill for medium-high heat. Remove the shrimp from the marinade, brushing off any excess. Grill the shrimp until cooked through, rotating once during the grilling process to char nicely on both sides, about 5 minutes total.

Toss the watermelon, papaya, and greens in a bowl, dress with the vinaigrette, and season with salt and pepper.

Transfer the fruit and greens to a platter, top with the shrimp, and sprinkle with toasted egusi seeds. Serve immediately.

COUSCOUS AND ROASTED FIGS
≪with≫ LEMON AYIB AND HONEY VINAIGRETTE

If you are doing a cookout and you need a side that's going to make everyone happy, this is the perfect dish. Everyone should try to make the Ethiopian fresh cheese called ayib. Adding the acid of lemon makes the cheese stand out with a good tart flavor. These flavors work for me very well—lemon, fig, and couscous are all delicious and have a very North African/Middle Eastern feel.

ACTIVE TIME: *20 minutes*
START TO FINISH: *35 minutes*
SERVES 4 TO 6 AS A SIDE DISH

LEMON AYIB

½ cup Ayib (page 294)

1 tablespoon grated lemon zest

1 teaspoon fresh lemon juice

1 tablespoon extra virgin olive oil

¼ teaspoon kosher salt

Pinch freshly ground black pepper

COUSCOUS SALAD

1 cup water

½ cup couscous

1 tablespoon honey

2 tablespoons extra virgin olive oil

1 cup halved mission figs

¼ teaspoon kosher salt

Pinch freshly ground black pepper

1 cup raw cashews

1 tablespoon Berbere Spice Brown Butter (page 277), melted

½ cup fresh parsley leaves and tender stems

¼ cup fresh mint leaves

1 tablespoon grated lemon zest

2 cups fresh sorrel leaves, watercress, or arugula, torn

½ cup Caramelized Honey Vinaigrette (page 281)

Preheat the oven to 375°F.

Make the lemon ayib: Combine the ayib, lemon zest, lemon juice, olive oil, salt, and pepper in a small mixing bowl and stir to mix. Cover with plastic and refrigerate until ready to use.

Make the salad: Bring the water to a boil in a small saucepan. Add the couscous, cover, remove from the heat, and set aside for 5 to 7 minutes. Fluff the couscous with a fork and transfer to a large mixing bowl. Set aside.

Whisk the honey and olive oil together in a small bowl. Add the figs and toss to coat. Spread out on a baking sheet in an even layer and season with the salt and pepper. Roast the figs until tender and lightly caramelized around the edges, 20 to 25 minutes.

Toss the cashews with the melted berbere butter and spread on a small baking sheet. Toast in the oven until fragrant and golden brown, 5 to 8 minutes. Remove from the oven and set aside to cool. Roughly chop when cool enough to handle.

Combine the cooked couscous with the cashews, parsley, mint, lemon zest, and torn sorrel leaves. Add ¼ cup of the honey vinaigrette and gently toss to coat.

To serve: Transfer the couscous salad to a large shallow bowl or platter, top with the roasted figs and lemon ayib. Drizzle with the remaining vinaigrette and serve immediately.

> *"Understanding how flavors traveled around the world...is super powerful."*

NYESHA ARRINGTON

Chef in Los Angeles, California

Former chef-owner of Native, in Santa Monica, past Top Chef *contestant*

Born in Los Angeles, California

Known for: Combining the many strands of LA culture on one plate

Weekends in Nyesha Arrington's childhood home meant chore time. She grew up in Gardena, tucked in the South Bay region of Los Angeles County, in a neighborhood shared by many Korean families. She'd wake to the crescendo of her father's funk music playlist. They jammed and they cleaned, Arrington and her younger sister moving through the household chore list and her parents, John and Janet, helping out and supervising. But no one cleaned on an empty stomach.

Breakfast often began with grits, toast, eggs, and bacon. Sometimes her father fixed his famous banana pancakes. Arrington favored his grits. Later, in the early 2000s, as Southern chefs began to embrace traditional foods in new ways, Arrington observed the emergence of milled grains in the Michelin-starred restaurants where she worked. The dishes were "polenta-like," plated with thoughtfully sourced, often pricey ingredients. It was a combination Arrington had not previously seen. "This is—grits!" she remembers thinking. The ones she enjoyed as a girl might not have been labeled "heirloom," but she was beginning to understand the cultural shift at play. Southern ingredients—even the modest ones—were now welcome at the fine dining table.

When she opened Native, her Santa Monica restaurant that celebrated Los Angeles produce and Arrington's African American and Korean heritage, she featured a dish with crispy hominy, white corn grit paste, and goat's milk butter made in-house. Arrington admits that when she first started cooking, she wouldn't have turned to grits as a base ingredient. But the dish was one of Native's most popular.

Both of Arrington's parents are from Los Angeles, but her father's African American heritage goes back to Mississippi and her mother's family comes from Korea. Arrington remembers the aroma of fiery, roasted chiles at her maternal grandmother's home in nearby Inglewood. Arrington named a featured condiment at Native after her—Aisoon sauce—a bright, soy blend made with peppers, scallions, garlic, and sesame. At the restaurant, she drizzled it over Wagyu beef tartare. At home, Arrington uses it to top off her one-pot stews made with collard greens or kale, lentils, and kimchi jjigae—using over-fermented pickled cabbage that's a bit too robust to serve as a meal starter, but perfect to balance out a rich, soupy dish. Her after-work mash-up is perhaps the best example of her cooking philosophy—in which ingredients from different cultures merge to bring out the best in one another.

COUNTRY-STYLE SPARE RIBS
«with» PICKLED GREENS SLAW

Nyesha goes back and forth between classic French cooking, Korean influences, and African American cuisine; that's why her food is so special. Ham hocks, pork jowls, and smoked turkey are often cooked with greens, and Nyesha grew up in Los Angeles loving kimchi, so what better way to celebrate both her African American and Korean heritage than with ribs and pickled greens? Nyesha, a runner-up for the America Bocuse d'Or cooking competition in France, is so devoted and focused on her food. She has all the French style, she grew up with Asian and African American cuisine, and she's also an LA girl. When you step back and look at what Nyesha's doing, you can't help but ask: Isn't she the definition of American cuisine?

ACTIVE TIME: 45 minutes

START TO FINISH: 2 to 3 hours, plus 4 to 12 hours to cure

SERVES 4

DRY BRINE AND RIBS

¼ cup packed dark brown sugar

4 cloves garlic, grated

1 tablespoon kosher salt

2 teaspoons coriander seeds

1 teaspoon cayenne pepper

¼ teaspoon smoked paprika

3 pounds country-style pork spare ribs

PICKLED GREENS SLAW

2 cups shredded carrots

1 cup diced pineapple

½ small green papaya, shredded

¼ cup Pickled Greens (Kimchi Style), chopped (recipe follows)

1 tablespoon toasted sesame seeds

1 cup fresh cilantro leaves and tender stems

Brine and cook the ribs: Combine the brown sugar, garlic, salt, coriander, cayenne, and paprika in a small bowl. Pat the ribs dry with a paper towel and rub the dry brine into the meat and the crevices. Place on a baking sheet, cover with plastic wrap, and allow to cure in the refrigerator for 4 to 12 hours.

Preheat the oven to 375°F. Wrap each rack in a double layer of foil, crimping edges to seal tightly. Place each foil packet on a rimmed baking sheet and bake until the meat is fork-tender at the thickest part but not falling off the bone, 2 to 3 hours.

Just before the ribs are finished cooking, make the slaw: In a large bowl, toss all the slaw ingredients together.

Turn the oven to the high broil setting. Unwrap the ribs from the foil package and reserve the juices by pouring into a measuring cup. Let cool slightly, then skim any fat off the top, and transfer the juices to a small saucepan. Reduce the juices over medium heat until the sauce thickens to coat the back of a spoon.

Place the ribs on a baking sheet and brush with the reduced sauce. Broil, turning occasionally, until caramelized and charred in spots, about 8 to 10 minutes. When cool enough to handle, cut the ribs and serve alongside the slaw.

PICKLED GREENS (KIMCHI STYLE)

ACTIVE TIME: *15 minutes*
START TO FINISH: *1 hour plus 2 to 7 days to ferment*
MAKES 1 (16-OUNCE) MASON JAR
(ABOUT 4 CUPS PACKED)

1 pound turnip greens (or other greens such as sweet potato, dandelion, mustard, or amaranth)

2 tablespoons kosher salt

1 small red onion, chopped

5 red Fresno chiles, stemmed

2-inch piece fresh ginger, peeled

4 cloves garlic, peeled

1 tablespoon dried shrimp powder (or fish sauce)

2 teaspoons locust bean powder

1 tablespoon red pepper flakes

Lay half of the greens in an even layer on a baking sheet and sprinkle with 1 tablespoon of the salt, carefully rubbing the salt into the leaves. Place the next layer of greens over the top and sprinkle and rub with another tablespoon salt. Cover the baking sheet with plastic wrap and allow the greens to sit for at least 1 hour. The greens will release liquid and reduce in volume. Rinse the greens in cold water several times to remove the salt and drain completely.

In a food processor, pulse the onion, chiles, ginger, and garlic into a coarse puree. Stir in the dried shrimp, locust bean powder, and pepper flakes. Pour this mixture over the greens and combine, making sure the greens are evenly coated with the aromatic mixture.

Pack the greens into a clean 16-ounce mason jar with a lid and cover. Allow to sit at room temperature to ferment for at least 2 days. After 2 days, you should see bubbles rising to the surface. Once this happens, carefully release any pressure by unscrewing the lid and resealing the jar. Refrigerate and allow to sit for another 2 to 3 days to deepen the flavor.

CRAB CURRY
⟪with⟫ YAMS AND MUSTARD GREENS

Bring this dish to a park cookout and pull out your bib. Get your groove on. Imagine someone is playing "Outstanding" by the Gap Band in the background. This dish is delicious—it will make you want to move.

ACTIVE TIME: *40 minutes*

START TO FINISH: *1 hour 20 minutes*

SERVES 4

2 tablespoons vegetable oil

1 large red onion, julienned

6 cloves garlic, thinly sliced

2-inch piece fresh ginger, peeled and finely chopped

2 teaspoons ground turmeric

1 teaspoon kosher salt

1 teaspoon ground cumin

¼ teaspoon cayenne pepper

2 curry leaves

2 tablespoons tomato paste

2 cans unsweetened coconut milk

1 cup water

1 Scotch bonnet (or habanero) chile, stemmed and finely chopped

2 sweet potatoes, peeled and cut into 1-inch pieces

2 cups packed mustard greens, chopped

2 ½ to 3 pounds crabs, cleaned, cooked, and cut into 3- to 4-inch pieces, or 1 pound lump crabmeat

FOR SERVING

2 cups cooked broken rice

2 tablespoons fresh cilantro leaves

1 Fresno chile, thinly sliced

Lime wedges

Heat the oil into a large 6-quart Dutch oven set over medium-high heat. When the oil shimmers, add the onion, garlic, ginger, turmeric, and salt and cook, stirring often and scraping up browned bits, until the onion is translucent, about 5 minutes. Add the cumin, cayenne, curry leaves, and tomato paste and cook until the paste darkens in color, about 3 minutes.

Add the coconut milk, water, Scotch bonnet chile, and sweet potatoes and bring to simmer. Decrease the heat, cover, and cook for 15 minutes, or until potatoes are almost tender.

Add the greens and continue cooking for 2 to 3 minutes. Add the crab and cook until heated through and the greens are wilted, 2 to 3 minutes more.

Serve over rice, topped with cilantro, sliced Fresno chile, and lime wedges.

> *"The story belongs to the people who tell it."*

THERESE NELSON

Writer and chef in Harlem, New York

Born in Newark, New Jersey

Influences: Edna Lewis, George Washington Carver, Anne Northrop

Therese Nelson was frustrated. She'd made her way through culinary school and had found interesting jobs in places like the Four Seasons where she'd acquired new skills. "But there was something missing," she says. She noticed a lack of African American professionals in her fine dining surroundings, especially in leadership positions. Nelson also wasn't seeing the food that had inspired her to plot a course as a professional cook in the first place. "It all seemed so strange," Nelson says.

Born in Newark, Nelson grew up attending summertime family reunions in Latta, South Carolina, where her parents are from. In high school, Nelson had set her sights on a career in computer engineering. But another career possibility emerged. "The Food Network was becoming a thing," Nelson says. "I remember seeing Tanya Holland," the African American Bay Area chef who appeared on the show *Melting Pot.* And then Nelson encountered Edna Lewis's 1976 masterwork *The Taste of Country Cooking* in her high school library. Lewis's singular voice described refined, Southern recipes that asked the reader to consider season and place—specifically, her birthplace of Freetown, Virginia. She wrote of blossomed seeds planted when the moon was light, the breads her community made, how salad ingredients evolved with the harvest. Springtime breakfast could be pan-fried shad, whole hominy, and corn pone with wild strawberry preserves. Summer lunch meant buttered green beans with chervil and steamed lamb's-quarters.

Nelson was enchanted. She grew up eating stewed lima beans, cubed steak with gravy, and sweet potatoes and yams, which was fine. But Lewis's food sounded dreamy and accessible. Maybe she could become a chef? Engineering suddenly seemed less compelling.

Nelson did cook professionally, but she still craved greater resources and acknowledgment for Black chefs and the wide impact of African American cooking. She never forgot the feeling that bubbled up when she read Edna Lewis—that there was more to Black cooking than what white-dominant fine dining institutions had presented to her. She launched the website Black Culinary History. There, she documented the stories of Black culinary figures, hoping to make them more visible. She rounded up reading lists from chefs Marvin Wood and Jennifer Hill Booker. She blogged about beloved chefs like Darryl Evans, who mentored talents like Duane Nutter and Todd Richards. Nelson wanted prospective Black culinary professionals to have easier access to the information that had eluded her.

Nelson eventually shifted to private chef work, and her writing on Black Culinary History landed her a role as the online magazine *Taste*'s cook-in-residence. In one of her essays, she described chemist and botanist George Washington Carver as the Beyoncé of the science world in early 20th-century Tuskegee. She wrote about vinegary hot sauce as the umami component to Black cooking. She celebrated Southern cakes and pies as "life-affirming blackness" in a piece that heralded the James Beard Award–winning Birmingham pastry chef Dolester Miles. She went on to link Miles's baking tradition to church fund-raising cookbooks, and those heirloom recipes to women like Anne Northrop, wife of Solomon Northrop of *12 Years a Slave,* herself a pastry chef, whose work took her across the country to prestigious households and businesses in the mid-1800s.

Nelson's mission is to see more African American identities credited on our national plate. "There's got to be more folks who are willing to do the work…folks who are dedicated to telling this story accurately," Nelson says. "The story belongs to the people who tell it."

The Harriet Tubman Memorial, known as "Swing Low," in Harlem

ROASTED CARROTS
≪with≫ AYIB AND AWAZE VINAIGRETTE

I'm inspired by Therese's website BlackCulinary-History.com, which celebrates the many different paths and stories of Black cooking. Here's a dish for her that tells part of my story.

Every culture has a sauce that amplifies every dish you add it to. In Ethiopia, it's awaze—it's our Sriracha. (There's another recipe for awaze on page 281.) Everyone has access to this sauce. It isn't super hot, but it still brings the heat and you can dip everything in it. By stretching it with other ingredients, the awaze gets lighter and becomes a vinaigrette. Berbere spiced butter is an essential part here. You get umami from the butter and sour from the lemon. It's something you find in every Ethiopian household. You have to make it: In the US, you can get the ingredients online or buy them from an Ethiopian restaurant.

ACTIVE TIME: *25 minutes*
START TO FINISH: *1 hour 15 minutes*
SERVES 6 TO 8

---

2 pounds carrots, cleaned and tops removed

4 tablespoons vegetable oil

1 orange, thinly sliced, each slice cut in half and seeds removed

½ teaspoon kosher salt, plus more for vinaigrette

¼ teaspoon freshly ground black pepper

2 tablespoons Berbere Spice Brown Butter (page 277), melted

3 tablespoons fresh lemon juice

1 tablespoon honey

2 teaspoons Dijon mustard

½ cup fresh parsley leaves and tender stems

¼ cup Ayib (page 294) or goat cheese

Preheat the oven to 400°F.

Spread the carrots in one layer on a baking sheet, drizzle with 2 tablespoons of the oil, add the orange, salt, and pepper, and toss to coat. Roast, tossing occasionally, until the carrots are tender and the orange slices are caramelized, 40 to 45 minutes.

To make the awaze vinaigrette: Combine the remaining 2 tablespoons oil, berbere butter, lemon juice, honey, Dijon, and a pinch of salt and pepper in a glass jar with a lid and shake until an emulsion forms, 10 to 15 seconds. Taste and adjust the seasoning as desired.

To serve, place the carrots on a platter, drizzle with the vinaigrette, and top with parsley and ayib. Serve immediately.

PORK AND BEANS
≪with≫ PIRI PIRI SAUCE

Nothing says summer more than a big tin-foil pan of barbecue pork and beans. They're usually cooked with bacon and a sweet, messy sauce of molasses, ketchup, mustard, and spice. Here, the twist is cooking them with piri piri sauce. The result is a dish similar in style to Brazilian feijoada, Ghanaian red red, and Nigerian ewa riro. Serve this as a stew with fried plantains, or pair it with a charred hot dog and potato salad. It's food therapy at its best.

ACTIVE TIME: *45 minutes*
START TO FINISH: *2 to 3 hours*
SERVES 4

1 pound boneless pork shoulder, cut into 2-inch pieces

1 teaspoon kosher salt

1 tablespoon vegetable oil

1 red onion, finely chopped

6 to 8 cloves garlic, peeled and smashed

1 habanero chile, halved

1½ cups honey beans (or black-eyed peas, pinto beans, or navy beans), soaked in 4 cups water overnight

1½ cups crushed canned tomatoes

3 cups vegetable or chicken stock

2 tablespoons red palm oil

2 cups thinly sliced greens (collards, kale, mustard, etc.)

½ cup garri (ground, fermented dried cassava), for sprinkling

Season the pork pieces generously with salt.

Heat the oil in a 6-quart Dutch oven or other large, heavy pot over medium-high heat until hot but not smoking. In batches if necessary, add the pork and brown well on all sides, 10 to 12 minutes. Remove the pork from the pot.

Add the onion to the pot and cook, stirring occasionally, until translucent, 5 to 7 minutes. Add the garlic and habanero and sauté, stirring frequently, for 1 minute. Return the pork to the pot along with any accumulated juices and add the beans with their soaking liquid, the tomatoes, and stock. Stir in the red palm oil and bring the mixture to a simmer. Reduce the heat to low and cover the pot with its lid.

Cook until the pork is tender and starts to pull apart when prompted with a fork, about 2½ hours. The beans should be plump and completely soft. Stir in the sliced greens, adjust the seasonings, and cook until the greens are just beginning to wilt, about 2 minutes.

Serve the stew in bowls with the garri sprinkled over the top, and a side of fried plantains.

> *"I had to help them understand the diversity of what it means to be an African American cook."*

TONI TIPTON-MARTIN

Author in Baltimore, Maryland

The first African American food editor of a major daily newspaper

Born in Los Angeles, California

Known for: Her books The Jemima Code *and* Jubilee

If you show up for lunch with Toni Tipton-Martin on a random afternoon, she won't bake you macaroni and cheese. She will likely whip up a Napa cabbage coleslaw with hints of soy, sesame, and scallions. And she will be the first to tell you: That's Black cooking, too.

African American cooking, Tipton-Martin says, has always evolved beyond its perceived limitations. More than a set of soul food dishes, what Black people eat has always been diverse and representative of place. She understood this as a nutrition writer for the *Los Angeles Times* in the late 1980s, and when she served as food editor at Cleveland's *Plain Dealer* in 1991—the first African American woman to hold such a position.

When she published *The Jemima Code* in 2015, a gorgeous, colorful annotated survey of more than 150 African American cookbooks spanning nearly two hundred years, the tome countered the mistaken, though widespread, belief that Black cooks contributed little authorship to dishes they prepared for others. Her work shows that African American chefs have been innovative, sought after, and emulated as far back as the earliest days of this nation.

Tipton-Martin was born and raised in Los Angeles, California. Her parents' families, from Texas and Louisiana, migrated West around World War II. By the early 1960s, they landed in View Park, an affluent Black neighborhood abutting Windsor Hills and Baldwin Park, where Black doctors, lawyers, and entertainers resided. In Tipton-Martin's childhood home, the South was present, but rarely discussed.

Like many households shaped by the Great Migration, parts of the family lore were painfully incomplete. Her father refused to talk about his mixed-race parentage. Her mother called Oklahoma City her native town, but while doing research Tipton-Martin discovered she was actually born in Paris, Texas. Like many Black families who made home in distant places, a fresh start for the future meant a hard stop to the past. "It's like the lineage begins in South LA and doesn't exist prior to that," Tipton-Martin says.

Food was Tipton-Martin's connection between the South and Los Angeles. Her mother made neck bones and smothered cubed steak for dinner. Flavors from Mexico enhanced homemade enchiladas, tacos, and meat loaf. "We would pool our allowance money and we'd make tacos for lunch. We'd walk to the store, come back, and fry the shells ourselves." Later, with *The Jemima Code,* she'd learn that Black cooks incorporating Mexican flavors wasn't new to her generation. Black cooking has always reflected its locality. Her childhood backyard was an urban garden, with a slope marked by fruit trees. The family picked avocados on the bottom of the hill, berries and classic garden vegetables covered the bottom.

When Tipton-Martin's maternal grandmother died suddenly, her mother linked the loss with rich, fatty soul food cooking—memory food. "It sent my mother into a health tailspin." She shifted the family to a mostly raw, vegan routine. By the time Tipton-Martin was in college at the University of Southern California, an outing with her mom meant fresh-squeezed orange juice, sesame seed sticks, carrots, and raisin snacks.

Later, as Tipton-Martin's stature as a journalist grew, she was surprised by white editors who tried to "correct" her recipe ideas based on their perception of Black cooking as heavy soul food. She'd suggest a lamb dish or an asparagus side, and an editor would redirect her to mac and cheese or sweet potatoes.

"It gave me a moment of pause. Am I being disingenuous to what it means to be a Black person in the food world?" she wondered. But Black cooking is more than checking a stereotypical box, "I had to help those editors understand the diversity of what it means to be an African American cook."

Books from Tipton-Martin's prized collection

BEETS
≪with≫ SAGE LEAF AND DUKKAH SPICE

Dukkah is a coarsely ground Egyptian and Middle Eastern spice blend composed of fennel, coriander, nuts, and benne seeds. Dukkah's name derives from the Arabic for "to pound," and it adds flavor as well as texture to dishes. It's a great rub for lamb, chicken, and vegetables. It's very fly and flavorful—a great spice rub. I like to put it on rice and couscous. You can throw it on anything and it's delicious. Sage creates a great flavor combo with the dukkah spice—it brings the herbaceous note that makes this dish work.

ACTIVE TIME: *30 minutes*
START TO FINISH: *1¼ hours*
**SERVES 4 AS A SIDE DISH*

ROASTED BEETS

1 pound small red or golden beets

¼ cup water

2 tablespoons sherry vinegar

2 tablespoons extra virgin olive oil

Kosher salt

DUKKAH

1½ teaspoons fennel seeds

1½ teaspoons coriander seeds

1 teaspoon cumin seeds

2 tablespoons raw cashews

2 tablespoons unsalted shelled pistachios

1½ teaspoons benne seeds (or sesame seeds)

¼ teaspoon kosher salt

2 tablespoons extra virgin olive oil

2 tablespoons fresh lime juice

1 small red onion, thinly sliced

¼ cup fresh sage leaves (or a mix of fresh basil and mint leaves), julienned, plus more for garnish

Kosher salt

Roast the beets (or see Note): Preheat the oven to 425°F. Combine the beets, water, vinegar, and olive oil in a medium baking dish; season with salt. Cover with foil and steam until the beets are tender, 40 to 50 minutes. Let sit until cool enough to handle.

Make the dukkah: While the beets are roasting, toast the fennel, coriander, and cumin seeds in a small skillet over low heat until fragrant, 2 to 3 minutes. Place the toasted seeds in a food processor with the cashews, pistachios, and benne seeds and pulse to grind coarsely. Season with the salt.

When cool enough to handle, peel the beets, quarter, and then toss with the olive oil, lime juice, onion, and sage in a large bowl; season with salt. Add half of the dukkah, toss, and transfer to a serving platter. Adjust the seasoning with more salt if necessary. Top the beets with remaining dukkah and additional sage leaves.

NOTE: You can also grill the beets. Preheat a grill to medium-high. Place the beets on a large piece of foil, drizzle with the vinegar and oil, and season with the salt. Wrap the beets in the foil, place on the grill, and let steam until the beets are tender, 45 to 50 minutes. Let sit until cool enough to handle.

TIGERNUT CUSTARD TART
≪with≫ CINNAMON POACHED PEARS

Tigernuts, also known as chufa, aren't really nuts; they're tubers that grow in the soil like a sweet potato. Turns out this newest fiber-rich superfood has been around for a long time: We've been eating and growing them for thousands of years. Likened to coconut in flavor, tigernuts are sweet with a nutty taste whether served raw, dried, or baked. Toni's expertise in African American cooking and her writing in this space—which has opened the door to many home cooks incorporating ingredients such as tigernuts into their cooking—inspired this dish.

ACTIVE TIME: 25 minutes
START TO FINISH: 1½ hours
SERVES 10 TO 12

1¼ cups sugar

2 tablespoons freshly squeezed lemon juice

3 cinnamon sticks

3 ripe pears, peeled, halved, and cored

¾ cup (1½ sticks) unsalted butter, room temperature

2 large eggs, room temperature

1 teaspoon vanilla extract

¾ cup tigernut flour

1 teaspoon kosher salt

¼ teaspoon ground cinnamon

⅛ teaspoon ground cardamom

⅛ teaspoon ground black pepper

Basic Tigernut Pie Crust (page 295), parbaked for 15 minutes

Bring 4 cups water, 1 cup of the sugar, the lemon juice, and cinnamon sticks to a simmer in a large saucepan over medium heat, stirring until the sugar dissolves. Add the pears and reduce the heat to low. Simmer until the pears are just tender, turning occasionally, about 20 minutes. Cool the pears in the syrup. Cover and refrigerate. Can be made 2 days ahead.

Combine the butter and remaining ¼ cup sugar in the bowl of a stand mixer with the paddle attachment and beat on medium speed until fluffy, 2 to 3 minutes. Add the eggs and vanilla and beat until combined.

Add the tigernut flour, salt, cinnamon, cardamom, and pepper and beat on low until just combined, 1 to 2 minutes.

Preheat the oven to 375°F.

Spread the custard filling in an even layer in the parbaked crust.

Remove the pears from the syrup and drain on paper towels for 2 to 3 minutes. Slice the pear halves crosswise into thin slices. Using a spatula, carefully lift each sliced pear half and place on the custard filling, with the narrow end of the pear facing the center of the tart, fanning the slices apart slightly as you work. Repeat with the remaining pear halves, spacing them evenly around the tart.

Bake the tart for 35 to 40 minutes, until the custard is set and golden brown. Transfer to a cooling rack and let cool at room temperature for 1 hour before removing from the pan and serving.

CRAB AND CHILE CHITARRA PASTA

Darrell and I cooked together all over. Darrell is Rastafarian, from Trinidad. He's always coming up with new ways to think about food and he loves dishes packed with flavor and texture. Take this dish, for example, where crabmeat and an uni (sea urchin) butter are folded into pasta. The crab provides a velvety feeling in the mouth, while basil contributes a brightness and freshness.

ACTIVE TIME: *15 minutes*

START TO FINISH: *35 minutes*

SERVES 4

4 ounces uni

1½ cups (3 sticks) unsalted butter, room temperature

½ teaspoon kosher salt

¼ teaspoon ground turmeric

1 pound chitarra pasta

8 ounces lump crabmeat

16 Calabrian chile peppers, stemmed and halved lengthwise

Small handful fresh basil leaves

Place the uni in the bowl of a food processor and process until smooth. Add the butter, salt, and turmeric and continue to process until well incorporated and smooth, 4 to 5 minutes, stopping to scrape down the sides of the bowl as needed. Set aside until ready to use.

Cook the pasta in a large pot of salted boiling water until al dente. Transfer to large bowl and toss with the uni butter.

Divide the pasta among four shallow bowls, top with the crabmeat, chile peppers, and basil, and serve immediately.

SEAFOOD STEW
《with》 CASSAVA DUMPLINGS

Tristen is our chef in Miami at Red Rooster Overtown. He's super talented, and a brother on his grind. His diverse influences include his Trinidadian roots, as well as his upbringing in the Carolinas and Texas. He's such a good cook. Everybody needs to watch out: The sky's the limit for Tristen.

Tristen is a young guy who's old school, so I think of him with this dish. It's a classic combination of prawns and pork, but the cassava dumplings make the stew feel brand-new.

ACTIVE TIME: *45 minutes*
START TO FINISH: *2 to 3 hours*
SERVES 4 TO 6

SEAFOOD STEW

8 large prawns, shells and tails on

4 cups water

2 tablespoons extra virgin olive oil

1 small yellow sweet onion, chopped

2 stalks celery, chopped

1 green bell pepper, stemmed, seeded, and chopped

4 cloves garlic, sliced

1 teaspoon red pepper flakes

1 teaspoon fennel seeds

1 bay leaf

1 (15.5-ounce) can whole peeled tomatoes

1 pound catfish, grouper, or snapper fillets, cut into 1-inch cubes

½ pound cooked crawfish tails

1 sprig fresh marjoram, picked

CASSAVA DUMPLINGS

½ cup coarse ground fermented cassava flour

½ cup all-purpose flour

2 teaspoons baking powder

2 tablespoons minced fresh chives

1 teaspoon kosher salt

½ teaspoon fresh cracked black pepper

¾ cup buttermilk

GARNISH

1 lemon, zest grated and lemon cut into wedges for squeezing

2 tablespoons chopped fresh parsley

1 tablespoon chopped fresh dill or tarragon

(Continued)

Start the stew: Peel and devein the prawns, leaving the tails on. Set the prawns aside and save the shells. In a medium stockpot, combine the shells with any trimmings from the onion and celery. Pour in the water and bring to a simmer. Simmer for 45 minutes, until all the flavors are extracted. Strain through a fine mesh strainer.

Heat the olive oil in a large pot over medium-high heat. Add the onion, celery, and bell pepper and sauté until softened and the onion is translucent, about 8 minutes. Add the garlic, red pepper flakes, and fennel and sauté until just fragrant, about 1 minute. Add the bay leaf and tomatoes, crushing with your fingers as you put them in, and then pour in the strained shrimp stock. Bring the pot up to a boil and allow to simmer until just slightly reduced, 12 to 15 minutes.

While the stew is simmering, make the dumplings: In a medium bowl, whisk together the cassava flour, all-purpose flour, baking powder, chives, salt, and black pepper until combined. Slowly stream in the buttermilk and whisk until the mixture forms a soft dough.

Lower the heat on the stew and fish out the bay leaf and discard. Add the dumplings by dropping teaspoonfuls of dough into the liquid until all dough has been used. Allow the dumplings to gently simmer and float to the surface, 18 to 20 minutes (the dumplings will thicken the stew as they cook). Gently add the seafood starting with the prawns, then the catfish fillets and finishing with the crawfish tails. Cook the seafood until the prawns turn pink and the catfish fillets turn opaque, 2 to 3 minutes per seafood. Add the chopped marjoram.

Combine the lemon zest, parsley, and dill in a bowl. Mix well. Divide the stew among four bowls and top each with herb garnish and a squeeze of lemon.

AYIB AND SWEET POTATO RAVIOLI
≪with≫ BERBERE SPICE BROWN BUTTER

Twenty-five years ago when I first visited Café Beulah, my first impression was, *"This restaurant is massive."* Although not huge in a physical sense, this restaurant had an enormous impact on the dining scene in New York and beyond.

Sitting between Broadway and Park Ave on 19th Street, Café B featured amazing art on the walls from Lorna Simpson and Low Country cooking, an experience that was the result of the precision of Chef Marvin Woods and the vision of restaurateur Alexander Smalls. You could tell there was a dialogue between the art and food. I had never experienced a restaurant that way. It was a huge influence on me, something I kept in mind as I began to open restaurants of my own. Alexander, who had The Cecil restaurant in Harlem and is an award-winning cookbook author, cooks food inspired by travels and the broad reach of the African diaspora. His contributions to Harlem and New York have been indispensable.

I've featured many variations of this dish at my restaurants over the years. It involves making ayib cheese—something some people are intimidated by. Truth is, all it takes is buttermilk or yogurt, warmed to a boil until the solids separate from the liquid, and then strained and lightly salted. With its mild flavor and a texture similar to cottage cheese, ricotta, or feta, ayib pairs nicely with the sweet potato in these raviolis.

ACTIVE TIME: *1 hour*
START TO FINISH: *1 hour 15 minutes*
SERVES 4 TO 6

1 pound sweet potatoes

½ cup pecans

¼ cup sliced fresh chives

¼ cup chopped fresh mint

1 tablespoon grated lemon zest

1 tablespoon yellow cornmeal, plus more for dusting

1 large egg yolk

½ cup strained Ayib (page 294)

Kosher salt and freshly cracked black pepper

¼ cup all-purpose flour, for dusting

8 fresh lasagna sheets

1 large egg plus 1 teaspoon water, lightly whisked

¼ cup Berbere Spice Brown Butter (page 277)

1 tablespoon freshly squeezed lemon juice

Preheat the oven to 375°F.

Wrap the sweet potatoes individually in foil and roast in the oven until tender enough to pull apart with a fork, about 45 minutes.

While the potatoes are roasting, spread the pecans in an even layer on a small baking sheet. Toast in the oven until fragrant, 6 to 8 minutes. Transfer to a cooling rack to cool completely. Once cooled, finely chop the pecans and combine in a small bowl with the chives, mint, and lemon zest. Set aside.

Remove the potatoes from the oven and allow to cool slightly. When cool enough to handle, scoop the flesh into a mixing bowl and mash until smooth. Add the cornmeal, egg yolk, and ayib. Season with salt and pepper to taste.

Dust a baking sheet with additional cornmeal and lightly dust a work surface with the flour. Lay a lasagna sheet on the work surface. Using a pastry brush, lightly brush the pasta dough with egg wash. Scoop the sweet potato filling in 1-tablespoon amounts, spacing

each about 1½ inches apart and creating two rows on the one sheet. Top with the remaining pasta sheet. Use your thumb to press and seal the area around each scoop of filling. Using a pastry cutter, cut the ravioli into 2½-inch squares and transfer to the cornmeal-dusted baking sheet.

Bring a large pot of water to a boil over high heat and season generously with salt.

Heat 1 tablespoon of the berbere butter in a large skillet over medium heat

Working in batches, add the ravioli to the boiling water and cook for 1½ to 2 minutes, until they float to the top. Use a slotted spoon to drain, then transfer the ravioli to the skillet. Gently toss to coat in the berbere butter and finish with a teaspoon of lemon juice. Repeat this process until all the ravioli have been cooked and coated in the berbere butter. Divide the ravioli evenly among plates and garnish with the herb and pecan mixture. Serve immediately.

LAMB WAT
《with》 FRIES AND CAULIFLOWER CHEESE SAUCE

Eden is an extraordinary home cook, and her family comes from Eritrea. Massawa, the restaurant run by her aunt Almaz, has been a destination in New York for East African food since 1988. Eden worked with me for about 15 years in various roles—early on, she was the glue that held our office together, and helped me with books and was a part of starting Red Rooster. Her husband, James Bowen, is my culinary director and leads an all-star team at Marcus B&P in Newark, New Jersey. His highest aspiration in cooking is to please Eden and his mother-in-law.

This is a late-night Ethiopian snack in honor of Eden, James, and their family. Wat is an Ethiopian and Eritrean spicy sauce that I typically serve over pasta at my restaurants, but here it is paired with lamb and crispy potatoes. Think of it as lamb stew layered over delicious fries. In East Africa, wat would be served with injera (page 79).

ACTIVE TIME: *1 hour*
START TO FINISH: *2 hours*
SERVES 6 TO 8

LAMB WAT

1 tablespoon olive oil

2 tablespoons Aged Butter (page 265)

1½ cups diced red onions

3 cloves garlic, coarsely chopped

½-inch piece fresh ginger, peeled and coarsely chopped

2 tablespoons berbere seasoning

1 teaspoon kosher salt

1½ pounds boneless lamb shoulder, cut into ¼-inch cubes

3 sprigs fresh thyme

½ cup canned crushed tomatoes

1 cup packed shredded kale

1 cup water

FRIES

2 large russet potatoes

Vegetable oil, for frying

CAULIFLOWER CHEESE SAUCE

1½ pounds cauliflower (about ½ head)

1 cup heavy cream

½ cup whole milk

2 cloves garlic, smashed

1 teaspoon kosher salt

½ cup shredded cheddar cheese

½ cup grated Parmesan cheese

Freshly ground black pepper

Unsalted butter, for the casserole dish

(Continued)

Make the lamb wat: Heat the olive oil and aged butter in a 4-quart Dutch oven and set over medium heat. Once the butter melts and the fat shimmers, add the onions, garlic, ginger, berbere, and salt. Cook, stirring frequently, until the onions are translucent, 4 to 5 minutes.

Add the lamb, thyme, tomatoes, kale, and water and bring to a simmer. Decrease the heat to maintain a simmer, cover, and cook for 1 hour, or until the lamb is tender.

Make the fries: Bring a large pot of water to a boil. Peel each potato and cut into 1-inch-long by ¼-inch-thick sticks. Rinse the potatoes in a colander under cold, running water for 5 minutes. Once the water boils, add the potatoes and cook for 30 seconds. Remove with a slotted spoon to a paper towel–lined cooling rack.

Heat ¼ inch vegetable oil in a large sauté pan or Dutch oven set over medium-high heat. Place clean, dry paper towels on the cooling rack. When the oil reaches 350°F, add the potatoes in a single layer and fry until golden brown, about 10 minutes. Do this in batches if necessary. Use a slotted spoon to transfer the potatoes to the rack. Set aside until ready to assemble.

Make the cheese sauce: Heat the cauliflower, cream, milk, garlic, and salt in a medium saucepan set over medium-high heat. Once the mixture simmers, decrease the heat to maintain a simmer and cook for 25 minutes, or until the cauliflower is tender.

Add the cheddar and Parmesan cheeses and stir until melted. Transfer to a food processor and puree until smooth. Taste and season with additional salt and black pepper to taste.

To build and serve: Preheat the oven to 400°F.

Butter a 2- to 3-quart casserole dish and place half of the potatoes in the dish. Top with the lamb mixture and then with half of the cheese sauce. Top that with the remaining potatoes and finish with remaining cheese sauce. Bake for 20 minutes, or until bubbly and heated through. Allow to cool slightly before serving.

BAKE AND SHARK ISLAND FISH SANDWICHES

Kingsley and I are like brothers. He's been working with me since we were both kids—since he was about eighteen and I was twenty. He's from St. Lucia, which is why he really understands how to make a good fish sandwich. King was the first young chef I sent to Charlie Trotter, before I sent him to France. His range of cooking is incredible. When we work together, I feel like I'm in a band. I riff on one delicious beat; he jams on another. Whatever I do, I hope King will be a part of it.

This sandwich takes many iterations throughout the Caribbean. The bread is often fried and the fish is the catch of the day; sometimes it's shark and sometimes it's not. This recipe, however, calls for skinless snapper and some homemade coconut buns. Take a bite and love it.

ACTIVE TIME: *40 minutes*
START TO FINISH: *45 minutes*
MAKES 4 SANDWICHES

4 large cloves garlic, peeled

2 limes, cut in half

2 tablespoons extra virgin olive oil

2 tablespoons soy sauce

2 teaspoons honey

2 teaspoons sriracha

4 (4-ounce) boneless, skinless snapper fillets

4 Coco Bread Buns (recipe follows), for serving

1 avocado, peeled, pitted, and sliced

8 slices tomato

4 pickled chile peppers

4 leaves Bibb lettuce

4 sprigs fresh cilantro

Heat a grill or grill pan to high.

Brush the garlic and lime halves lightly with a small amount of the olive oil. Place on the grill and cook until both the garlic and lime are slightly charred, 8 to 10 minutes. Finely chop the garlic and set it and the limes aside.

Combine the remaining olive oil, the soy sauce, honey, and sriracha in a small bowl and whisk to combine. Brush the snapper on all sides with half of the glaze, reserving the rest for serving.

Grill the snapper for about 4 minutes on each side, or until just cooked through.

To serve, place each snapper fillet on a coco bread bun. Top with chopped grilled garlic, a squeeze of grilled lime juice, and some of the remaining glaze. Then top each with a slice of avocado, two slices tomato, one pickled chile, one leaf lettuce and one sprig cilantro. Serve immediately.

(Continued)

COCO BREAD BUNS

ACTIVE TIME: *35 minutes*
START TO FINISH: *2 hours 30 minutes*
MAKES 10 BUNS

½ cup unsweetened coconut milk	2 (¼-ounce) packages active dry yeast
1 cup whole milk	3½ cups all-purpose flour
½ cup water	
½ teaspoon ground coriander	¼ cup granulated sugar
2 whole cloves	1 teaspoon kosher salt
3 tablespoons coconut oil	3 tablespoons unsalted butter, melted
	Nonstick spray

Combine the coconut milk, milk, water, coriander, cloves, and 1½ tablespoons of the coconut oil in a small saucepan set over medium heat. Bring to a boil, remove from the heat, cover, and set aside to steep for 10 minutes. Remove the lid and let cool to 110°F to 120°F.

Once the milk has cooled, transfer to the bowl of a stand mixer with the dough hook attachment, add the yeast, and combine on low speed for 1 minute. Set aside until foamy, to 10 minutes.

In a medium bowl, whisk together the flour, sugar, and salt. Add the dry mixture to the liquid mixture and combine on low speed. Once the flour is incorporated, increase the speed to medium and mix for 5 minutes, or until the dough begins to pull away from the sides of the bowl. Cover with plastic wrap and set aside in a warm dry place to rise until doubled in size, about 1 hour.

Combine the remaining 1½ tablespoons coconut oil and the melted butter in a small bowl and set aside. Spray a baking sheet or cake pan with nonstick spray and set aside.

Turn the dough out onto a countertop and divide into ten equal pieces, about 3 ounces each. Shape a piece of dough into a ball. Using a rolling pin, roll the ball into a 6-inch round disk and brush with the coconut oil and butter. Fold the disk in half, brush again, and place in the prepared pan. Repeat until all buns have been shaped. Cover with a towel and set aside in a warm, dry place for 20 to 30 minutes, until the dough has almost doubled in size.

Preheat the oven to 375°F.

Bake the bun for 20 minutes, or until golden brown and cooked through. Allow to cool slightly before serving. Store at room temperature in an airtight container for up to 3 days.

KITFO «with» BERBERE SPICE BROWN BUTTER

When I want to come up with the Ethiopian menu, I always ask my wife Maya for her take. Truth is, I'm not even allowed in the kitchen at home when Maya and her sisters are cooking Ethiopian food. Her sisters and cousins, who fly in from DC, Toronto, and London, think what I do is "cute." No matter how long I've been cooking, they don't consider me an Ethiopian chef who cooks Ethiopian food. And every time we are in Ethiopia, Maya's mom stuffs our bags with food, because she doesn't fully believe we have real food in America. Butter, cheese, it's all crammed inside our suitcases, and I'm the one who's nervous about going through customs at JFK. Her mom just looks at me and says, "What's your problem? Get on board."

On big days and special occasions, even Maya has to step aside to let her older sister Alema set the record straight in the kitchen. Kitfo is an Ethiopian beef tartare, cooked lightly or eaten raw. It is a specialty of the Gurage people, Maya's tribe of Southwest Ethiopia. Maya and her sisters make kitfo with enormous pride for special occasions, family gatherings, feasts, and holidays. The word means "finely chopped," and it is true to its name, a mixture of finely diced beef, spices, chili powder, and warm butter. Minced raw beef recipes like steak tartare aren't only enjoyed in Europe. Kifto has been around for centuries.

ACTIVE TIME: *30 minutes*
START TO FINISH: *30 minutes*
SERVES 8 TO 10 AS AN APPETIZER

1 pound trimmed chilled beef tenderloin

2 tablespoons Berbere Spice Brown Butter (page 277), plus more melted for serving

¼ teaspoon ground cardamom

¼ teaspoon freshly ground black pepper

1 shallot, minced

2 cloves garlic, grated

Grated zest of 1 lemon

1 tablespoon fresh lemon juice

½ teaspoon kosher salt

Flatbread chips

Slice the tenderloin into ¼-inch-thick slices. Cut each slice into ¼-inch strips and then into ¼-inch cubes.

Heat the berbere butter in a small saucepan set over medium-low heat. As soon as it melts, add the cardamom and black pepper and cook until just fragrant, about 1 minute. Add the shallot and grated garlic and cook, stirring frequently, until softened, 1 to 2 minutes.

Transfer the mixture to a medium mixing bowl and allow to cool slightly. Add the beef, lemon zest and juice, and salt and toss to combine. Drizzle with more berbere butter just before serving with flatbread chips.

ZAZA'S DORO WAT RIGATONI

This is my son Zion's favorite dish. As I'm cooking this, I always think, "Wow, here I am making Ethiopian food for my son and he's still gumming on graham crackers." It's just amazing to me. Zaza (that's what he calls himself when he is running around the house) is going to grow up to be a herring and mackerel boy, and he will definitely also be a doro wat kid. Maya and I are building our family bond through food.

This chicken stew just gets better and better the longer it sits, and you end up with a dish that you can enjoy more the second time around, two or three days later. When we're cooking at home, we like to add butternut squash to the mix. I eat doro wat stew for breakfast with a poached egg, and for lunch Maya serves it with rigatoni, which is basically this recipe. It starts as a main dish, but it becomes a delicious leftover. So good.

ACTIVE TIME: *45 minutes*
START TO FINISH: *2½ hours*
**SERVES 6 TO 8*

DORO WAT

5 pounds chicken leg quarters (about 4), skinned

2 teaspoons kosher salt

¼ teaspoon freshly ground black pepper

2 large red onions, peeled and quartered

1 (2-inch) piece fresh ginger, peeled and sliced

8 cloves garlic, peeled

½ cup (1 stick) unsalted butter

1 teaspoon ground fenugreek

2½ tablespoons berbere seasoning

1 (28-ounce) can crushed tomatoes

SQUASH

1 butternut squash, peeled and cut into ½-inch cubes

1 tablespoon extra virgin olive oil

1 teaspoon kosher salt

¼ teaspoon freshly ground black pepper

1 pound rigatoni, cooked until al dente

⅓ cup ayib (page 294)

Freshly grated Parmesan, for garnish

Fresh basil leaves, for garnish

Make the doro wat: Season the chicken with the salt and pepper and set aside at room temperature.

Place the onions, ginger, and garlic in a food processor and pulse until the consistency is a chunky puree.

Heat the butter and fenugreek in a large, 8- to 10-quart Dutch oven set over medium-high heat. Once the butter has melted, add the onion mixture and stir to combine. Decrease the heat to low, cover, and cook, stirring occasionally, until the onion is melted and caramelized, about 45 minutes.

Preheat the oven to 350°F.

Add the berbere and stir until fragrant, 2 to 3 minutes. Add the tomatoes, stir to combine, and bring to a simmer, about 5 minutes. Place the chicken in the pot and spoon the sauce over the chicken. Cover and braise in the oven until the chicken is cooked through and tender, about 1 hour.

Make the squash: Combine the squash, olive oil, salt, and pepper in a large mixing bowl and toss to coat well. Transfer the squash to a baking sheet and spread into a single layer. Roast next to the chicken for the last 30 to 35 minutes, tossing occasionally, until the squash is tender.

To serve: Place the cooked pasta into a large serving bowl. Add the sauce from the chicken and the squash and toss to combine. Place the chicken on top, dot with the ayib, and garnish with freshly grated Parmesan and torn basil leaves.

GOOD VIBES CURRY GOAT

Jamaica has so much good food because it has so many influences. And Tiffany, the pastry chef at Red Rooster, knows Jamaican cuisine. She's an amazing pastry chef, but she's also a wonderful cook. When she cooks for the staff meal, everybody lights up. We still talk about the day she made the curried goat that inspired this recipe.

ACTIVE TIME: *45 minutes*
START TO FINISH: *3½ hours*
SERVES 4 TO 6

3 pounds bone-in goat stew meat	crushed tomatoes
1 teaspoon kosher salt	¾ cup Green Curry Paste (recipe follows)
½ teaspoon freshly ground black pepper	1 cup unsweetened coconut milk
¼ cup vegetable oil	2 cups water
1 large yellow onion, chopped	1 pound gold potatoes, cut into 1-inch cubes
6 cloves garlic, grated	3 cups cooked rice
1 (15-ounce) can	Pikliz (page 30)

Season the stew meat with the salt and pepper. Heat the oil in a large 6-quart Dutch oven set over medium-high heat. When the oil shimmers, add the meat, in batches if necessary, and brown on all sides, about 5 minutes. Transfer the browned meat to a bowl.

Once all the meat is browned, add the onion to the pot and cook until translucent, 4 to 5 minutes. Add the garlic and continue cooking for 1 to 2 minutes, until fragrant. Return the meat to the pot and add the tomatoes, ½ cup of the curry paste, the coconut milk, and water. Stir to combine and bring to a simmer. Decrease the heat to maintain a simmer, cover, and cook for 1½ to 2 hours, until the meat is just tender. Add the potatoes and continue to cook for another 30 minutes, or until potatoes are cooked through and tender. Stir in the remaining ¼ cup curry paste and serve over rice with the pikliz.

GREEN CURRY PASTE

ACTIVE TIME: *30 minutes*
START TO FINISH: *30 minutes*
MAKES 1½ CUPS

2 pieces lemongrass, trimmed and coarsely chopped	2 jalapeño chiles, stems removed
1-inch piece fresh ginger, peeled and cut in half	Grated zest and juice of 2 limes
3 cloves garlic, peeled	6 whole white peppercorns
3 small bunches fresh cilantro	4 whole black peppercorns
4 serrano chiles, stemmed and seeded	1 teaspoon cumin seed
	3 tablespoons vegetable oil

Place the lemongrass, ginger, garlic, cilantro, chiles, lime zest and juice, peppercorns, cumin, and oil in the carafe of a blender and pulse to combine until a paste forms, 3 to 4 minutes.

PORTLAND PARISH LAMB PIE

This lamb pie is simply a leftover stew with rice and peas baked under a pie crust. You lay pie dough on top of the stew, bake it, and now have a new dinner to serve—good to go. Tiffany is Jamaican and her ancestors are from Portland, a parish in Jamaica. This pie celebrates her and them.

ACTIVE TIME: *1½ hours*
START TO FINISH: *4 hours*
SERVES 8 TO 10

CURRIED LAMB

1½ pounds boneless lamb stew meat

1 teaspoon kosher salt

¼ teaspoon freshly ground black pepper

2 tablespoons vegetable oil

½ large onion, chopped

3 cloves garlic, grated

1 cup canned crushed tomatoes

⅓ cup Green Curry Paste (page 136)

½ cup unsweetened coconut milk

½ cup water

PASTRY DOUGH

2½ cups all-purpose flour

1 teaspoon kosher salt

½ teaspoon sugar

1 cup (2 sticks) unsalted butter, cut into small cubes and chilled

¾ to 1 cup cold water

TO FILL THE PIE

3 cups Rice and Peas (page 53)

1 large egg plus 1 teaspoon water, beaten

STEAMED CABBAGE

2 pounds cored cabbage, shredded

1 teaspoon kosher salt

½ cup water

½ cup (1 stick) unsalted butter

3 carrots, peeled and shredded

1 red bell pepper, cored and diced

2 cloves garlic, minced

1 Scotch bonnet (or habanero) chile, stemmed and seeded

1 tablespoon fresh ground black pepper

½ cup white wine vinegar

1 tablespoon honey

2 teaspoons soy sauce

(Continued)

Make the lamb: Season the stew meat with salt and pepper. Heat the oil in a large 6-quart Dutch oven set over medium-high heat. When the oil shimmers, add the meat and brown on all sides, about 5 minutes. Transfer the browned meat to a bowl. Do this in batches if necessary to prevent overcrowding the pan.

Once all the meat is browned, add the onion to the pot and cook until translucent, 4 to 5 minutes. Add the garlic and continue cooking for 1 to 2 minutes, until fragrant. Return the meat to the pot. Add the tomatoes, curry paste, coconut milk, and water and stir to combine. Bring to a simmer. Decrease the heat to maintain a simmer, cover, and cook for 1 to 1½ hours, until the meat is just tender.

Make the dough: Whisk together the flour, salt, and sugar in a medium mixing bowl. Using a pastry blender, fork, or your fingers, work in the butter until it is the size of peas. Add the water, beginning with ¾ cup, and stir until a dough forms, adding more water as needed. Shape the dough into a ball, wrap in plastic, and refrigerate for 30 minutes. Roll the dough into a shape slightly larger than the dish you will bake the pie in.

Assemble and bake the pie: Preheat the oven to 425°F.

Butter a 2-quart casserole dish. Place the rice and peas in the dish and top with the lamb. Using your rolling pin, transfer the dough to the top of the casserole dish and pinch to seal around the edges. Brush the crust with the egg wash. Bake for 25 to 35 minutes, until the crust is golden brown.

Make the cabbage: Combine the cabbage, salt, and water in a large saucepan set over medium-high heat. Cover and cook until the cabbage shrinks down by half, about 15 minutes.

Add the butter, carrots, bell pepper, garlic, chile, black pepper, vinegar, honey, and soy sauce and stir to combine. Decrease the heat to low, cover, and cook, stirring occasionally, until the carrots and peppers are tender, about 20 minutes. Remove the chile before serving.

Serve the lamb pie with the cabbage.

Red Rooster, past and present: From left, Tiffany Jones, Edward Brumfield, Jaqueta Tucker, Almira Session, Tiana Gee, and Marcus Samuelsson

OKRA AND CREEK SEAFOOD STEW

Yewande is on the rise. She's a star; she's already been on the front page of the *New York Times* food section and is at work on a book. She works with me on recipes, including most of the ones in this book. She was born in Berlin, Germany, raised in Lagos, Nigeria, moved to New Jersey when she was 16, and now lives in Brooklyn. She's like many Black chefs with a foot in the US, who travel to Africa for learning and inspiration.

Serve this stew over the Rice and Peas (page 53), garnished with fresh tomatoes, sliced scallions, parsley, and a squeeze from a lemon wedge. Or, it's a stew—so eat it with fufu (page 293), sometimes referred to as "swallow." Traditionally it is eaten with your hands. Break off a piece of the fufu and scoop up some of the stew with it. You can also serve the stew over couscous.

ACTIVE TIME: *1 hour*
START TO FINISH: *3½ hours*
SERVES 6 TO 8

6-ounce piece smoked ham hock

2 tablespoons extra virgin olive oil

1 small green bell pepper, stemmed, seeded, and finely chopped

2 stalks celery, finely chopped

1 yellow onion, finely chopped

6 cloves garlic, thinly sliced

1 teaspoon ground cayenne

1 (28-ounce) can crushed tomatoes

4 fresh thyme sprigs

2 fresh bay leaves

4 cups chicken stock

2 cups water

8 ounces okra, stemmed, cut in half lengthwise, and then into 1-inch pieces

1 pound large shrimp, peeled and deveined

Kosher salt and black pepper

Soak the ham hock in 2 cups hot water, ideally for 1 hour. Drain.

Heat the olive oil in a large Dutch oven or stockpot set over medium heat. Add the green pepper, celery, and onion and sauté until softened, 8 to 10 minutes, stirring frequently. Add the garlic and cayenne and cook until fragrant, about 1 minute. Add the can of tomatoes with their liquid, the thyme sprigs, and bay leaves. Add the soaked ham hock, chicken stock, and water and bring to a simmer. Lower the heat, cover, and continue to cook, adding more water if necessary, until the ham hock is tender, about 45 minutes.

Remove and discard the ham hock, bay leaves, and thyme sprigs. Continue cooking until the soup is reduced by half, about 45 minutes. Add the okra, cook for 10 minutes, and add the shrimp. Cook for an additional 1 to 2 minutes, until shrimp are just tender. Remove from the heat and season to taste with salt and pepper.

SMOKED DUCK
⟪with⟫ SORGHUM-GLAZED ALLIUMS

Sorghum is one of the oldest known grains in the world. Researchers believe it originated in northeast Africa and moved along trade routes to many countries. As part of the import economy that accompanied enslaving Africans, traders brought many foods to the Americas, including sorghum. Sorghum syrup was once a popular, low-cost sweetener used in the deep South. Like honey or molasses, sorghum syrup has an earthy sweetness, though it tends to be thinner in viscosity and a little more sour.

ACTIVE TIME: *1 hour*
START TO FINISH: *4 to 6 hours*
SERVES 4

2 tablespoons coriander seeds, toasted and crushed

1 tablespoon kosher salt, plus more to taste

4 duck legs

Hickory chips

2 whole garlic bulbs, halved crosswise

1 cup duck or chicken stock

2 tablespoons sorghum syrup (or maple syrup or honey)

1 tablespoon grated orange zest

¼ cup fresh orange juice

30 pearl onions, peeled

10 scallions (about 1 bunch), root ends trimmed

10 stalks green garlic (about 1 bunch), root ends trimmed

1 bunch fresh thyme

Freshly ground black pepper

(Continued)

In a small bowl, combine 1 tablespoon of the crushed coriander seeds and the salt. Use a sharp knife to puncture the skin of the duck legs through the fat layer on both sides of each leg. Season the duck legs with the coriander mix, place in a freezer bag, seal, and refrigerate for 4 hours, or overnight.

To cold-smoke the duck, if using a backyard smoker, smoke over hickory chips at 400°F for 20 minutes. If using a handheld smoking gun, thoroughly cover meat in a closed container with smoke. Allow to infuse for 20 minutes.

Preheat the oven to 300°F.

Heat a Dutch oven, large enough to fit all four legs, over medium heat. Brush off any excess seasoning and place each leg skin side down in the pot. Cook and allow the fat to render, about 10 minutes. Flip the legs, add the garlic bulbs, cut side down, and brown for 1 minute. Add the thyme sprigs and stock. Cover the pot and move to the oven. Allow the duck to braise slowly in its fat and juices until the meat is tender and the leg bone moves freely in its joint, about 3 hours.

Make the sorghum glaze while the duck is braising: Combine the sorghum, orange zest and juice, and remaining 1 tablespoon crushed coriander seeds in a small saucepan. Heat over low heat until just beginning to simmer, 5 to 6 minutes. Remove from the heat.

Once the duck is cooked and completely tender, let cool slightly and remove from its liquid. Allow to drain on a baking rack set in a baking sheet. Increase the oven to 400°F.

Place the duck legs in the oven and roast until the skin is a deep golden brown, 15 to 20 minutes.

In the meantime, remove the herbs and garlic from the pot and drain off all but 2 tablespoons of the rendered fat. (Reserve the rendered fat, it will keep refrigerated for up to a month.) Over medium heat, add the pearl onions to the pot. Cook, turning frequently, until a deep golden brown on all sides and tender, 5 to 6 minutes. Add the scallions and green garlic and cook for 1 minute, until just beginning to wilt. Lower the heat, pour in the sorghum glaze, and cook until slightly reduced and the alliums are coated. Remove the pot from the heat and season with salt and pepper.

Serve this family style in the pot.

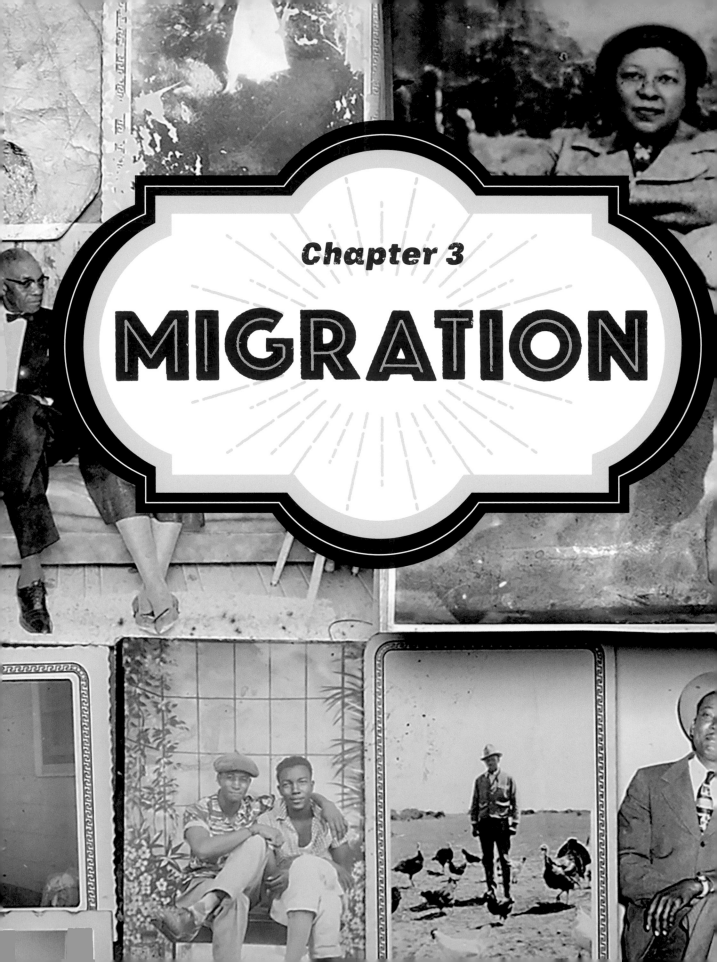

MIGRATION

Chapter 3

The influence of the American South—
the Great Migration and beyond.

IN HONOR OF:

CHERYL DAY, chef, Savannah, GA

Baobab-Buttermilk and Broiled
Peach Popsicles

Chicken Kofta with Charred Okra Salad
and Yogurt Sauce

Sweet Wild Berry Pie with C&C Crumble

ANDRÉ HUESTON MACK, winemaker,
New York, NY

Leftover Wine Spiced Chocolate Cake
with Mulled Wine Raspberries

DONNA PIERCE, writer, Chicago, IL

Auntie's Layer Cake with Pecan and Mango

Donna's Pull-Apart Fresh Dinner Rolls

FRED OPIE, historian, Boston, MA

Broken Rice Peanut Seafood Stew

Next Day Grits

Hoecakes

JOE STINCHCOMB, bartender, Oxford, MS

Mar Cocktail/The Bowie

Bullock Fries

Spiced Lemon Chess Pie

MATTHEW RAIFORD, chef-farmer, and
JOVAN SAGE, herb alchemist, Brunswick, GA

Spicy Grilled Garden Egg Salad

Chilled Watermelon and Red Pepper Soup
with Pickled Berries

ALBERTA WRIGHT, chef, New York, NY

Sunday Roast Chicken
with Chickpeas and Couscous

ED BRUMFIELD, chef, New York, NY

Papa Ed's Shrimp and Grits

Citrus Scallops with Hibiscus Tea

MELBA WILSON, chef, New York, NY

Bird and Toast

Fried Chicken and Waffles with Piri Piri Glaze

Throughout my career as a chef and restaurant owner, I've thought a lot about migration, and done my share of it. I have been shaped by moving from one country, one culture, to another. The food traditions that make up my day-to-day are a mix of what I've carried with me and what I've picked up in a new place. It's more than just my cooking—it's my life.

Migration is a constantly evolving and modern story. My son, Zion, is a New Yorker by birth, and Harlem has been my home for two decades. But I also want to make sure he grows up with love and respect for the Ethiopian heritage shared by his mother and me, and the values I got from my Swedish parents. Every day I'm presented with a host of choices—what do I bring forward, what do I allow to live in the past?

In the United States, the South has been center stage for the conversation about migration: both as destination and point of departure. Large-scale movements to and from the South have shaped this book, and the work of the people highlighted in it. I am thinking of the forced migration of millions of African people to the country that would become the United States beginning in 1619, and the domestic Second Middle Passage that tracked with economics-driven shifts into more cotton production and newly acquired territory. I think of the decades-long Great Migration that took African American people to metropolitan centers throughout other regions of the country in search of financial stability and social and political freedom in the middle of the twentieth century. And I think of what economists describe today as a reverse Great Migration, as many young African Americans now seek opportunity and a better quality of life in Southern cities and suburban neighborhoods.

This mass movement—this migration—continues to shape our food. That's why I've come to think of the American South as not only a geographical region, but a state of mind. Because of how deeply the idea of America has depended on African and African American people and cultures, I'd argue there's a version of the South anywhere you find Black people. And food in the South is still very much West and Central African cooking reinterpreted, remixed, in America.

This chapter takes a broad view of movement and seeks to call out the inspiring and creative results of journeys from one place to another. Los Angeles–born Cheryl Day finds home and comfort in her bakery in Savannah, Georgia. André Hueston Mack and Joe Stinchcomb were military kids who moved all over. André now makes Oregon wine and owns a ham bar in Brooklyn, and Joe is bringing mixology in dialogue with African American history, continuing in the vein of Tom Bullock, one of the first authors of a cocktail book in the US. Donna Pierce in Chicago still feels tied to her Mobile, Alabama, heritage, carrying those recipes forward. Fred Opie is connecting the dots between the past and present in the academic setting, after previous generations moved north. And Matthew Raiford grew up with a desire to escape the South—but returned to Georgia as a chef and farmer, working with his partner Jovan Sage, who settled in the South by way of the Midwest.

But in the broader tale of the history of migration, there's also something left behind. It's plain to see how much—and who—has been left out of America's food story, when you look at professional kitchens, many culinary school programs, and food media that continue to minimize the contributions of Black creators to the world's foodways. It's past time to change that narrative.

Black food is American food. It's not one straight arrow through history. It is diverse by its nature, mixed in its birth, fought about, argued over, imitated, and loved. Let's complicate our understanding of how we got to where we are today. Thomas Jefferson is credited with bringing French cooking to America, but let's remember it was Jefferson's enslaved cook, James Hemings, who actually trained to be a chef in Paris.

Food always keeps moving. So do people. Our hearts and minds should also be open to heading somewhere new, more equitable, more beautiful, and more delicious. Let's migrate toward a new American food story that recognizes all of us.

"Pies, biscuits, cakes all remind me of different people."

CHERYL DAY

Baker-owner of Back in the Day Bakery in Savannah, Georgia

Born in Sherman Oaks, California

Author of five definitive Southern baking cookbooks, including The Back in the Day Bakery Cookbook

Known for: Signature biscuits, party cakes, seasonal pies, and bars

At Back in the Day Bakery, regulars know the right move: arrive early. At the popular baked goods and coffee shop owned by Cheryl and Griffith Day, visitors can be certain that everything will taste great, and that the baked goods will sell out by late afternoon. Back in the Day is known far beyond Savannah for its arsenal of buttermilk biscuit sandwiches, cinnamon buns, vanilla old-fashioned cupcakes, seasonal fruit hand pies, Mexican chocolate brownies, and lavender shortbread cookies.

Day's mother introduced her to baking in their Sherman Oaks kitchen, tucked in a neighborhood of Los Angeles. As a young girl, she also spent summers in Tuscaloosa, Alabama, with her maternal grandmother, learning the craft of cakes and biscuits.

The flaky, fruit-filled Queen of Tarts is one bakery item Day named for her mother, Janie Queen Brown, who died when Day was twenty-two. During World War II, Brown took a clerical job with the US Army that helped her leave small-town Dothan, Alabama. She wound up in Los Angeles where she married Day's father, Lonnie, and they had two daughters. Brown worked full-time as a social worker and still made dinner for Day and her sister every night, meals like roast chicken and vegetables. Day's father was a production photographer for Desilu Productions, best known for classic TV shows like *I Love Lucy* and *The Untouchables*. Big personalities filled the house on weekends, from actor friends to people in transition that Brown encountered in her role as social worker.

Even as a kid, Day observed that the act of baking seemed to slow down time. She appreciated the peaceful silence inherent in baking—the mechanics of rolling, pinching, flouring; repeat. When Day baked with her mom, they shared a distinct connection. Of Brown's many go-to treats, she had mastered the lemon meringue pie. But after she passed, Day couldn't approach the recipe.

"Even after having the bakery for years, I would never make it," she says. The food memory was precious, if fragile, and Day feared her interpretation wouldn't hold up to her mother's original.

Admissions like that are hard to believe, coming from such a talent. Day credits her baking and entrepreneurial chops to a line of distant relatives who cooked for a living. She treasures an epistolary journal her mother left behind with pieces of family history. One of Day's Alabama kin had a general store where they sold scratch biscuits and gingerbread squares.

Day's connection to her family's past is part of what lured her from California to the South. Hours away from big cities like Atlanta, Day enjoyed the lifestyle—she adjusted to a more even-paced rhythm that gave her time to think and dream. This breathing room allowed Day the space to return to her mother's lemon meringue pie, decades after Brown's death. Day wanted to include the recipe

in a cookbook and the fear of failing was no longer strong enough to deter her.

"I remember making it and I sliced it, and it was like, 'oh my god'—this is my mom. This is my mom's pie. How I was able to recreate it, I have no idea."

Maybe after years of professional baking, Day had finally acquired the skills to make her mother's perfect pie. She's too humble to say what is more likely true—that she had the know-how all along, the legacy of cherished hours spent with her grandmother and mother whose knowledge lives on.

BAOBAB–BUTTERMILK AND BROILED PEACH POPSICLES

The baobab is one of the world's most treasured trees, and it's been a veritable tree of life for the people of Africa, its native home. It can grow as large as a tall building, live for thousands of years, survive fire, and hold up to 60,000 gallons of rainwater in its trunk. The baobab fruit is lemony and floral in taste. It is typically dried and turned into a powder that can be added to lemonade, smoothies, or frozen treats.

ACTIVE TIME: *10 minutes*

START TO FINISH: *20 minutes, plus 6 to 12 hours to freeze*

MAKES 10 POPS

1 pound ripe peaches (2 to 3), halved and pitted

3 tablespoons dark amber honey (like buckwheat or wildflower)

2 teaspoons extra virgin olive oil

1 teaspoon kosher salt

1¾ cups buttermilk

¼ cup full-fat yogurt

3 tablespoons baobab powder

Pinch of kosher salt

Preheat the oven to the high-broil function.

Toss the peach halves with 1 tablespoon of the honey, the olive oil, and salt on a rimmed baking sheet. Spread the peaches in an even layer, cut side up. Broil until the peaches are just tender and lightly caramelized around the edges, about 10 minutes. Remove from the heat and allow to cool. Once cool enough to handle, peel off the skins and roughly chop the roasted flesh. Set aside.

Using an immersion blender or in a blender, combine the buttermilk, yogurt, baobab powder, remaining 2 tablespoons honey, and salt by whizzing together.

Assemble the Popsicles: Alternately pour the buttermilk mixture and spoon some of the chopped peaches into each of ten ice pop molds. Begin and end with the buttermilk mixture, leaving ¼ inch room on the tops of each mold. Snap the lids of each mold on and freeze until the pops are fully set, 6 to 12 hours.

CHICKEN KOFTA
《with》 CHARRED OKRA SALAD AND YOGURT SAUCE

Okra, in all of its many preparations, is so closely identified with the American South that cooking it or seeing it on a menu always makes me think of returning there. For me, this dish is all about the charred okra salad, and the dynamic it brings to whatever you pair it with. Made with corn, herbs, and lime juice for brightness, it enlivens grilled meats of all kinds, such as the chicken kofta in this dish. Serve them with a yogurt dressing and Grilled Chickpea Flatbread (page 218).

ACTIVE TIME: *30 minutes*
START TO FINISH: *45 minutes*
MAKES 12 KOFTA

2 pounds ground chicken thighs

1 onion, grated

1 teaspoon ground coriander seed

½ teaspoon ground cumin

½ teaspoon Aleppo pepper

⅛ teaspoon ground cinnamon

⅛ teaspoon ground allspice

1 tablespoon kosher salt

1 teaspoon cracked black pepper

½ cup chopped fresh cilantro

¼ cup chopped fresh mint

2 tablespoons vegetable oil, plus more for brushing

1 cup yogurt

Grated zest of 1 orange

2 tablespoons fresh orange juice

Charred Okra Salad (recipe follows), for serving

Preheat a grill (or griddle pan) to medium-high and make sure the grates are cleaned and lightly oiled.

Combine the chicken and onion with the ½ teaspoon of the coriander, the cumin, Aleppo, cinnamon, allspice, salt, black pepper, ¼ cup of the cilantro, and the mint in a large mixing bowl. Mix just enough to incorporate ingredients, then add the oil. Allow the meat to rest in the refrigerator for at least 10 minutes.

To make the yogurt dressing, in a small bowl, whisk the yogurt with the remaining ½ teaspoon coriander, remaining ¼ cup cilantro, and the orange zest and juice and season with salt and pepper. Refrigerate the dressing until the kofta is ready.

Form the chicken mix into small patties, about 2 tablespoons each. Shape each patty tightly around a single short skewer or into a ball with your hands. Grill the kofta, turning once, until they are slightly charred and cooked through, 6 to 8 minutes per side.

Serve the kofta with the yogurt dressing and okra salad.

CHARRED OKRA SALAD

ACTIVE TIME: *15 minutes*

START TO FINISH: *40 minutes*

SERVES 4 TO 6 AS A SIDE DISH

¼ cup vegetable oil, plus more for brushing grill grates

1 pound okra

2 large ears corn

1 teaspoon kosher salt

1 cup cherry tomatoes, halved

½ small red onion, julienned

2 tablespoons fresh lime juice

¼ cup chopped fresh cilantro leaves and tender stems

¼ cup chopped fresh mint leaves

Preheat a grill (or griddle pan) to high and make sure the grates are cleaned and lightly oiled.

Toss the okra and corn with the oil and salt. Grill the corn for 8 to 10 minutes, until it is tender and slightly charred. Set aside to cool slightly. When the corn is cool enough to handle, Cut the kernels from the cob. Transfer to a large mixing bowl.

Grill the okra for 5 to 6 minutes, until slightly charred but not completely cooked through or mushy. Set aside to cool. When cool enough to handle, slice in half lengthwise and add to the corn.

Add the tomatoes, onion, lime juice, cilantro, and mint and toss to combine. Serve immediately.

SWEET WILD BERRY PIE
≪*with*≫ C&C CRUMBLE

This is a dessert that screams at you, "Put some cream on me!" Cassava is the root of a leafy shrub also known as yuca (not the same as yucca). It can be ground into cassava flour, and tapioca comes from extracting the starch in pulp form. It's one of the most used crops in the world. Hopefully more Americans will begin to cook with it. A coconut and cassava topping brings a crunchy and delicious flavor to this pie. I'm inspired by Cheryl's bakery and how her food honors the women in her family.

ACTIVE TIME: *15 minutes*
START TO FINISH: *1½ hours*
MAKES ONE 9-INCH CRUMBLE

CRUMBLE TOPPING

½ cup cassava flour (or tapioca flour)

1 cup large-flake coconut

½ cup granulated sugar

2 teaspoons baking powder

Grated zest of 1 lime

1 teaspoon kosher salt

½ cup (1 stick) unsalted butter, cold, cut into 1-inch pieces

1 large egg yolk

BERRIES

6 cups assorted wild berries (blackberries, blueberries, huckleberries, strawberries, raspberries)

½ cup granulated sugar

2 tablespoons cassava flour (or tapioca flour)

Grated zest of 1 lime

2 tablespoons fresh lime juice

Pinch of kosher salt

1 teaspoon cracked black pepper

Make the topping: Combine the tapioca flour, ½ cup of the coconut flakes, the sugar, baking powder, lime zest, and salt in a food processor. Pulse to combine. Add the cold butter and pulse until the mixture resembles coarse crumbs. Transfer to a medium bowl and add the yolk and the remaining ½ cup coconut. Mix together with your hands to form loose crumbles. Set aside in the refrigerator.

Preheat the oven to 375°F.

Prepare the berries: Combine the berries, sugar, tapioca flour, and lime zest and juice in a large bowl. Season with salt and black pepper.

Transfer the fruit and all the juices to a 2½-quart baking dish. Set the dish on a rimmed baking sheet. Top with the crumble topping and bake until the juices are bubbling and the topping is golden brown, 50 to 60 minutes. Let the crumble cool and set for at least 1 hour before serving.

ANDRÉ HUESTON MACK

Owner and winemaker at Maison Noir, and & Sons Ham Bar in Brooklyn, New York

Largest producer of wine by an African American vintner

Born in Trenton, New Jersey

Known for: Named Best Young Sommelier in America by the Chaine des Rotisseurs

Even after becoming head sommelier at Manhattan's luxury Per Se restaurant, André Hueston Mack understood that he was the last person in the room some customers would expect to know about wine. "I would hear the table say, 'Yeah, we'd love to speak with the sommelier.' I would approach the table and say, "So hey guys, we ready to talk about wine?" And they would say, 'We're waiting for the sommelier.'"

Mack refused to allow being underestimated to dilute his interest in wine. He founded Maison Noir in 2007, its portfolio of wines from the Willamette Valley in Oregon meeting at the nexus of delicious and accessible, with a tongue-in-cheek branding approach that draws from popular culture. "O.P.P." or "Other People's Pinot" Noir is a nod to the classic hip hop jam from Naughty by Nature. "Love Drunk" is the brand's rosé; "Knock on Wood" their chardonnay.

The company leases six vineyards, produces tens of thousands of cases of wine per year and distributes throughout the US and globally, which makes Mack the biggest African American wine producer in the United States. His wines, perhaps due to their playfulness, are sometimes overlooked the way he was on the dining room floor. Mack doesn't mind. "People taste them and they're like, 'Wow, this is great, it overdelivers.'"

Mack was born in Trenton, New Jersey, to parents who served as officers in the US Army. Moving was constant. He's lived in Killeen, Texas; Atlanta; Gräfenberg, Germany; Fort Leavenworth, Kansas; Annapolis, Maryland; San Antonio; and Oklahoma City. Bouncing around meant that Mack was always adjusting to a new social atmosphere. His family ate lots of rice, which Mack credits to their Red Springs, North Carolina, heritage, and they enjoyed seasonal produce. But in new friend groups, he distanced himself from ideas of Black cooking that carried more weight than was fair for a young boy to bear. "Soul food wasn't cool to my friends. It was kind of a shame thing. It'd be like, 'You probably eat fried chicken every night.' And oh man, I wish I could....But that became a derogatory thing. Now that the South has reclaimed its food, you have all these other people running around talking about how good fried chicken is. It's funny how the tides have turned."

Mack initially pursued a short-lived career in finance, only to realize he missed the banter and energy of the restaurants he'd worked in during college. A couple of years in, he took a severance package that bought him paid time on the couch. He'd watch back-to-back episodes of the sitcom *Frasier* and became a fan of the Seattle therapist and his pompous brother who shared a love for good wine. Their geeky interest was inspiring.

"The greatest foil to pretension is humor. I felt by watching the show if I could arm myself with a few comedic anecdotes. That would break the ice and I would feel more comfortable walking into a wine shop."

Mack set out to work at the Palm in San Antonio, where he cultivated his palate through staff wine tastings and after-hours research. "I studied wine every single night. My first sommelier job was at a steak house right next door to the Palm. The next sommelier job I had was in Napa at the French Laundry."

After four years of sommelier work, during which time Mack had acquired a list of accolades, he formed his company. It was originally called Mouton Noir, or "black sheep." He says, "I wanted to continue to learn about wine, and I felt like the only way to do that was to make my own."

Mack launched his company around the same time as a new guard of chefs was taking hold in New York. "There was a shift in the dynamic of what chefs could be. They worked for the masters to learn the techniques, but they wanted to do it on their own terms." Mack wanted to make wines for those restaurants. "That's why our wines look the way they do."

In 2020, Mack opened & Sons, a ham bar in Brooklyn that celebrates American-made country ham, from hickory-smoked to salt-cured. Served thinly sliced like their European counterparts, customers can pair ham tastings with a deep-cut wine list that Mack curated over years of collecting.

Every now and then he takes stock of his life. "Not that I ever thought for one second that I would be the largest producer of wine made by an African American in this country—from watching *Frasier*."

LEFTOVER WINE SPICED CHOCOLATE CAKE «with» MULLED WINE RASPBERRIES

Black people's contribution to the world of beverages should not be overlooked: Nathan "Nearest" Green created what we now know as Jack Daniels whiskey; Tom Bullock was a bartender who became the first African American to write a cocktail book; and now we've got André. He is the largest African American seller of Pinot Noir in the country. However, he did not grow up on a winery and his parents did not own a lot of land. This is how he got there: He called up all the wineries he knew and said, "I can blend a wine for you. Do you have grapes you are not selling?" Almost all of them said "no," until he found a winery in Oregon to partner with, and now he produces tens of thousands of cases of wine a year. His story shows that an African American can start a winery and open the door for other people behind him. If anyone has leftover wine, it will be André—and that's why it's a main ingredient in this cake!

ACTIVE TIME: *35 minutes*
START TO FINISH: *1 hour 35 minutes*
MAKES 10 TO 12 SERVINGS

2 cups leftover red wine

½ cup granulated sugar

1 cinnamon stick

3 cardamom pods

3 whole cloves

1 teaspoon ground ginger

Grated zest and juice of 1 orange

Grated zest and juice of 1 grapefruit

6 ounces raspberries

½ cup pitted cherries, coarsely chopped

¼ cup slivered almonds

1 cup all-purpose flour

½ cup cake flour

⅓ cup cocoa powder

1 teaspoon baking soda

½ teaspoon kosher salt

⅓ cup coconut oil

½ cup packed brown sugar

2 large eggs, room temperature

1 cup heavy whipping cream

¼ cup powdered sugar

¼ cup mascarpone, room temperature

Grated zest of ½ lemon

(Continued)

Combine the wine, granulated sugar, cinnamon, cardamom, cloves, ginger, orange zest and juice, and grapefruit zest and juice in a small saucepan set over medium-high heat. Bring to a boil and cook until reduced to 2 cups, 10 to 15 minutes. Strain and transfer 1 cup to a medium bowl; add the raspberries, cherries, and almonds and stir to combine. Set aside to cool slightly. Reserve the remaining cup wine to use in the cake batter.

Preheat the oven to 375°F. Grease a 9-inch round cake pan and set aside.

Whisk the all-purpose flour, cake flour, cocoa powder, baking soda, and salt in a small bowl until combined. Place the oil and brown sugar in the bowl of a stand mixer with the paddle attachment and mix on high speed for 2 to 3 minutes, until lightened in color. Add the eggs one at a time, beating well after each addition.

With the mixer on low speed, add the flour mixture in three batches, alternating with the remaining 1 cup reduced wine, beginning and ending with the flour and mixing until just incorporated.

Pour the batter into the prepared pan and bake for 35 to 40 minutes, until the cake is cooked through and a toothpick inserted into the center comes out clean. Set the cake, in the cake pan, on a cooling rack for 10 minutes. Run a knife around the cake to release from the pan and turn the cake out of the pan to cool on the rack.

Whisk the whipping cream and powdered sugar in the bowl of a stand mixer with the whisk attachment until soft peaks form. Add the mascarpone and lemon zest and continue whisking until stiff peaks form.

Spread the wine-soaked berries on the cake, top with whipped cream, and serve.

NATIONAL BLACK THEATRE'S
NSTITUTE OF ACT ON ARTS
2031 NATIONAL BLACK THEATRE WAY

The exterior of Dr. Barbara Ann Teer's
National Black Theater in Harlem

"The story that I wanted to tell was of my culture."

DONNA PIERCE

Writer and editor in Chicago, Illinois; Harvard Nieman Foundation fellow

Born in Poplar Bluff, Missouri

Former food editor at Chicago Tribune and past columnist at Chicago Defender

Known for: Documenting African American culture through food

When Donna Pierce started at the *Chicago Tribune* in 2002 as assistant food editor and director of the test kitchen, her new role was a dream come true. She'd been the features editor for a city paper in Columbia, Missouri, where her "Flavors of Home" column had garnered attention. In her first year at the *Tribune*, she wrote a feature about Juneteenth, the celebration that commemorates the June 19, 1865 abolition of slavery in Texas, two years after Abraham Lincoln signed the Emancipation Proclamation. The gathering brings together family, friends, and homemade meals, and Pierce found much to share with readers.

The following year, she pitched another Juneteenth story. "My editor said, 'Well, you already did one.' I said, 'We do a July 4th story every year.'" The contradiction incensed Pierce. Both Juneteenth and July 4th are celebrations of independence that are inherent to American history. But somehow, the judgment was that only one deserved to be retold for readers year after year. Pierce set out on a path to further document African American culture through food: "I began to realize that the story that I wanted to tell was of my culture." She observed that publications across the white-dominant media tended to generalize, disregard, or diminish the contributions of Black cooks.

Six years later, Pierce transitioned to the work that fulfills her today. She writes about the lives of lesser known, or outright forgotten, African American culinary figures. Pierce's adventures in the archives earned her a spot at Harvard University's Knight Visiting Nieman Fellowship. She's celebrated trailblazers like Freda DeKnight, *Ebony* magazine's first food editor, who brought glamour and nuance to the publication's post-World War II pages.

Pierce finds as much joy digging into the records as she does carrying the torch for her own family tree, folks who came from Mobile, Alabama, and New Orleans. Of her generation, she's the one in the family who learned the old recipes, which she says sparked glimmers in the eyes of her great-aunts. "Now I get the glimmer from the next generation," she says.

While she fleshes out the histories of African American food writers and cooks, she's inspired to share the untold stories of her own family's history. Pierce traces her paternal and maternal great-grandfathers to the Wintzell's building in Mobile, the site of Wintzell's Oyster House. "This was a totally Black-created, Black-owned business," Pierce says.

From New Orleans and Mobile, Pierce's parents made it to Columbia, Missouri, where they brought recipes for dishes like homemade rolls, gumbo, date nut bread spiked with pecans, and for special treats, pralines or charlotte russe—a mold of sponge-like cake set with cream and lined with ladyfingers. Oyster loaf was another showstopper— white bread hollowed-out, filled with fried oysters, buttered, then roasted. But the hallmark dish for Pierce is her mother's poppyseed bread cake. It's now a holiday tradition. People from all corners of Pierce's life expect to receive a gifted loaf, down to the doorman of her Chicago condo. It's an end-of-year challenge she's delighted to have. "I have to bake at least a dozen at a time," she says.

Photos from Pierce's family collection

AUNTIE'S LAYER CAKE
《with》 PECANS AND MANGO

Donna is my Chicago auntie, and like all good aunties, she's taught me so much. Her love and knowledge of Black culture and our journey is incredible. This lady is impeccable. She inspired me to create this cake, made with brown butter and pecans and layered with a mango topping

ACTIVE TIME: *1 hour*
START TO FINISH: *About 2¾ hours*
MAKES ONE THREE-LAYER, 8-INCH CAKE
(10 TO 12 SERVINGS)

CAKES

Nonstick spray

¾ cup (1½ sticks) butter

6 large eggs

1½ teaspoons vanilla extract

¾ cup granulated sugar

2 cups cake flour

1 teaspoon kosher salt

¾ cup toasted pecans, finely chopped

MANGO TOPPING

1 (1-ounce) package gelatin

2 tablespoons cold water

5 large egg yolks

1 cup mango puree

2 tablespoons cornstarch

1½ cups heavy cream

¼ cup whole milk

1¼ cups granulated sugar

2 teaspoons kosher salt

1 cup (1 stick) unsalted butter

1 mango, sliced, for garnish

Make the cakes: Preheat the oven to 325°F. Spray three 8-inch round cake pans with nonstick spray and line the bottom of each pan with a circle of parchment paper.

Heat the butter in a small saucepan over medium heat until foaming and bubbling and the milk solids begin to caramelize (turn brown) on the bottom of the pan, about 8 minutes. Remove from the heat and set aside.

In the bowl of an electric mixer with the whisk attachment, whip the eggs and vanilla on high until foamy and pale yellow in color, 2 to 3 minutes. Decrease the mixer speed to low and add the sugar a little at a time. Once all of the sugar has been added, increase the speed to high and whip until the sugar is incorporated and the mixture is foamy, 4 to 5 minutes.

In a separate bowl, sift together the flour and salt. Add one-third of the flour to the egg mixture and gently fold in using a rubber spatula. Repeat the process until all the flour has been incorporated.

Add the nuts and the cooled brown butter and fold to incorporate.

Divide the batter evenly among the prepared pans and bake until golden brown and cooked through, 25 to 30 minutes. Let cool on a cooling rack for 10 minutes. Run an offset spatula around the edges of the pans to loosen the layers and invert onto the cooling rack. Allow the cakes to cool completely, then peel off the parchment before building the cake.

Make the mango topping: Bloom the gelatin in the cold water and set aside.

Whisk together the egg yolks, mango puree, and cornstarch in a medium mixing bowl and set aside.

Combine ½ cup of the heavy cream, the milk, sugar, and salt in a saucepan. Set over low heat and stir until the sugar dissolves. Drizzle the warm cream into the egg mixture while whisking continuously. Return the mango and cream mixture to the saucepan, and cook over medium-low heat, stirring continually and scraping the bottom of the pot to prevent scorching. Continue to cook until the mixture thickens enough to coat the back of a spoon, 7 to 8 minutes.

Remove from the heat, add the bloomed gelatin and butter, and stir until melted and combined. Strain the curd through a fine mesh strainer into a bowl and cover with a piece of plastic wrap pressed directly on the surface. Refrigerate until cool but not set, 35 to 40 minutes.

When ready to build cake, whip the remaining 1 cup heavy cream to soft peaks and fold into the mango curd.

Assemble the cake: Place one cake layer on a stand or cake board. Top with about a third of the mango topping and spread to the edges of the cake. Place the second layer over the topping and top with half of remaining topping, spreading in a similar manner. Top with the third layer, spread the remaining topping in a smooth even layer and smooth any that oozes out the sides. Refrigerate the cake for at least 30 minutes before serving.

Before serving, garnish the top with fresh mango slices.

DONNA'S PULL-APART FRESH DINNER ROLLS

Starting in the early 1900s, the Black migration over the course of the following six decades resulted in six million African Americans leaving the South. Like Donna's own family, who left Mobile for Missouri, many African Americans brought along Southern food traditions, like recipes passed down from elders. There's nothing better than slathering hot rolls with pecan prune butter, which has a decadent sweetness and can be devoured for breakfast or lunch.

ACTIVE TIME: *45 minutes*
START TO FINISH: *3½ hours*
MAKES 16 WARM ROLLS

1 tablespoon active dry yeast

1¼ cups warm milk (110°F)

2 large eggs, lightly beaten

3 tablespoons honey

3 cups all-purpose flour

1 cup teff flour (or whole wheat or millet flour)

2 teaspoons kosher salt

4 tablespoons (½ stick) unsalted butter, plus more for brushing pan, softened

¼ cup Pecan Prune Butter (recipe follows), softened, plus more for serving

Sprinkle the yeast over the warm milk in a small bowl. Allow to stand until foamy, about 5 minutes.

In the bowl of an electric or stand mixer, combine the yeast mixture, eggs, and honey. In a medium bowl, combine the all-purpose flour, teff flour, and salt with a whisk. Fit the electric mixer with a dough hook, add the flour mixture, ½ cup at a time, and knead on medium-low speed until all the flour is incorporated. Add the unsalted butter and knead until incorporated and a slightly sticky dough is formed, 3 to 4 minutes. Transfer the dough to a bowl, cover with a clean linen, and allow to rise in a warm place until doubled in size, about 45 minutes. Punch the dough down and allow to rest for 10 minutes.

Prepare a 9- by 13-inch baking pan or a 10-inch round baking dish by brushing generously with softened unsalted butter. On a lightly floured surface, divide the dough into 16 pieces (about 2 ounces each). With a cupped palm, roll each piece of dough into a smooth, tight ball. Place the rolled dough pieces in the prepared baking pan with no space between each roll. Cover and allow to double in size for another 45 to 60 minutes.

Preheat the oven to 350°F.

When the rolls have doubled in size, generously brush the tops with some of the softened pecan prune butter. Bake until golden brown, 35 to 40 minutes, rotating once for even color. Remove the rolls from the oven and brush tops again with remaining pecan prune butter. Serve warm with additional pecan prune butter.

PECAN PRUNE BUTTER

MAKES 2 CUPS

2 tablespoons chopped pecans

¼ teaspoon ground cinnamon

¼ teaspoon ground ginger

¼ teaspoon kosher salt

6 pieces prunes, diced

1 tablespoon maple syrup or honey

1 pound (4 sticks) unsalted butter, cut into cubes, at room temperature

Cook the pecans, cinnamon, ginger, and salt in a sauté pan over medium until the nuts are toasted. Add the prunes and honey and cook for a few minutes, until caramelized. Let cool for 10 minutes. Fold into the butter until incorporated.

Form the butter into a roughly 4-inch log and roll it up in plastic wrap, then parchment paper. Chill in the freezer for at least 2 hours.

> *"This is a system controlled by gatekeepers that don't look like us. Unless you write the history…about people like us it's not going to get done."*

FRED OPIE

Professor of history and foodways at Babson College in Boston, MA

Born in Tarrytown, New York

Influenced by:
Books by Frederick Douglass, Malcolm X

African American history *is* American history, but it's been sidelined so often, one might not expect to find a professor of African American history and foodways at a college known for producing tomorrow's business leaders. But there's possibly no better place for Fred Opie than Babson College, where he asks his students, future executives, to expand and challenge historic perceptions of the United States that have left out the crucial contributions of Black people.

Opie connects the dots between the past and present. In courses and a host of books, he presents the diverse cultures of the African diaspora and unpacks food as a symbol in politics and civil rights. Students enthusiastically recommend his course to their peers. "Most of them are unaware of how big Africa is as a continent and are unaware of how many staples within the US food system, from rice to peppers to watermelon to coffee, come from Africa," Opie says. "They are blown away."

In his book *Southern Food and Civil Rights: Feeding the Revolution,* he shows how food was a constant presence in African American led social justice movements from the early twentieth century to Black Lives Matter. In *Hog and Hominy: Soul Food from Africa to America*, he traces the development of soul food. In the collection *Zora Neale Hurston on Florida Food: Recipes, Remedies & Simple Pleasures,* he documents the acclaimed author's ethnographic writing on Black communities throughout Florida. Still more of Opie's work dives into Caribbean and Afro Latinx communities where food, labor, and policy intersect. His research has made him a resource on platforms like PBS and NPR.

Opie was born and raised in the Hudson Valley, after previous generations migrated from North Carolina and Virginia. His family lived among Italian, German, and Jewish communities. His father was a corrections officer at Sing Sing prison, and his mother worked as a restaurant host. She participated in anti-apartheid protests, and worked with the NAACP. "A lot of the movement meetings would occur at our house and they always occurred around food," he says.

One day Opie's mother handed him a copy of the autobiography of Frederick Douglass (Opie's full name, Frederick Douglass Opie, pays homage to the influential leader). Opie was moved by Douglass' ability to learn to read and write under threat of death, his escape from enslavement, and his ability to become one of the foremost public intellectuals, orators, and abolitionists of the nineteenth century.

His introduction to Douglass spurred an interest in other Black figures like W.E.B. DuBois and Malcolm X. The self-directed nature of X's and Douglass' education made an impression on Opie, who discovered the importance of developing his own reading list while a graduate student at Syracuse University.

Around the same time, he noticed that aging relatives had been diagnosed with diabetes, high blood pressure, and cardiovascular issues. Opie had just started to live on his own and cook for himself. He reflected on the southern-style meals he enjoyed at his grandmother's home as a kid, and realized how much time and ingredients went into those recipes. He also considered the effect of so much celebration food on his family's health. "I started thinking about how I ate. And how was it affecting these older relatives around me and Black people in general."

He listened to Dick Gregory on the radio, the comedian whose incisive wit was grounded in issues of Black political identity. Gregory educated Black people about radical shifts in their diet and rejected the American industrialized food economy as an act of resistance. Gregory's words led Opie to Dr. Alvenia Fulton, a Chicago nutritionist and columnist whose vegetarian lifestyle and teachings reached many (she advised celebrities of her day like Redd Foxx, Roberta Flack, and Mahalia Jackson).

"A passion of mine is to teach people in our community about food that you can eat well and food that can taste good," he says. "We're in a stressful situation in a racist society. And then we don't have high octane in our tank. So that is part of the mission of my work."

Babson College's campus

BROKEN RICE PEANUT SEAFOOD STEW

When I think about West African culture and its links to Black Americans, this is the dish that springs to mind. Broken rice, a result of the laborious milling process, was once rejected as unworthy of trade. But over time, communities around the world that got "stuck" with broken rice learned to value it and even prefer it—as in Senegal, for example. South Carolina's Low Country was famous for its rice crop, made possible by the forced migration and enslavement of rice farmers from modern-day Sierra Leone, Liberia, and Gambia, among other areas. These rice experts weren't credited as such, but they were sought after for their skill and were responsible for South Carolina's booming economy. The ingenuity of Black cooks helped turn broken rice or "middlins" into a tasty staple of Southern cooking. It's now in high demand among chefs today, resulting in some mills purposefully breaking the rice hull to ensure they have available stock to sell.

ACTIVE TIME: *45 minutes*
START TO FINISH: *1½ hours*
SERVES 8 TO 10

½ cup Caroline Gold rice grits (or basmati rice)

1 cup ¼-inch cubed peeled sweet potato

3 tablespoons extra virgin olive oil

2 medium red onions, finely chopped

2 Fresno chiles, stemmed and finely chopped

1-inch piece fresh ginger, finely chopped

4 cloves garlic, finely chopped

1 tablespoon fermented shrimp paste

2 cups unsweetened coconut milk

1 (14-ounce) can crushed tomatoes

2 cups clam juice

1 cup chicken stock

2 tablespoons peanut butter

½ cup crabmeat

8 whole cherrystone clams

8 shrimp (26 to 30 per pound), peeled and deveined

1 pound salmon collars or other leftover fish, cubed

1 teaspoon fish sauce

Juice of 3 limes

2 cups coarsely chopped mustard greens

¼ cup chopped toasted peanuts, for serving

Rinse the rice grits and sweet potato in a fine mesh strainer under cold water until the water run clears, 3 to 4 minutes. Set aside.

Heat the olive oil in a large pot set over medium-high heat. When the oil shimmers, add the onions, chiles, ginger, and garlic and cook for 4 to 5 minutes, until the onions are translucent. Add the rice grits, potatoes, and shrimp paste and cook for 3 minutes, stirring continually.

Add the coconut milk and tomatoes and simmer for 10 minutes. Add the clam juice and chicken stock and simmer another 10 minutes.

Add the peanut butter, crab, clams, shrimp, and salmon and stir to combine. Simmer an additional 3 minutes, or until the seafood is just cooked through. Add the fish sauce, lime juice, and mustard greens and stir to combine just until the mustard greens have slightly wilted. Serve garnished with toasted peanuts.

NEXT DAY GRITS

You don't have to come from the American South to understand the glory of grits; soul-warming porridges are popular all over the world. In Asia, grits are called congee; in Italy, they're called polenta; in East Africa, ugali; in South Africa, pap; and in West Africa, fufu. But in the United States, we know this staple simply as grits, and we have Native American people like the Muskogee to thank—hominy is a precursor to grits. Whether you just stir in a pat of butter or get fancy and add scallions and shrimps, grits are always good. And for those of you who I have seen sprinkle Lawry's Seasoned Salt (or sugar!) on a bowl of grits...alright, fine. I won't tell. People make grits as they always have and should do!

ACTIVE TIME: *30 minutes*
START TO FINISH: *50 minutes*
SERVES 4

2 cups leftover cooked grits

1 cup unsweetened coconut milk

1 cup chicken stock

4 cloves garlic, minced

1-inch piece fresh ginger, peeled and minced

1 tablespoon soy sauce

2 tablespoons white vinegar

1 cup ¼-inch diced leftover dark meat chicken

1 cup chopped mustard greens

Kosher salt

Four 4-minute poached eggs

4 tablespoons shredded cheddar cheese

Rinse the grits in a fine mesh strainer under cool water, avoiding pressing on the grits, for 2 to 3 minutes, until the grains separate.

Transfer the rinsed grits to a medium saucepan and add the coconut milk, chicken stock, garlic, and ginger. Bring to a simmer over medium-high heat, 8 to 10 minutes.

Add the soy sauce, vinegar, chicken, and mustard greens and stir to combine. Cook for 1 to 2 minutes, until the chicken is heated through and the greens are slightly wilted. Season to taste with salt. Divide among four bowls and serve topped with a poached egg and 1 tablespoon grated cheese.

HOECAKES

Fred is a history professor who knows a great deal about the foodways journey of African Americans. He writes that enslaved farmers from Africa used the iron field hoe to cook hoecakes. He says that cooking corn in this way calls back to practices of baking corn bread wrapped in banana leaves in Angola and other nearby countries.

ACTIVE TIME: *20 minutes*
START TO FINISH: *25 to 30 minutes*
MAKES 8 TO 10 (3-INCH) HOECAKES

1 cup cornmeal

1 tablespoon sugar

1 teaspoon baking powder

½ teaspoon kosher salt

1 large egg, beaten

1 cup plus 1 tablespoon buttermilk

2 tablespoons bacon grease, plus extra for cooking

Sorghum syrup, for serving

Place the cornmeal, sugar, baking powder, and salt in a small bowl and whisk to combine. Combine the egg, buttermilk, and bacon grease in a separate small bowl and whisk to combine.

Add the liquid mixture to the dry ingredients and stir to combine.

Heat a cast iron skillet over medium heat and add a teaspoon of bacon grease. When it shimmers, scoop 2-tablespoon portions of batter into the pan and spread to make approximate 3-inch cakes. Cook until golden brown and crispy, 2 to 3 minutes per side.

Repeat until all of the batter is cooked. Serve the warm hoecakes with sorghum syrup.

*"They'd be like, 'Which one was better?'
And we'd just say, 'They're both really good!'"*

JOE STINCHCOMB

Bar director at Saint Leo's in Oxford, Mississippi

Born in Zweibrücken, Germany

Awarded the Sam Bealls Fellowship by the Blackberry Farm Foundation, which recognizes young hospitality leaders

Known for: Boozy drinks that reflect Black pop culture and history with symbolic ingredients

Not long after graduating from college at the University of Mississippi, Joe Stinchcomb got the opportunity to launch the bar program at Saint Leo, an Italian restaurant that would garner a James Beard semifinalist nomination for its wood-fired pizzas and small plates. He dove in headfirst.

Stinchcomb found he had a knack for developing drink menus that play off of pop culture—his culture. The Grown Simba references a J. Cole track, personified with gin, yellow chartreuse, and dry egg white shake. I'm Not Your Negroni takes the traditional Italian drink, but infuses the gin with grains of paradise (native to Africa), before adding Campari and sweet vermouth. It's a hat tip to James Baldwin and the heralded documentary about his work, *I Am Not Your Negro*.

Stinchcomb is always looking for ways to incorporate African American history, both behind and beyond the bar, as riff, homage, celebration, and inquiry. He is particularly proud of the Bullock and Dabney, his creation that references the Mint Julep and the Corpse Reviver, made with bourbon, citrus, and Bénédictine. The cocktail is named for influential Black bartenders of the early twentieth century. Tom Bullock, the first-known African American author of a cocktail recipe book, and John Dabney, who was born enslaved and managed to pay for his freedom, and that of his wife's and mother's, through the gratuities he earned making drinks.

Stinchcomb will be the first to admit what a nerd he is, that he spends a lot of time digging deep into history. It's a habit he built as a middle child in a six-kid family—you had to know how to amuse yourself. He spent most of his early childhood on military bases. Aaron, his father, was in the Air Force. Stinchcomb was born in Germany and lived in Oklahoma City; Billings, Montana; Lancaster, California, and the Mississippi Gulf Coast all before middle school. Most of the kids he encountered were white, which he didn't really notice until the family moved to Fayetteville, Georgia, a suburb just south of Atlanta that was home to significantly more African Americans than he'd been around before. That's the first time he realized that the way he ate at home was how many of his friends ate, too.

"It was no longer like, 'You don't have this?' Asking for things at other people's houses had changed."

Most days, meals for the family of eight were made up of the dishes Joe's parents ate growing up, like fried chicken, collard greens, and mashed potatoes. But Aaron often referenced cookbooks and asked local friends and colleagues for recipe ideas, so his cooking was inspired by their changing surroundings. It'd be schnitzel one day and curry goat the next. Aaron was a deacon and hosted a crawfish, shrimp, and crab boil every year for the church crowd, where he would boil fifteen pounds of each, then add potatoes and corn.

"One time he cooked durian," Stinchcomb remembers, when they lived on the Gulf Coast and were introduced to produce that was popular among the southeast Asian cultures that made up much of the area. "He just loves to cook things that are unusual for Black culture. He exposed me to different foods and different cultures." Aaron was always adding something new to the family palate, like dragonfruit or jackfruit. When he tried durian, with its distinct, often pungent, aroma and custard-like texture, it was not a universal hit. "He hated it, but I loved it. I still do."

Stinchcomb's mother, Carol, didn't seek out new ingredients so much. But she still had her fun in the kitchen. On holidays in Oklahoma City, she and her sister, Cynthia, would make duplicate courses then ask the family to vote for the best. It was all in good spirits. Sort of. "It'd be a cook-off," Stinchcomb says. "My aunt would do a caramel cake and my mom would do the honey bun cake. It was our version of *Chopped*."

"They'd be like, 'Which one was better?' And we'd just say, 'They're both really good!'"

Stinchcomb says he still can't get the intel on the honey bun cake. His mom won't give it up. "It was like a pound cake. She'd put cinnamon-sugar swirl in there to make it look like a honey bun and glazed icing over it. Man!"

The playful but celebratory approach to food and culture Stinchcomb saw from his family and their travels helped shape his approach to a career of making drinks. As a bar director at a restaurant, Stinchcomb creates menus that connect with the food, but can stand apart from it too. He's widely sought after beyond his home-base bar. To celebrate the 118th birthday of Harlem Renaissance poet Langston Hughes, the Schomburg Center for Research and Black Culture in New York invited him to curate drinks inspired by the period to a sold-out crowd. Within minutes, not a drop was left.

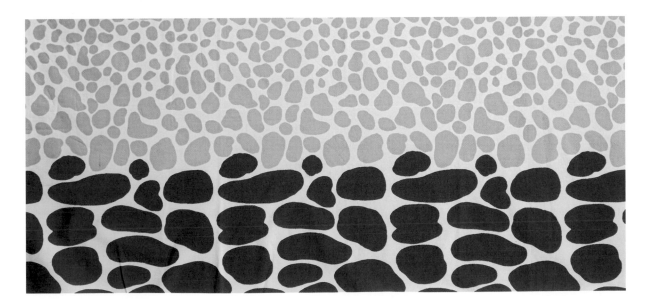

MAR COCKTAIL/THE BOWIE

Robert R. Bowie was a Black bartender who, along with a group of Washington, DC's, top Black barmen, founded the exclusive Mixologist Club in 1889. Historians have found information about the Black bartender members, who gained wealth and fame behind the bar, even before Prohibition. We named this cocktail after mar, the word for honey in Ethiopia. It's so nice to see that, just like in cooking, diversity is happening behind the bar. This cocktail is in honor of him. Raise a glass.

ACTIVE TIME: *10 minutes*
START TO FINISH: *15 minutes*
MAKES 4 COCKTAILS

1 cup Champagne

½ cup gin

½ cup mead

Juice of 2 limes

2 tablespoons honey simple syrup (recipe follows)

¼ teaspoon berbere seasoning

2 sprigs fresh thyme

8 fresh mint leaves

Combine the Champagne, gin, mead, lime juice, simple syrup, berbere, and thyme sprigs in a large cocktail shaker and fill with ice. Shake for 20 to 30 seconds.

Serve over ice with two mint leaves in each glass.

HONEY SIMPLE SYRUP

ACTIVE TIME: *10 minutes*
START TO FINISH: *30 minutes*
MAKES ¾ CUP

½ cup water

2 tablespoons sugar

2 tablespoons honey

Combine the water, honey, and sugar in a small saucepan set over high heat and stir until the sugar dissolves. Set aside to cool. Refrigerate in an airtight container for up to 1 month.

BULLOCK FRIES

Bar food is such an important part of the bar experience. The snacks should be salty and delicious, like French fries and nuts. This dish brings a ton of flavor with extra crispiness and the zest of lemon. When I think of this recipe, I imagine myself sitting at a bar in St. Louis, talking to Tom Bullock, who was a brilliant bartender and in 1917 became the first African American to write a mixology book, called *The Ideal Bartender*.

To turn this into a meal, serve alongside the catfish (page 246), with the yaji (suya spice) aioli (page 290) for dipping.

ACTIVE TIME: *30 minutes*
START TO FINISH: *40 minutes*
SERVES 4

2 cups vegetable oil

1½ pounds sweet potatoes, peeled and cut into 2-inch sticks

2 cups white wine vinegar (optional)

4 cloves garlic, minced

½ cup fresh rosemary sprigs, chopped

Grated zest of 1 lemon

Kosher salt and fresh cracked black pepper

In a deep pot over medium-high heat, bring the oil to 220°F. Place a baking rack in a baking sheet. If you can, soak the sweet potatoes in the vinegar for about 30 minutes before cooking to make them extra crispy. Dry them on a towel before frying.

Working in batches to avoid crowding the pot, add the sweet potatoes and fry until just cooked through, about 5 minutes. Remove the potatoes, drain, and allow to cool on the rack on the baking sheet.

In a medium bowl, toss the garlic, rosemary, and lemon zest. Season with salt and some cracked black pepper.

Bring the temperature of the oil up to 400°F and fry the potatoes a second time, this time aiming for a golden-brown color, 5 to 6 minutes. Drain on the baking rack.

Toss the fries while still warm with the garlic mixture.

SPICED LEMON CHESS PIE

If you're from the South, you're likely familiar with chess pie. It's a deliciously sweet and gooey dessert that is made into plain buttermilk, chocolate, and lemon versions. Theories vary on the name's origins. But we know that for hundreds of years, it was Black women doing much of the culinary and domestic labor in households in the US. Perhaps those stories are for their descendants to tell. Joe's mother and aunt throw down in the kitchen during holidays. If I ever had the chance to join the dessert competition, here's what I'd put in the mix.

You can make the pie dough up to 3 days ahead; keep it refrigerated.

ACTIVE TIME: *30 minutes*
START TO FINISH: *1½ hours, plus time to chill dough*
MAKES ONE 10-INCH PIE (8 TO 10 SERVINGS)

PIE DOUGH

½ cup powdered sugar, plus more for dusting

2¼ cups all-purpose flour

1 teaspoon kosher salt

½ cup (1 stick) cold unsalted butter, cut into pieces

1 large egg yolk

6 tablespoons cold water

FILLING

3 large eggs

3 large egg yolks

1½ cups granulated sugar

2 teaspoons kosher salt

1 teaspoon grains of paradise, cracked

1 tablespoon grated lemon zest

¼ cup fresh lemon juice

¾ cup full-cream buttermilk

½ cup (1 stick) unsalted butter, melted

Powdered sugar, for dusting

Whipped cream, for serving

Make the dough: In a medium bowl, combine the powdered sugar, flour, and salt. Work in the cold butter and blend until clumpy. Mix in the egg yolk and cold water. Using your hands, combine just until the dough comes together in clumps. Gather the dough into a ball and flatten into a disk. Wrap in plastic and chill for at least 2 hours.

Roll out the chilled dough on a floured surface to a 12-inch round. Using the rolling pin, transfer the dough into a 10-inch pie dish and fit in. Trim any overhang to 1 inch above the rim. Fold the trimmed overhang under and crimp around the edges of the dish.

Preheat the oven to 350°F.

Line the pie dough with parchment paper and fill with pie weights or dried beans. Bake until the crust is lightly browned around the edge and beginning to firm up, 15 to 20 minutes. If necessary, remove the pie weights and parchment halfway through the bake to lightly brown the bottom. Press the bottom down with the back of a spoon if the crust bubbles. Allow the crust to cool completely before filling.

Make the filling: Whisk together the eggs, yolks, granulated sugar, salt, grains of paradise, and lemon zest and lemon juice in a medium bowl. Stir in the buttermilk and melted butter.

Pour the filling into the cooled pie shell. Bake until the filling is golden brown and puffed and jiggles slightly when the pie pan is moved, about 40 minutes. Cool the pie completely before slicing. Serve topped with a dusting of powdered sugar and some whipped heavy cream on the side.

> "My mom was the one who taught me that a recipe was a guide. You have to taste." "How do we find we find ways to heal and reclaim all these different pieces?"

MATTHEW RAIFORD

Chef and farmer at Gilliard Farms in Brunswick, Georgia

Born in Bridgeport, Connecticut

James Beard semifinalist for Best Chef Southeast for The Farmer & The Larder

Influenced by: His Nana, who asked, and kept asking, when he'd come back to the family land

JOVAN SAGE

Herbalist at Gilliard Farms in Brunswick, Georgia

Born in Kansas City, Missouri

Former Director of Network Engagement for Slow Food USA

Known for: Building her herbal healing practice from an understanding of how social injustice affects individuals and their bodies

It seems rare, if not impossible, to encounter Matthew Raiford without Jovan Sage, or her without him, at least in regard to their work. The chef who became a farmer, and the food-focused community advocate who developed expertise in herbal medicine are nearly inseparable. The world, especially the American South, is better for it.

At Gilliard Farms in Brunswick, Georgia, Raiford and Sage adapted acreage that has been in Raiford's family for six generations into an independent, sustainable, organic operation where they host dinner events, cultivate chickens (with hogs on the way), and farm various vegetables and herbs. Much of the latter are featured as part of the Sage's Larder online offering, which includes her custom flower essences, tea blends, and other holistic body care.

While Raiford and Sage have lived on the family land for years, it hasn't always been the main driver of their business. Raiford had earned a James Beard semifinalist nod for their restaurant The Farmer and the Larder, which opened in 2015 in downtown Brunswick. Locals and travelers en route to St. Simon or Jekyll Island made it a part of their routine. They'd opened a second restaurant in 2018 before ultimately opting to close both that same year. They felt a pull to shore up their resources and focus more intently on Gilliard.

Jupiter Gilliard, Raiford's maternal great-great-great-grandfather, a formerly enslaved farmer, bought 476 acres in 1874, not long after emancipation. Bits and pieces have been parceled off among various family members over the generations, but Raiford and his sister Althea co-own twenty-eight acres between them. As a boy, Raiford knew he was getting the heck out of the South. Though he was born in Bridgeport, Connecticut—where his father was from and where his parents met—Brunswick and nearby Jekyll Island had realistically only been integrated for a few years by the time he was a teen. He didn't see a future for himself there. Raiford started thinking about culinary school but his father discouraged him: "You'll never get the status that you want."

He was trying to protect his son from the disappointment he'd experienced. A professionally trained baker in the northeast before moving the family down to Brunswick around 1968, Raiford's father couldn't find work as a baker in the area. None of the white-owned bakeries would hire him.

"My dad would make puff pastry dough and he'd make these amazing apple turnovers when I was a kid," Raiford says. "Next to those apple turnovers would be cathead biscuits." Raiford remembers decadent cakes too—German chocolate and red velvet. "That was his thing."

Eventually, his father found work as a longshoreman and saved his baking skills for the family, but the obstacles to his preferred vocation, the one he'd trained for and was passionate about, were heartbreaking.

Sage grew up in the Midwest but describes her upbringing as "very Southern."

"I come from a place where we throw parades for our cows. The American Royal, the World Barbecue Championship, that's my childhood." Her father was a truck driver; her mother a secretary who had been raised by Sage's grandmother as part of the Nation of Islam. "We would go to get our bean pies. Kansas City is an international city—I grew up eating Israeli food, Mexican, Peruvian. German sauerkraut and potato salad. I took it for granted. I assumed this has got to be what it's like everywhere."

Influenced by her truck-driving father's travel mugs, Sage started drinking coffee at the age of ten, and by the time she was a young teen, started frequenting the indie- and punk-fueled coffee shop scene. She studied critical race theory, went into organizing, and eventually moved to New York. Her work varied from supporting safe educational environments for youth and queer communities, political organizing, teaching kids about sustainable food practices, to eventually coordinating the Slow Food chapters in the US and building partnerships with growers. Her interest in plants as medicine emerged from discovering her ancestry, speaking to family elders, and studying native traditions of healing. "How do we find ways to heal and reclaim all these different pieces from slavery, to the genocide that happened here? We look to the past."

She and Raiford met in Turin, Italy, at the international Slow Food conference. After time in the Army, culinary school, and multiple chef jobs, he'd been executive chef of catering for the House of Representatives in Washington, DC, but decided it was time to come back home, back to Brunswick, back to the land.

Sage eventually left New York for the small port city. It's now home. She converts plants into healing elixirs and other recipes as a health coach and doula, her broader empathy for larger communities funneled into meaningful and intimate exchanges with individuals. The farm that she and Raiford operate is, of course, governed by nature, and Raiford knows to follow its lead.

"My mom was the one who taught me that a recipe was a guide. You have to taste," he says, recalling the shrimp creole he used to make with stewed tomatoes and rice. "The pepper that came out today might not taste the same way the pepper did the last time. The tomatoes might not be as sweet, they might be a little more acidic. I learned that whole taste and feel thing, between her and my grandmother."

SPICY GRILLED GARDEN EGG SALAD

Black people have always farmed. In the US, I've noticed that African farmers now living in the US (some of them as refugees) are using social media to sell crops native to their homelands. The West African eggplant, or "garden egg," featured in this egg salad is one such crop that I've seen making the rounds. Matthew and Jovan use their deep knowledge of the land and their commitment to community to honor their families' legacies and contribute to the folks around them. This recipe celebrates them.

ACTIVE TIME: 15 minutes
START TO FINISH: 30 minutes
SERVES 6 TO 8

1 cup thinly sliced red onion (about ½ an onion)

4 tablespoons fresh lemon juice

Kosher salt and freshly ground black pepper

1 pound West African eggplants (garden egg), halved lengthwise if large

3 tablespoons vegetable oil

1 teaspoon honey

1 tablespoon dried shrimp powder (optional)

1 clove garlic, finely grated

1 bird's-eye chile, sliced

4 heirloom tomatoes, cut into 1-inch slices, seeds removed

¼ cup scent leaves (or basil), julienned

¼ cup fresh cilantro leaves and tender stems

Preheat the grill to medium-high heat.

Toss the onions in a bowl with 1 tablespoon of the lemon juice. Season with salt and let sit for 10 minutes to quick pickle. Drain.

Toss the eggplant slices with the oil and season with salt and black pepper. Grill the eggplant for 2 to 3 minutes a side, or until you get good grill marks.

Make the dressing: In a small bowl, whisk the remaining 3 tablespoons lemon juice, the honey, shrimp powder if using, garlic, and chile.

Arrange the warm grilled eggplant slices with the tomatoes and drained onions on a platter. Spoon the dressing over the salad and toss on the herbs. Season to taste with salt and cracked black pepper.

CHILLED WATERMELON AND RED PEPPER SOUP «with» PICKLED BERRIES

One of my and Zion's favorite things to do in the summer, when it is super hot out, is to take a bite of cool watermelon. My son is more into the shape of the melon and figuring it out: It is round and green and makes a nice thump when he hits it. For him that's summer and that's what this dish is all about. A chilled soup with watermelon and berries, made to refresh you. One day I have got to take Zion to Matthew and Jovan's farm to run around and play.

ACTIVE TIME: 30 minutes

START TO FINISH: 4½ hours or overnight

PICKLED BERRIES

¼ cup sherry vinegar

1 tablespoon granulated sugar

2 teaspoons yellow mustard seeds

2 whole Selim pepper pods (or black cardamom pods)

2 cups whole seasonal berries (such as raspberries, blueberries, and blackberries)

1 small shallot, sliced ¼ inch thick

SOUP

4 cups cubed seedless watermelon

2 medium red bell peppers, roasted, seeded, and peeled

2 large ripe tomatoes, seeded and diced

1 medium cucumber, peeled, seeded, and diced

Grated zest and juice of 1 lime

2 tablespoons extra virgin olive oil, plus more for drizzling

1 tablespoon sherry vinegar, plus more to taste

Kosher salt and freshly ground black pepper

¼ cup scent leaves (or a mix of fresh basil and mint leaves), torn

Make the pickled berries: Heat the vinegar, sugar, mustard seeds, and Selim in a small pot over low heat, stirring to dissolve the sugar, 1 to 2 minutes. Remove from the heat and allow the syrup to cool slightly. Mix the berries and shallot in a medium heat-proof bowl. Pour the syrup over the berries and gently crush a few. Let stand while you make the soup.

Make the soup: Puree the watermelon, roasted peppers, tomatoes, and cucumber in a blender until smooth, 1 to 2 minutes. Stir in the lime zest and juice, olive oil, and vinegar. Season to taste with salt, black pepper, and additional sherry vinegar if desired. Chill the soup for at least 4 hours or overnight.

Divide the chilled soup among four to six bowls and garnish with the scent leaves, pickled berries, and an additional drizzle of olive oil.

SUNDAY ROAST CHICKEN
«with» CHICKPEAS AND COUSCOUS

Alberta Wright owned Jezebel, which was one of my inspirations for Red Rooster, and that place was fabulous. Located in Manhattan, near the southeast corner of West 45th and 9th Avenue, Jezebel was right across the street from where I lived. I've never seen anyone host like Alberta. Whether she was seating a celebrity, even Denzel Washington or Madonna, Alberta was always the real star in that dining room. She had style. She set the restaurant up like you had just walked into a Southern lady's home. Once you were there, she surrounded you with her warmth.

When I think about Alberta's history—her fierceness combined with her incredible charm and grace, I am humbled by how much she accomplished, when she started with very little. She had an eighth-grade education, but she ended up opening a Jezebel in Paris. I am reminded that there are so many Albertas out there, a whole lineage of Black queens who won't be told what they can't do—they are charming, hardworking, talented—even if most of them don't get acknowledged. I was very lucky to have Alberta as a mentor. In fact, I wouldn't be in Harlem without her.

She died in 2015. I remember my last conversation with her. She was living in Harlem and we were standing on the terrace outside of Red Rooster, watching people walk back and forth. She leaned over to me and whispered, "I'm coming back, Marcus. I'm coming back."

ACTIVE TIME: *30 minutes*
START TO FINISH: *1 hour 15 minutes*
SERVES 4 TO 6

1 whole chicken, innards removed

½ cup Berbere Spice Brown Butter (page 277), cut into cubes

1 small bunch fresh parsley, chopped

1 small bunch fresh cilantro, chopped

8 to 10 stems fresh sage, chopped

1 tablespoon plus 1 teaspoon extra virgin olive oil

2 teaspoons kosher salt

1 teaspoon freshly ground black pepper

1 red onion, chopped

2 cloves garlic, minced

1 (14-ounce) can chickpeas

½ cup pitted black olives

1 (14-ounce) can crushed tomatoes

1 teaspoon ground cumin

1 teaspoon ground turmeric

½ cup red wine

⅔ cup couscous

Grated zest and juice of 1 lemon

4 chicken livers

(Continued)

Preheat the oven to 400°F.

Using your fingers and starting at the neck of the chicken, gently separate the skin from the meat of the breasts, just enough to slide half of the berbere butter in between the skin and the breast. Take half of all of the herbs and distribute them under the skin and inside the cavity of the chicken. Rub the chicken all over with 1 tablespoon of the olive oil and season with half of the salt and pepper.

Place the chicken in a medium roasting pan and roast until the skin is golden brown, juices from the thigh run clear when pricked with a knife, and the internal temperature of the thickest part of the thigh registers 165°F, 45 to 60 minutes. Remove the bird from the oven and allow to rest at least 10 minutes before carving.

In the meantime, heat the remaining berbere butter in a medium Dutch oven set over medium heat. When the butter has melted, add the onion, garlic, and remaining salt and pepper and sauté until the onion is beginning to brown, about 10 minutes.

Add the remaining herbs, the chickpeas, olives, tomatoes, cumin, turmeric, and red wine and stir to combine. Decrease the heat to low, cover, and cook for 20 minutes. Add the couscous and the lemon zest and juice and stir to combine. Remove from the heat, cover, and set aside for 5 to 10 minutes, until the couscous is tender.

Heat the remaining 1 teaspoon olive oil in a small sauté pan set over medium heat. When the oil shimmers, add the chicken livers. Cook for 4 to 5 minutes, just until cooked through. Slice the liver and stir into the chickpea couscous mixture.

Carve the chicken and serve with chickpeas and couscous.

PAPA ED'S SHRIMP AND GRITS

Ed is the executive chef at the Rooster. He's my man. He's a major part of what we do. He's put Rooster on fire. His mix tape dinners are legendary: He creates dinners based on rap and R&B music, with Nas, Biggie, Missy Elliott, and Wu Tang in mind. It's so beautiful; diners are invited to eat a soulful story on a plate. And of course, when Raekwon the Chef, of the Wu Tang Clan, came and performed, he and Ed tore it up.

When I think about a Southern dish like shrimp and grits, I'm reminded of the mood that jazz and church give me, and of how universal these feelings are. These dishes are eaten all over the world, just like hip-hop is heard all over the world.

Ed's parents grew up in the South, so he can teach us about shrimp and grits, about gumbo. Food like this points to a culture, to art, to music. I didn't grow up in America, so when I listen to Ed, I'm learning not only from a chef's point of view. I'll say, "Ed, what do you remember about eating at home?" Then I sit back, taste, and listen.

ACTIVE TIME: *45 minutes*
START TO FINISH: *1 hour*
SERVES 4 TO 6

GRITS

2 cups water

1 cup heavy cream

4 tablespoons (½ stick) unsalted butter

1 cup stone ground grits

4 ounces white cheddar cheese, shredded

Kosher salt

GUMBO SAUCE AND SHRIMP

3 tablespoons vegetable oil

¼ cup small-diced celery

¼ cup small-diced red onion

¼ cup small-diced red bell pepper

4 cloves garlic, minced

1 teaspoon kosher salt

½ teaspoon freshly ground black pepper

4 ounces ground chorizo

1 (14-ounce) can crushed tomatoes

8 ounces small-diced fresh okra

1 tablespoon smoked paprika

1 teaspoon cayenne pepper

2 cups fish stock

2 tablespoons apple cider vinegar

12 large shrimp, tail on, peeled and deveined

Make the grits: Combine the water, cream, and butter in a medium saucepan set over medium-high heat. Once the liquid comes to a simmer, add the grits and whisk to combine. Decrease the heat to low and cook, stirring frequently, until the grits are tender and creamy, 20 to 25 minutes. Remove from the heat and stir in the cheese until melted. Taste and adjust seasoning with salt as desired.

Make the sauce: Heat the vegetable oil in a large saucepan or Dutch oven set over medium-high heat. When the oil shimmers, add the celery, onion, red pepper, garlic, salt, and pepper and cook, stirring frequently, until the onions are translucent, 3 to 4 minutes. Add the chorizo and cook for 4 to 5 minutes, stirring frequently. Add the tomatoes, okra, paprika, and cayenne and continue cooking for 4 to 5 minutes, stirring frequently. Add the stock and vinegar and bring to a simmer. Decrease the heat to low, cover, and cook, stirring occasionally, for 20 to 25 minutes, until the vegetables are tender and the mixture has thickened slightly.

Add the shrimp and stir to combine. Continue to cook 4 to 5 minutes, until the shrimp are cooked through. Serve the shrimp and sauce over the warm grits.

CITRUS SCALLOPS ⟨*with*⟩ HIBISCUS TEA

This dish is like ceviche but with hibiscus tea. For me the hibiscus links Senegal to the Caribbean islands, representing a whole arc of tradition. It's an acidic seafood dish, with the narrative of Africa and the Caribbean on complete display. It's an elegant dish that uses dried hibiscus (or sorrel, referring to the sepals of the hibiscus plant) that gives a nod to Ed's range. He pulls from his personal ties to the South and his fine dining training. And he lives in Brooklyn where there's a huge Caribbean population.

ACTIVE TIME: *20 minutes*
START TO FINISH: *1½ hours*
SERVES 4 AS AN APPETIZER

2 tablespoons dried sorrel (hibiscus) leaves

1 cup water

½ cup macadamia nuts, roughly chopped

1 tablespoon plus 2 teaspoons extra virgin olive oil

1 pound dry packed large scallops, sliced into 6 pieces each

¼ teaspoon kosher salt

Juice of 1 lemon

¼ cup fresh parsley leaves

Place the sorrel leaves and water in a small saucepan, cover, and bring to a simmer over high heat. Remove from the heat and set aside to steep for 1 hour. Strain the tea and refrigerate until chilled.

Preheat the oven to 350°F.

Toss the nuts with 2 teaspoons of the olive oil and spread on a baking sheet. Place in oven and roast until the nuts are golden brown, 8 to 10 minutes. Set aside to cool.

Season the scallop slices with salt and drizzle with the remaining 1 tablespoon olive oil and the lemon juice.

To serve, place 2 tablespoons hibiscus tea in each of four bowls. Place the scallops in the bowls, making sure some of each scallop is touching the tea. Garnish with the roasted macadamia nuts and parsley leaves. Serve immediately.

BIRD AND TOAST

Melba is an amazing lady, a community leader and a very dear friend of mine. She opened her restaurant, Melba's, in 2005 in Harlem, long before it was chic or cool. She has served the neighborhood through good and tough times, always finding a way to keep the lights on, which as restaurant owners is sometimes hard to do. In nearly every city and every town in America, there's an iconic restaurant known for good Southern-style food. The fried chicken trend has taken the country by storm, but it's hard to compete with the originals, usually owners of legendary restaurants in African American communities, like Melba or her late aunt Sylvia Woods of Harlem's Sylvia's.

This dish is a play on another icon and another chicken trend: One of the most magical restaurants in America is Prince's Hot Chicken Shack in Nashville, which is indisputably the birthplace of hot chicken. Despite the electrifying spices—or maybe because of them—customers come back for more. This recipe uses black pepper, berbere spice, and cayenne pepper for a good kick. You can use brioche toast with this recipe, but in Nashville they use white bread. Nashville's hot-style chicken is famous all over the country, and although the original is too good to duplicate, it's a great jumping-off point for inspiration.

ACTIVE TIME: *45 minutes*
START TO FINISH: *4 hours 15 minutes*
SERVES 8

CHICKEN AND BRINE

1 quart water

¼ cup kosher salt

2 tablespoons sugar

1 tablespoon soy sauce

3 sprigs fresh thyme

1-inch piece fresh ginger, peeled and sliced

2 bay leaves

1 Scotch bonnet (or habanero) chile, stemmed and halved

8 boneless, skin-on chicken thighs

2 cups ice

SPICE MIX AND GLAZE

2 tablespoons cayenne pepper

1 tablespoon berbere seasoning

2 teaspoons light brown sugar

2 teaspoons paprika

2 teaspoons garlic powder

1 teaspoon kosher salt

1 teaspoon freshly ground black pepper

3 tablespoons honey

1 tablespoon soy sauce

½ teaspoon fish sauce

Peanut oil, for frying

8 (½ -inch) slices brioche, toasted

1 tablespoon unsalted butter

3 tablespoons Chicken Liver Mousse (page 22)

Pickled Peaches (page 252), for garnish

Brine the chicken: Combine the water, salt, sugar, soy sauce, thyme, ginger, bay leaves, and chile in a large container and stir until the salt and sugar dissolve. Add the chicken and ice. Cover and refrigerate for 3 hours.

Make the spice mix and glaze: Combine the cayenne, berbere, brown sugar, paprika, garlic powder, salt, and pepper in a small bowl and whisk to combine.

Combine ½ teaspoon of the spice mix with the honey, soy sauce, and fish sauce in a small bowl and whisk to combine. Set the glaze aside.

Fry the chicken and finish the dish: Remove the chicken from the brine, rinse, and pat dry. Season the chicken on all sides with the remaining spice mix.

Heat 1 inch peanut oil to 325°F in a large Dutch oven set over medium-high heat. Gently place four thighs in the oil and fry for 6 to 7 minutes, until the chicken reaches an internal temperature of 165°F. Remove to a paper towel–lined cooling rack and tent loosely with foil. Repeat with remaining thighs.

In the meantime, lightly coat one side of each toast with butter and spread with about 1 teaspoon chicken liver mousse. Slice each thigh into three or four pieces, depending on the size, and set on top of the mousse. Drizzle with the honey glaze and serve, garnished with a pickled peach.

A mural outside the National Black Theater in Harlem

FRIED CHICKEN AND WAFFLES
«with» PIRI PIRI GLAZE

A native New Yorker with strong ties to South Carolina, Melba likes to say she was "born, bred, and buttered" in Harlem. Her aunt is Sylvia Woods of Harlem's Sylvia's. Chicken and waffles originated in Harlem when jazz musicians wanted something delicious after playing all night. It's a dish that perfectly reflects Melba and her Harlem roots.

Note: This recipe may seem intimidating, but if you make the glaze first, then boil the sweet potato for the waffles while frying the chicken, you can keep the chicken warm in the oven while making the waffles.

ACTIVE TIME: *1 hour*
START TO FINISH: *3 hours*
SERVES 4 TO 6

PIRI PIRI GLAZE
Piri Piri Marinade (page 287)
¼ cup honey
2 tablespoons extra virgin olive oil

FRIED CHICKEN
1½ cups buttermilk
1 tablespoon Frank's RedHot sauce
8 small boneless, skinless chicken thighs
2 teaspoons kosher salt
1 cup all-purpose flour
¼ cup cornmeal
1 tablespoon cornstarch
1 teaspoon garlic powder
1 teaspoon paprika
Peanut oil, for frying

WAFFLES
1 small sweet potato, peeled and cubed
1½ cups whole wheat flour
¼ cup sugar
1 tablespoon baking powder
½ teaspoon kosher salt
½ teaspoon ground cinnamon
Pinch ground nutmeg
1¼ cups half and half or vanilla coconut milk
4 tablespoons (½ stick) unsalted butter, melted and cooled slightly
3 large eggs, separated
Nonstick cooking spray, for waffle iron
1 cup Pikliz (page 30)

For the glaze: Whisk together the marinade, honey, and olive oil in a small bowl and set aside.

Make the fried chicken: Whisk together the buttermilk and hot sauce in a bowl large enough to hold the chicken. Add the chicken and toss to coat. Cover and refrigerate for at least 2 hours or up to 6 hours.

Preheat the oven to the warm setting or 200°F. Place a cooling rack inside a baking sheet, cover with paper towels, and set in the oven.

Remove the chicken from the marinade and season on all sides with 1 teaspoon of the salt.

Combine the flour, cornmeal, cornstarch, garlic powder, paprika, and remaining 1 teaspoon salt in a shallow dish or bowl. Toss the chicken, one thigh at a time, in the mixture and set aside.

Heat ¼ inch oil in a large cast iron skillet set over medium-high heat and bring to 350°F.

Carefully add the chicken, a few pieces at a time, so as to not overcrowd the pan. Fry for 4 to 5 minutes, until golden brown. Turn the chicken over and continue cooking until the other side is golden brown and the chicken reaches an internal temperature of 165°F, about 5 minutes. Transfer the chicken to the prepared rack in the oven and repeat until all of the chicken has been cooked.

For the waffles: Place the sweet potato in a medium saucepan, cover with water, and bring to a boil over high heat. Cook until the potatoes are fork tender, 15 to 20 minutes. Drain the potatoes and mash until smooth. Set aside to cool slightly.

Place the flour, sugar, baking powder, salt, cinnamon, and nutmeg in a large mixing bowl and whisk to combine.

Combine the sweet potatoes, half and half, butter, and egg yolks in another bowl and whisk to combine.

Place the egg whites in a third bowl and beat until stiff peaks form.

Add the liquid mixture to the dry ingredients and stir to combine. Do not overmix. Fold the egg whites into the batter until minimal streaks of white are showing.

Heat a waffle iron. Spray with nonstick spray. Once hot, pour one-fourth of the batter into the waffle iron.

Close the lid and cook until golden brown and cooked through, 4 to 5 minutes. Transfer the cooked waffles to the oven to keep warm. Repeat until all the batter has been used.

Top each waffle with two chicken thighs, drizzle with the piri piri glaze, and serve with pikliz.

Chapter 4
LEGACY

Old and new journeys from Africa to the Americas and stories of Black figures in food reclaiming their history.

IN HONOR OF:

BJ DENNIS, chef, Charleston, SC

Corn and Crab Beignets with Yaji (Suya Spice) Aioli

Grilled Snapper
with Goober Pea Marinade and Moyo

JESSICA B. HARRIS, historian, Brooklyn, NY

Saffron Tapioca Pudding
with Amaro Marinated Strawberries

Chicken Neck Soup with Oyster Mushrooms

KWAME ONWUACHI, chef, Washington, DC

Braised Goat Shoulder
with Locust Bean and Chili Oil

Pots de Crème with Benne Seed Praline
and Roasted Pineapple

Grilled Chickpea Flatbread with Lentil Dal

LEAH CHASE, chef, New Orleans, LA

Leah Chase Gumbo

MASHAMA BAILEY, chef, Savannah, GA

Chilled Corn and Tomato Soup

Fish Cakes with Birmingham Greens Salad

Pepper Broth with Beef Heart

MICHAEL TWITTY, writer, Washington, DC

Grilled Short Ribs in Piri Piri Marinade

Bean Fritters

Mangú with Eggplant Escabeche

RODNEY SCOTT, pitmaster, Charleston, SC

Rodney's Ribs with Baked Cowpeas

Rodney's Hushpuppies with Peanut Succotash

CARLA HALL, chef and television host, New York, NY

Kelewele Crusted Catfish with Yucca Fries
and Garden Egg Chow Chow

HERB WILSON, chef, Miami, FL

Montego Bay Rum Cake

JEROME GRANT, chef, Washington, DC

Boston Bay Jerk Chicken with Plantains

MARVIN WOODS, chef, Atlanta, GA

Collard Green and Fresh Cheese Salad

MICHAEL ADÉ ELÉGBÈDÉ, chef, Lagos, Nigeria

Callaloo and Bitter Greens Salad
with Smoked Fish and Egusi Seeds

Ginger and Hibiscus Flower Granita

Taro and Millet Croquettes

PATRICK CLARK, chef, Washington, DC

Short Ribs with Get Up Sauce and Green Beans

PIERRE THIAM, chef, Lagos, Nigeria, and New York, NY

Farro in Jollof Sauce

Fonio Stuffed Collards with Pepper Sambal
and Sauce Moyo

JAQUETA TUCKER, sous chef, New York, NY

Spiced Butter-Poached Shrimp and Potatoes

ROBLÉ ALI, chef, New York, NY

Teff and Brown Butter Biscuits with Shaved
Country Ham

LAUREN VON DER POOL, chef, Los Angeles, CA

Sea Moss Delight Smoothie

It was the late '90s and I was cooking at Aquavit in New York when the legendary Black restaurateur and civil rights activist Leah Chase came to see what the young buck chef was doing there. I was so nervous when she came into the restaurant, but she broke the ice. We started to talk about crayfish, something we had both cooked many times, about food, about Africa. Before she left, she told me, "Whatever you do, aim high. Keep pushing. Keep teaching."

One thing about the moment we're in—the *movement* we're in—is that I see more and more young Black people wanting to become food professionals. That tells me something important: restoring authorship leads to greater aspiration.

The legacy Black cooks inherit in this country is inextricably tied to the systemic racism, history of enslavement, and policies that have harmed Black families, creators, and entrepreneurs for centuries. For so long, the authorship and ownership of Black food has been ripped away from its creators. Without authorship, there becomes no reason to celebrate food from a cultural perspective because the link between the two is erased. How can you aspire to something that you never see recognized?

Now, Black foodways in the United States and around the world are being studied with new vigor and interest, and Black excellence in the culinary arts is starting to be recognized widely. Today there are Black chefs, writers, sommeliers, and others transforming the food world—all of us standing on the shoulders of Leah and her husband, Dooky, building on the legacy of people like Edna Lewis and Sylvia Woods and other iconic African American restaurateurs.

Black cooks have always been in this profession. But none of us would be here without those who came before.

This chapter honors those cooks and their foodways. That story starts on the continent of Africa, and was carried to this country through the enslavement of Africans. Yet Africa itself, the root of so much beloved food and ritual shared by people around the world, has often been excised from the narrative.

Take "French-roasted" coffee—where the location and style of a finishing touch on a coffee bean is more common to discuss than the farmer who grew the coffee in Ethiopia. People love Belgian chocolate—but there is no cacao growing in Belgium. Let's *also* celebrate the origin of that bar of chocolate in the Congo, which was under Belgian colonial rule. African American culture has influenced the world. Why aren't okra and peanuts acknowledged on the same level as Parmesan cheese or olive oil?

The chefs and writers in this chapter are restoring the Black authorship of American food. BJ Dennis is raising up the Gullah Geechee cuisine in the Low Country of South Carolina. Perhaps no one has done more than Jessica B. Harris to shed light on the connection between African and American foodways. Kwame Onwuachi is finding a path forward for his cooking by looking at his past. Mashama Bailey is extending Edna Lewis's legacy of Southern cooking and storytelling. Michael Twitty is showing all kinds of Americans just how African they are. And Rodney Scott's whole-hog barbecue continues the long-held practice of pit cookery perfected by enslaved Black pitmasters.

Learning about young and elder food icons will help us to aspire, and to inspire. As we become more capable of noticing the ways in which Africa has been left out, we can bring it back in. If the United States can embrace kimchi and nigiri sushi, we can learn to eat fufu. Jollof rice deserves to be in the same conversation as paella or jambalaya. Pho has become an important part of the food story here, and fish pepper soup, a staple of Nigeria and other countries, ought to be just as present. Why do we accept one food but treat another as too different to try? We ought to unpack that. This book is one step in that direction.

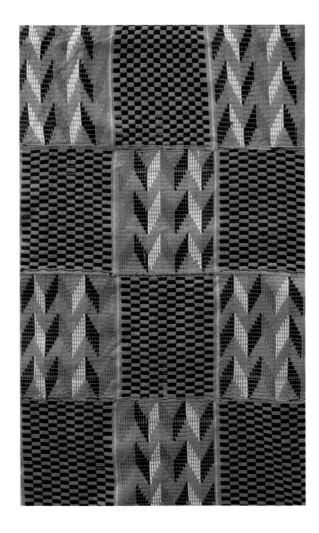

BJ DENNIS

Chef of Gullah Geechee cuisine in Charleston, South Carolina

An ambassador of African ancestral culinary traditions in the Low Country

Born in Charleston, South Carolina

Known for: Local pop-ups and national dining events that celebrate fresh seafood, heritage grains, and local agricultural practices of the Gullah Geechee

To hear BJ Dennis tell it, "the culture" has always been in him, even when he wasn't paying any mind. The culture is his people, living in body and in spirit on and near the Sea Islands. The culture is their Creole language still very much in use today. That culture was present, even when he was selling stewed chicken and rice out of his home as boxed lunches, without much thought for what the dish meant.

Dennis had grown up hearing stories from his grandfather about Gullah Geechee foodways in Charleston, around Daniel Island and across the creek in Clement Ferry. Those stories line the foundation of Dennis' work: he cooks the food of a nation of West African descendants located in the coastal region from North Florida up to North Carolina. He rattles off dishes that make up his upbringing: okra soup, okra rice, field peas, and lima beans. Salmon patties. Shrimp and crab rice, shrimp and crab perlou. Gumbo with blue crab.

Long conversations with his grandfather have become guideposts in his understanding of a personal and national history. "The full range of stories of what we were cooking for ourselves as enslaved and free people have never been told," Dennis says. Food holds the mystery of lost traditions; it's also the gateway to rediscovering them.

"Granddaddy, he was old-school Gullah Geechee," Dennis says. "He could hunt, he could fish. But his main love was his garden." The elder Benjamin Dennis tried to instill that love in his grandchildren, and tasked them with picking okra, and cleaning whatever came from the fishing creek: croaker, whiting, sea bass, tiny sweet shrimp, crab, and small sand sharks coming through inlets.

Dennis didn't grasp the widespread influence of his heritage until he left Charleston in his mid-20s. He moved to St. Thomas in the Virgin Islands, where he was surprised to note a deep knowledge and appreciation for his heritage. He'd hear the same construction of language, the same accent, a key observation in what has sometimes been described as an insular culture, in part due to Gullah Geechee communities' geographic placement. For a young man who'd never left Charleston before, finding home so far away had a huge impact. He met chefs on St. Thomas who proudly cooked their homeland cuisine. He also saw that on a majority Black island, professional kitchens were still heavily influenced by a white European aesthetic. "I was lucky to work with chefs who really got it, who were cooking their West Indian food and saying, 'This is our culture.'" Dennis saw that Black island cookery could hold its own in professional kitchens so often lauded as hallowed ground for French traditions. But the African roots of Low Country food—its ingredients and the people who developed it—had its traditions too. And those recipes deserved center stage as much as anyone's.

After several years, Dennis returned to Charleston to cook in major restaurants and worked alongside chefs who'd done the fine dining circuit in New York. But something was missing. "Where the flavor? Where the culture?" People were coming to Charleston for the cuisine, he says, but the people who made the cuisine weren't represented. "We getting all these accolades in the city, the city gets all this press, but the one thing that made, that built this city up to this point ain't getting no love."

He launched a series of pop-up events and now works as a personal chef and caterer cooking "culture food." He introduced Anthony Bourdain to Gullah Geechee food in an episode of *Parts Unknown*. He rediscovered a rare type of African rice in Trinidad and was written up in the *New York Times*. He is gratified to affirm stories from his grandfather with his own research and that of his friend and prolific historian David Shields.

"To see it in print, it makes it valid for others," Dennis says. "To see those foods that I'd been told or heard of...written [about] in the 1700s and 1800s..." He trails off. When you come from a history that was systematically erased, when its authors risked their lives for a chance at literacy, such records are profoundly important. "We forgot about the old wild greens we used to eat. The herbal medicines...There's so much out here."

Dennis's cooking and research is driven by a thirst for reeducation. Centuries ago, Gullah Geechee people grew their own rice, descendants of rice growers in present-day Sierra Leone, Liberia, and Guinea. The cuisine was driven by produce and seafood, rich and full of deep flavor. "One of my biggest battles is when people talk about 'slave food is killing us.' But dude, what is really slave food? Do you know what enslaved people really were growing on their own plots? Do we know about the indigenous? Do we know about the Africans that grew their rice here, grown by our people for their personal consumption...Do we know about the vegetables, the greens that we ate?"

Dennis wants to know. To find the answer, he reads, he asks questions, and he keeps cooking.

Scenes from Charleston

CORN AND CRAB BEIGNETS
«with» YAJI (SUYA SPICE) AIOLI

BJ Dennis grew up in Charleston, picking okra and fishing in the creeks for shrimp and crabs. The crab beignets here are paired with an aioli made with yaji, the ultra-popular West African spice blend.

ACTIVE TIME: *30 minutes*
START TO FINISH: *About 1 hour*
MAKES ABOUT 24 BEIGNETS

4 tablespoons (½ stick) unsalted butter

2 cups fresh corn kernels (from 2 ears)

2 tablespoons chopped fresh chives

1½ cups all-purpose flour

½ cup cornmeal

2 teaspoons baking powder

½ teaspoon ground cayenne

1 teaspoon kosher salt

1 cup buttermilk

1 large egg

8 ounces lump crabmeat

Vegetable oil, for frying

Yaji (Suya Spice) Aioli (page 290)

Melt the butter in a medium sauté pan set over medium heat. Add the corn and cook until softened slightly, 3 to 4 minutes. Transfer to a large mixing bowl, stir in the chives, and set aside until cool.

In a separate bowl, whisk together the flour, cornmeal, baking powder, cayenne, and salt.

Add the buttermilk and egg to the corn and stir to combine. Add the flour mixture and stir to combine. Add the crabmeat and fold to combine.

Heat 1½ inches oil in a large pot or deep fryer to 375°F. Place a paper towel–lined cooling rack in a baking sheet and set aside.

Using a tablespoon measure or a ½-ounce scoop, carefully place scoops of batter into the oil, four or five at time. (Work in batches to avoid overcrowding the beignets in the oil.) Fry, turning frequently, until the beignets are golden brown and cooked through the center, 5 to 7 minutes. Transfer the cooked beignets to the prepared cooling rack to drain and cool slightly.

Serve warm with the aioli for dipping.

GRILLED SNAPPER
≪with≫ GOOBER PEA MARINADE AND MOYO

In the Deep South, the goober, a boiled peanut and an African culinary staple, is everything, or can be anything; Civil War soldiers even used it to make coffee. But the peanut is not a nut, it's a legume that flowers above the ground, and fruits below it. Resourceful and brilliant cooks, those Southern grandmas and great aunties used the goober to create cheesecakes, make stews, put together a delicious oyster soup, and much more. Peanuts and South Carolina, where BJ lives, go hand in hand.

ACTIVE TIME: *30 minutes*
START TO FINISH: *4 hours to overnight*
SERVES 2

¼ cup smooth peanut butter

½ cup Roasted Red Pepper Sambal (page 288)

1 (2 pound) whole white fish, cleaned, with head on (like croaker, red snapper, whiting, sea bass, or flounder)

Kosher salt

2 limes, 1 thinly sliced (about ⅛ inch thick), 1 juiced

10 fresh thyme sprigs

¼ cup fresh parsley leaves and tender stems

½ cup fresh cilantro leaves and tender stems

1 lemongrass stalk, trimmed and cut crosswise into 3 pieces

¼ cup plus 1 tablespoon vegetable oil or other neutral oil

½ cup Sauce Moyo (page 289)

Fresh mint and basil leaves, for garnish

Combine the peanut butter and sambal, adding a teaspoon of water if the mixture is too thick: It should be the consistency of a spreadable paste.

Score the fish by cutting a slash lengthwise down to the bone, then crosswise in two places, repeat on the other side. Season the fish cavity and skin with salt and spread 2 tablespoons of the peanut paste inside the cavity. Stuff the cavity with some of the lime slices (reserve a few for garnish), the thyme, parsley, and cilantro. Smash the lemongrass stalk with the back of a knife and stuff into the fish cavity. Spread the remaining peanut paste all over the surface of both sides of the fish, making sure to get some into the cuts. Place the fish on a small baking sheet, cover with plastic wrap, and marinate in the refrigerator for up to 4 hours, or overnight.

Remove the fish from the refrigerator and allow to come to room temperature, 20 to 25 minutes. Preheat a gas grill or a griddle pan to high.

Scrape off any excess paste from the surface and drizzle both sides of the fish skin with the remaining ¼ cup oil. Place the fish on the grill and cook until blistered, charred in spots, and just cooked through, 4 to 5 minutes per side. Transfer the fish to a platter and serve garnished with sauce moyo, remaining lime slices, and fresh mint and basil leaves.

> *"I may eat choucroute or a leg of lamb with lavender and garlic, but I still am very much rooted in African American traditions."*

JESSICA B. HARRIS

Historian, editor, author, former professor in Brooklyn, New York

Author of My Soul Looks Back, High on the Hog, The Africa Cookbook, Iron Pots & Wooden Spoons, *and other books*

Born in Queens, New York

Known for: Making the legacy of African diaspora foodways in America visible through scholarship and a singular writing voice

In late April 2019 on a brightly lit stage at Chelsea Piers in New York City, Dr. Jessica B. Harris received a standing ovation from hundreds of chefs, editors, journalists, and celebrities as she was inducted into the James Beard Foundation Cookbook Hall of Fame. The award honored her ground-paving work in the study and celebration of African diaspora foodways.

Harris has authored a dozen books, written for magazines like *Food & Wine, Essence, Gourmet*, and *Saveur*, served as advisor to the Museum of Food and Drink in New York and the Southern Food and Beverage Museum in New Orleans, is a founding member of the Southern Foodways Alliance, curated the acclaimed restaurant menu at the Smithsonian's National Museum of African American History and Culture, and held a myriad of board and chair positions—all while she completed a 50-year tenure as a professor of English at Queens College.

When the JBF crowd finally quieted down, Harris' speech began with typical wit and candor: "I was in food before food was cool. I was *definitely* in food before food was diverse," she said to a rush of chuckles and agreement.

Harris' work, framed by a historian's lens, laid the foundation for this very cookbook to exist. She received her Ph.D. in performance studies, focusing on the French-language theater of Senegal, and brought the same level of rigor to her documentation of food history. In *Iron Pots & Wooden Spoons: Africa's Gifts to New World Cooking*, she wrote about how Caribbean, Cajun, and Creole dishes emerged from West and Central Africa; and summarized how places like Brazil and New Orleans ("the northern Caribbean"), spotlight ingredients that form the basis of those cuisines. In *High on the Hog: A Culinary Journey from Africa to America,* she traces the evolution of cooking that began on the African continent and transformed the food of the Western hemisphere. In her memoir *My Soul Looks Back*, she captures the social energy of New York City with beloved friends and fellow Black Intelligentsia like Maya Angelou, James Baldwin, and Toni Morrison. Each chapter ends with a recipe, from caldo gallego, a white bean soup, to roasted lamb doused in a spicy mint sauce.

Harris' professional contributions are representative of the Black cultures that have shaped her. She divides the year between multiple residences: a brownstone in Brooklyn, a family home in historic Oak Bluffs on Martha's Vineyard where she's spent summers for six decades, and a house in New Orleans' Marigny.

In Oak Bluffs, where generations of Black professionals and artists have vacationed and lived, Harris says, "People know each other. People knew my mother and my father and can talk about them. My butcher, I've known since he was a kid." When on island, she sources her vegetables from the farmers' market; her fish from the markets in Menemsha. "A sense of place in recipes is driven by the ingredients," she says. In New York, she's a regular at Sahadi's, where she loads up on provisions from Domaine Houchart rosé in the warm months to assorted olives, cured meats, and cheeses. In New Orleans, she seeks Creole tomatoes for a salad with sliced onions or grilled with bacon for breakfast. She spent a good portion of her time in the Crescent City with another titan of American cuisine, Leah Chase. They knew each other "for the better part of 27-28 years, which is a fair piece of road. She knew my mother, and after she died, she said, 'I've decided I'm going to take you on.' She became like my advising auntie."

There are some foods Harris doesn't attempt to make: Her mother's biscuits and mac and cheese. "Home is so inflected with nostalgia." She cleaned out her mother's freezer after she'd passed away. "Every year at Thanksgiving, I'd break off a piece and nuke it."

Her measured approach to savoring the past is the pulse of her work. For that contribution, the JBF named her the Lifetime Achievement Award recipient the following year. Chefs, writers, recipe developers, and foodways scholars reference Harris' still-growing tome of writing. From the podium where she accepted her Hall of Fame award, Harris said of the African ancestors who forged new lives under unspeakable conditions, whose work and creativity originated American cuisine: "They ate the slop that they were given, foraged and fished, hunted to add to that diet, and gradually turned the proverbial and often literal sow's ear into something lush, tasty, and profound."

One of artist Faith Ringgold's mosaics at the 125th Street Station in Harlem, titled "Flying Home: Harlem Heroes and Heroines"

SAFFRON TAPIOCA PUDDING
《with》 AMARO-MARINATED STRAWBERRIES

I don't know if anyone has done more in this country to link the food of the African Diaspora to American culture than Jessica Harris. Her books show how Africa and American food are connected. I'm so glad she has been getting acknowledged by the James Beard Awards and other institutions. This recipe contains tapioca, which can be found throughout West Africa, part of a cuisine that Jessica knows well. For some of us, tapioca brings to mind those chunky pearls floating in the popular bubble tea, but for others, tapioca pudding is our first reference. You can buy small tapioca pearls at Asian stores or specialty food shops. As far as taste, tapioca is a blank slate, which is why the roasted strawberries, flavored syrup, and juice in this recipe makes for an extra flavorful treat.

ACTIVE TIME: *15 minutes*
START TO FINISH: *35 minutes*
SERVES 6 TO 8

---

1 quart whole strawberries, hulled

½ cup sugar

1 tablespoon amaro liqueur, such as fernet

Grated zest of 1 orange

2 tablespoons fresh orange juice

1 cup small pearl tapioca

1 pinch saffron threads

½ teaspoon kosher salt

1½ cups whole coconut milk

Edible flowers, for garnish

Preheat the oven to 400°F.

Toss the strawberries and ¼ cup of the sugar in a bowl and spread in an even layer on a baking sheet. Roast until the strawberries are tender and any juice is beginning to thicken and reduce slightly, about 20 minutes. Remove from heat and allow to cool slightly in the pan. Transfer the roasted berries to a bowl, add the amaro, orange zest, and juice and toss gently to combine.

In a large saucepan, bring 4 cups water to a boil. Stir in the remaining ¼ cup sugar, the pearl tapioca, saffron threads, and salt. Cook on low heat, stirring frequently, until the pearls are tender, 15 to 20 minutes. Remove from the heat and stir in the coconut milk. Serve the pudding warm, or allow to cool and chill in the refrigerator.

To serve, divide the tapioca pudding among serving bowls, top with the strawberries and amaro syrup, and garnish with edible flower petals.

CHICKEN NECK SOUP
≪with≫ OYSTER MUSHROOMS

Sometimes being resourceful with food is a result of frugality or limited means. But it's often also because the dish ends up being the most delicious thing as a result. Take chicken necks, for example: They make a wonderful stew and broth while putting your roast chicken leftovers to work. For many people in the world today, eating chicken isn't just about unwrapping cutlets from shrink wrap any given day. For some, it means walking out into the yard, eyeing a particular bird, then slaughtering it themselves—hours of work for potentially one meal.

Jessica is a cherished chronicler of African foodways throughout the diaspora. Her experiences have taken her all over the world and she's wined and dined with the best of them. Jessica, through her work, honors so many unsung Black figures whose names we don't know, who shaped Southern food and changed the course of American cooking. This comforting recipe is a small tribute to their ingenuity.

ACTIVE TIME: *45 minutes*
START TO FINISH: *3 hours*
SERVES 4 TO 6

1 tablespoon vegetable oil

1 pound chicken necks (or chicken carcass and bones from Sunday Roast Chicken, page 188)

2 large yellow onions, cut into 2-inch pieces

1 large leek, green tops reserved and cut into 2-inch pieces, white and light green parts thinly sliced

2 large carrots, cut into 2-inch pieces

4 fresh thyme sprigs

2 fresh bay leaves

1 Scotch bonnet (or habanero) chile

2-inch piece fresh ginger, halved lengthwise

1 head garlic, halved crosswise

2 ears sweet corn on the cob, husked and cut crosswise into 1-inch pieces

Kosher salt

8 ounces oyster mushrooms, cleaned and torn into 2- to 3-inch pieces

¼ cup fresh cilantro leaves and tender stems, for garnish

¼ cup thinly sliced scallions, light and white green parts only, for garnish

2 limes, sliced into wedges for squeezing

Heat the oil in a large heavy pot over high heat. Add the chicken necks and sear until a deep brown on all sides, about 15 minutes. Cover with enough water to come 2 to 3 inches above the chicken (about 12 cups). Bring to a boil, lower the heat, and simmer on low for at least 1½ hours, until the chicken necks are breaking down and softened at the joints. While simmering, add more water, about 6 cups or as necessary, to keep the chicken completely submerged.

Add the onions, green tops of the leeks, carrots, thyme, bay leaves, chile, ginger, and garlic. Simmer for another 40 minutes, until the vegetables are tender and the herbs have given off their oils.

Strain out all the solids and return the broth to the pan. Add the pepper soup spice and corn pieces and season with salt. Simmer until the corn is tender, about 10 minutes. Add the sliced leeks and oyster mushrooms and simmer until just tender, about 1 minute. Remove from the heat and adjust the seasoning if necessary.

Spoon the soup into bowls to serve. Top with cilantro, sliced scallions, and a squeeze of lime.

A spread of dishes reflecting cuisines Harris has documented over the years

> *"The inspiration I'm drawing from is the dynasty of my childhood."*

KWAME ONWUACHI

Chef in Washington, DC

Author of Notes from a Young Black Chef: A Memoir

Born in the Bronx, New York

Food memory: Grew up helping his caterer mother make Southern Creole classics

Kwame Onwuachi was named after three Kwame's. His father, Patrick, saw that Onwuachi's grandfather, also Patrick, had befriended thoughtful, powerful men with the name. First, there was the Ghanaian revolutionary and first prime minister Kwame Nkrumah who would visit Onwuachi's grandfather's house in Nigeria. Then there was Pan African activist Kwame Ture (formerly Stokely Carmichael), whom the elder Patrick mentored at Howard University. And there was his father's best friend Kwame Olatunji, son of the great drummer Baba Olatunji. Onwuachi drew from this familial storytelling when the InterContinental Hotel invited him to open a restaurant to help anchor The Wharf, a multibillion-dollar commercial development in Washington, DC. He had two thoughts. First: Yes, absolutely. The second: Who was he as a chef now and what would he cook?

"I definitely retreated to what I was used to, modern American cuisine, French techniques, and so on," Onwuachi says of his early ideas for the space. Fresh off the sudden closure of Shaw Bijou, his highly anticipated debut met with mixed reviews and investor issues, Onwuachi wanted to distinguish his cooking in a creatively sustainable way.

The answer, he realized, was looking back at him in the mirror. He was Kwame, a Bronx-born beneficiary of a culturally rich lineage: West African, Afro Caribbean, and Black American Southern. His mother was born in Beaumont, Texas, with Creole family based in nearby Ville Platte, Louisiana. His father is Jamaican and Nigerian. His stepgrandfather was from Trinidad. He grew up hearing about grandparents and great-grandparents who owned restaurants. His earliest food memories are a baby-friendly pureed version of egusi soup. Its distinctive flavor comes from ground melon seeds and bitter leaf cooked down in crayfish. "The answer," he says, "was me."

The new restaurant wouldn't feature Americanized riffs on French cuisine. So long to the days of forcing a ginger nuoc cham gel into a dish with rat's tail radishes. He'd make versions of his culture's classics, a reflection of the dishes that shaped his upbringing: jollof rice, gumbo, red stew with chicken, and fufu. Kith and Kin launched in 2017 to robust enthusiasm. He won the James Beard

Award for Rising Star Chef in 2019, and announced his departure in 2020 with hopes of one day owning his own business.

As a child, Onwuachi assisted with his mother's home-based catering business. She cooked jollof rice, jerk chicken wings, and shrimp étouffée for her clients. "It's funny," he says, "I found an old menu of my mother's, and it's very similar to the menu that I had at Kith and Kin." When his mother visited the restaurant, she told a bartender, "This is all my food." it was true, Onwuachi agrees. For him, it was the highest form of praise.

BRAISED GOAT SHOULDER
《with》 LOCUST BEAN AND CHILI OIL

Kwame's journey is amazing. He links West Africa, the Caribbean, and America to create dishes that will make you step back and bow down. He's only thirty, but his dishes give a nod to the past while reaching toward the future. He's had an incredible couple of years, and all the awards and the accolades are deserved. I'm really excited and proud of Kwame, and his rise really shows that the next generation of great American chefs is here. His memoir, *Notes From a Young Black Chef*, is terrific. Keep cooking, Chef.

Serve the braised goat over the Farro in Jollof Sauce (page 260) or simply with Grilled Chickpea Flatbread (page 218).

ACTIVE TIME: *45 minutes*
START TO FINISH: *6 to 8 hours*
SERVES 8 TO 10

2 tablespoons vegetable oil

1 (5- to 6-pound) bone-in goat shoulder

Kosher salt

1 head garlic, cut crosswise in half

3 large carrots, cut into 2-inch pieces

1 large onion, roughly chopped

2 stalks celery, cut into 2-inch pieces

1 (15.5-ounce) can whole peeled tomatoes

1 habanero chile

10 fresh thyme sprigs

2 fresh rosemary sprigs

2 bay leaves

4 cups beef stock

½ cup Locust Bean and Chili Oil (page 286)

Heat the oil in a large Dutch oven or heavy-bottomed pot over medium-high heat. Season the goat shoulder on all sides generously with salt. Sear the shoulder on all sides until browned, 18 to 20 minutes. Remove the shoulder and set aside, keeping any rendered fat in the pot.

Preheat the oven to 325°F.

Sear the garlic, cut side down, in the rendered fat until golden brown, about 2 minutes. Remove and set aside. To the same pot, add the carrots, onion, and celery and sauté until the vegetables are just softened and translucent, about 8 minutes. Crush the tomatoes in the can with your hands, then pour into the pot along with the chile. Bring up to a simmer. Make a bouquet garni with the thyme, rosemary, and bay leaves by tying them together with butcher's twine, then add to the pot. Pour in the stock, stir to combine, and bring to a boil. Return the goat shoulder and garlic to the pot, cover, and transfer to the oven. Braise until the meat is tender but doesn't fall apart, 3 to 4 hours. Let cool slightly.

Once the goat is cool enough to handle, remove it from the pot, pull all the meat off the bone, and tear into bite-sized pieces. Discard the bone. Remove the solids from the pot and discard, then skim off any fat, leaving the flavorful braising liquid. Return the meat to the pot and cook, uncovered, over medium heat, until the sauce has reduced to an almost syrupy consistency, about 12 minutes. The meat should be tender enough to pull with a fork and the collagen from the bones will have helped thicken the sauce. Remove from heat and toss the goat pieces with the chili oil until evenly coated.

POTS DE CRÈME ⟨with⟩ BENNE SEED PRALINE AND ROASTED PINEAPPLE

The term pot de crème refers to little jars or pots of cream. Traditionally the French dessert features custardy chocolate with a helping of cream on top. Here we use crunchy praline sprinkled over the dense custard. Benne seeds have a nutty taste and deep West African lineage, and are derived from the same plant as sesame seeds but have a stronger flavor.

ACTIVE TIME: *40 minutes*
START TO FINISH: *4½ hours*
SERVES 4

POTS DE CRÈME

1 cup heavy cream

1 cup whole milk

½ teaspoon vanilla extract

½ teaspoon kosher salt

3 large egg yolks

⅓ cup packed brown sugar

2 tablespoons raw benne seeds (or sesame seeds)

BENNE SEED PRALINE

½ cup packed brown sugar

¼ cup water

½ cup raw benne seeds (or sesame seeds)

1 tablespoon unsalted butter, plus extra for pan if needed

1 teaspoon kosher salt

½ teaspoon baking soda

ROASTED PINEAPPLE

1½ cups fresh pineapple cut into ½-inch pieces

1 tablespoon brown sugar

2 teaspoons canola oil

2 Selim peppers, crushed in mortar and pestle or the back of a knife (or 4 green peppercorns)

Pinch kosher salt

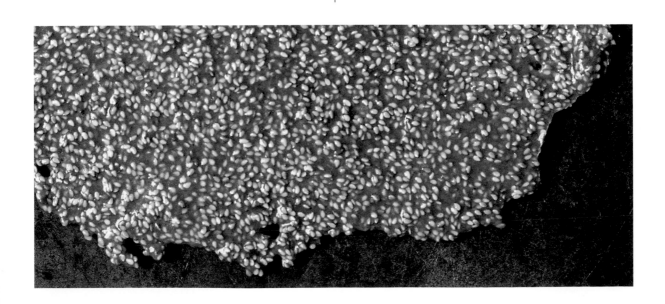

Make the pots de crème: Preheat the oven to 325°F. Add ½ inch of hot water to a 9- by 13-inch cake pan and place in the oven as it preheats.

Heat the cream, milk, vanilla, and salt in a small saucepan set over medium heat and bring to a bare simmer.

Place the yolks and brown sugar in a medium heatproof bowl and whisk to combine. Gradually, while whisking continually, add the warm milk mixture until incorporated.

Pour the mixture through a fine mesh strainer into a small bowl and add the benne seeds. Stir to combine. Divide the mixture evenly among four 6-ounce ramekins. Carefully set the ramekins into the pan of water and bake for 35 to 40 minutes, until set around the edges, but still slightly wobbly in the middle.

Remove from the oven and transfer the ramekins to a wire rack to cool slightly. Refrigerate until completely chilled, about 3 hours.

Make the benne seed praline: Line a baking sheet with a nonstick silicone liner or butter well. Set aside.

Combine the brown sugar and water in a small saucepan. Set over high heat and stir just until the sugar dissolves. Then stop stirring and begin swirling the pan. Continue to swirl and cook until the mixture takes on a deep amber color and reaches 300°F.

Remove from the heat and using a heatproof spatula or wooden spoon, stir in the benne seeds, butter, salt, and baking soda. Once the butter has melted, working quickly, pour the mixture onto the prepared baking sheet and spread into a thin layer. Allow to cool completely.

Once cool, break the brittle into small pieces and chop into a coarse crumble to use on top of the pots de crème. Any unused brittle may be stored at room temperature in an airtight container for up to 3 days.

Roast the pineapple: Preheat the oven to 375°F.

Place the pineapple, brown sugar, canola oil, crushed Selim peppers, and salt in a small mixing bowl and toss to combine. Transfer to a small baking sheet or metal pan and spread evenly. Roast in the oven for 20 to 25 minutes, until the pineapple is slightly brown, tossing occasionally.

To serve: Serve each pot de crème topped with roasted pineapple and praline crumbled on top.

GRILLED CHICKPEA FLATBREAD
⟪with⟫ LENTIL DAL

Here I'm giving a nod to Kwame's Jamaican side. Jamaican food often pulls in Indian influences. This is road food to me. Imagine you are driving from Kingston to Boston Bay to get the original jerk—that's a five-hour drive and as you look out the window, you're listening to incredible music and watching the views go by, and then you stop for road food. I've driven that road many times and never have I stepped inside a restaurant. Ginger juice, DJs on the corner, kids kicking soccer balls—it's all happening on the roadside. Driving that road, I think, "I see the links to Africa; I see the links to China, to Italy, to India." Everything and everyone is represented. All you have to do is look around or, better yet, stop and stretch your legs. This dish fits in perfectly during that moment: It may read India, but it's from Jamaica, showing how layered the culture there truly is.

ACTIVE TIME: *30 minutes*
START TO FINISH: *2 to 3 hours*
MAKES 8 FLATBREADS

2½ teaspoons active dry yeast

1 cup warm water (about 110°F)

2½ cups all-purpose flour

2 cups chickpea flour

1 teaspoon kosher salt

½ cup whole milk yogurt

2 tablespoons Berbere Spice Brown Butter (page 277), melted, plus more for brushing

Lentil Dal with Seasonal Vegetable Sauté (recipe follows)

In a small bowl, dissolve the yeast in the warm water and sprinkle a pinch of the flour over the surface. Set aside until bubbles begin to appear on the surface, about 5 minutes.

In a separate bowl, combine the all-purpose flour, chickpea flour, and salt. Pour in the yeast mixture, yogurt, and berbere butter. Combine with a wooden spoon until a shaggy dough forms. Turn the dough out onto your counter or work surface and knead into a smooth dough, about 8 minutes. Place in the bowl, cover with a damp cloth, and let rise until doubled in size, about 45 minutes.

Place the dough on a lightly floured work surface and divide into eight pieces. Cover with a piece of plastic and let rest for 10 minutes.

Heat a grill or griddle pan to medium-high heat. Pick up a piece of dough and using your hands, gently stretch into an 8-inch oblong piece. You can use a rolling pin too. Place the dough directly on the grill or griddle pan. Cook until nicely charred on one side, flip, and cook the other side, about 5 minutes total. Remove from heat and brush the surface with more of the berbere butter.

Repeat the process until all the dough has been cooked. Serve with the lentil dal.

LENTIL DAL ⟪with⟫ SEASONAL VEGETABLE SAUTÉ

ACTIVE TIME: 45 minutes
START TO FINISH: 1 hour 30 minutes
MAKES: 6 to 8 servings (9 cups)

2 tablespoons extra virgin olive oil

1 small yellow onion, chopped

3 cloves garlic, minced

1 (2-inch) piece fresh ginger, peeled and minced

2 teaspoons ground turmeric

1 teaspoon ground cumin

1 teaspoon ground cayenne

4 plum tomatoes, chopped

4 cups vegetable stock

1 cup mung beans

1 cup yellow lentils

1 (15.5-ounce) can unsweetened coconut milk

GARNISH AND SERVING

2 tablespoons Berbere Spiced Brown Butter (page 277)

2 cups assorted seasonal baby vegetables (field peas, carrots, radishes, okra, turnips, whatever is readily available), cut into 2-inch pieces

Juice of ½ lemon

¼ cup fresh mint leaves

2 tablespoons fresh dill

Kosher salt and freshly cracked black pepper

Fresh Ayib (page 294) or yogurt

Heat the olive oil in a medium stockpot or Dutch oven over medium heat. Add the onion and sauté until softened and translucent, about 2 minutes. Add the garlic and ginger and cook until fragrant, about 1 minute. Add the turmeric, cumin, and cayenne and cook, stirring frequently, until toasted and fragrant, about 1 minute. Stir in the tomatoes and cook until they turn bright red and begin to soften. Pour in the vegetable stock.

Drain the mung beans and add to the pot. Increase the heat to high and bring up to a simmer. Reduce the heat to low and simmer until the mung beans are just tender, about 30 minutes. Drain the lentils of their liquid and stir into the pot. Bring back up to a simmer and cook until the lentils are completely tender, the mung beans are beginning to break down, and the dal is beginning to thicken, about 30 minutes. Stir in the coconut milk and simmer for another 10 minutes to allow the flavors to meld.

Make the garnish: While the dal simmers, in a large sauté pan, heat the berbere butter over medium heat. Add the vegetable mix and sauté until the vegetables are just tender and golden brown. Add the lemon juice, remove from the heat, and stir in the mint and dill. Season to taste with salt and black pepper.

Ladle warm dal into a bowl, spoon the vegetable mix on top, and serve with a dollop of fresh ayib along with the Grilled Chickpea Flatbread (previous page).

> *"I'm grateful for everything I do. I'm grateful for every breath I take. I'm grateful for everything I see, every person I meet. But that doesn't mean I have to put up with mediocre things."*

LEAH CHASE

Former chef-owner of Dooky Chase's Restaurant in New Orleans, Louisiana

Was a civil rights icon, patron of African American artists, recipient of James Beard Foundation Who's Who of Food and Beverage in America, received honorary degrees from Tulane, Dillard, Johnson & Wales, and Loyola universities

Born in New Orleans, Louisiana

Known for: Offering Black customers the respect and finesse of fine dining and making Dooky Chase's a safe meeting place for activists

At ninety-five years old, Leah Chase still got to work in her kitchen by 7:30 a.m., overseeing the menu at Dooky Chase's, the Creole restaurant and New Orleans institution at which she held court for more than seventy years. Under her leadership, the brick building on Orleans Avenue in Treme endured through eras as a fine restaurant rich with ambience and care, created for Black people by Black people.

Dooky Chase Sr. opened the bar and casual restaurant in 1941, selling sandwiches and lottery tickets to fellow Black patrons. Chase married his son, jazz orchestra bandleader Dooky Jr. in 1946, five years after she'd moved to New Orleans from Madisonville, where she was raised and graduated from high school. She was twenty-three years old. The couple quickly took over, led by Chase's "high mind" of big ideas that her mother used to warn would cause trouble one day.

Some of those ideas included a move to white tablecloth service with place settings and multiple course meals, considerations that weren't readily accessible to Black diners who wished to eat out in late-1940s New Orleans. Chase wanted to offer African American clientele a place where they could eat food they loved, like gumbo, greens and yams, grilled fish with a crabmeat sauce, and chicken Creole with jambalaya. But she also wanted for her people what white folks had on the other side of town—an elegant, dignified experience of enjoying good food and company. A little panache. She learned to value simple gestures like a "double underline," so a diner's food dish always sat framed within a larger plate. A little thing like that, she said, showed "we always paid attention to people."

Like so many young folks of her time, Chase understood the import of the civil rights movement, not solely for the long-term social and political justice hopes, but for the immediate and practical impact of asserting one's rights in the face of inequity. New Orleans was deeply segregated—it still is, truthfully. But Dooky Chase's was one of few businesses known to host integrated groups in spite of the law. At considerable risk of violence, Chase and her family hosted voter registration workers, NAACP members, and political figures in need of private meeting space, and activists like Martin Luther King, Jr. Leaders of the movement have got to eat.

In the 1970s Chase began collecting paintings by Black artists like Jacob Lawrence and Elizabeth Catlett and she decorated the restaurant with those pieces. Works spoke to her not because of how they looked, but because of how they made her feel. Her inclinations caused confusion at first. This was a place to dine, after all, not a gallery. But there were few places for Black artists to show in those days. "I put it up in here where people could see it," she says. Today, the restaurant dining rooms—one painted a bold, golden yellow, the other crimson red—are revelatory destinations in themselves for the several dozens of works joyously displayed to her liking, including a portrait of Tupac Shakur by her grandson ("That caused a little controversy") Over the years, Dooky Chase's has welcomed figures from Duke Ellington to Beyoncé, to presidents George W. Bush and Barack Obama.

So much of Black America's political organizing through the centuries occurred in spaces that have gone unmarked, in buildings that have been razed in that all-too-American tendency to rewrite history. Dooky Chase's is representative of so many Black-owned businesses that were built to serve their communities and far exceeded the call. Diners come to eat the food, yes. But they also come to pay homage.

It's easy to forget Chase wasn't always an icon. In fact, she was once a country girl from just across Lake Pontchartrain, who liked to gaze at rainbows. Her mother, Hortensia Lange, managed the household of fourteen children; her father Charles Lange, was a master caulker in a New Orleans shipyard back when industry boats were still constructed from wood. Chase believed her parents met in New Orleans. "Back then, you didn't ask your parents anything. Whatever they told you, it was it."

Breakfast was a humble biscuit with jelly, a cup of cocoa or coffee. "We better bring back that 90 or 100 on that report card because Daddy wasn't going to tolerate anything else. And you had to do that on biscuit and coffee." Her mother typically cooked one-pot meals: string beans and rice, greens and rice, beans and rice. The family couldn't afford meat, so they didn't eat it, unless it was hog-killing time. Hortensia stretched every meal. She'd take bones and make a rich broth, then steep garden vegetables inside. The first course at dinner was the strained broth, course two the reserved vegetables. A taste of sweet always closed the family meal. Hortensia, averse to unnecessary dishes, would instruct the family, "Turn your plate over," and serve slices of pie.

"We were poor, true," Chase said. "I was happy."

In strawberry season they made jellies and jams out of too-ripe fruit on the bush. Charles had a talent for making strawberry wine. "When you were little, you got a glass of water and a spoon of wine. Put a little sugar in that and that's what you ate with your dinner. As you got older, the water got less in the wine."

Chase moved to New Orleans at sixteen to attend high school and live with extended family. She became enamored with the different cultures and cuisines she encountered, like Chinese and Italian. Spaghetti and meatballs was a favorite dish, which she enjoyed with red gravy or brown gravy. "We creolize our food."

Chase greeted her evenings with a cocktail—please, no wine until dinner is served. "Go color my Sprite. Put some Crown Royal in it," she'd say. And then she'd head off to bed musing on how to perfect her craft. "I never go to bed without taking up some kind of book on this industry...You gotta keep on," she said. "I'm going to study hard and keep going."

When Chase was little, her mother used to call the children over when a rainbow was visible. "We would stand there in that yard looking at the rainbow. You know what I was thinking? 'I can walk there.' You feel like, 'I can get to the end of that rainbow.' You can walk and walk, you're never going to get to the end of that rainbow. But you gotta keep walking and if that's your goal, you keep walking. And you may not make it all the way but you'll come close."

Mrs. Chase died on June 1, 2019. She was 96.

LEAH CHASE GUMBO

No one has inspired me more than Leah Chase. Nobody. When I say she's a driving force for me, I get frustrated because that's an understatement. I remember two weeks after Hurricane Katrina in New Orleans, I called Ms. Leah. She was eighty-one and I was calling just to check in. How could she bounce back from this natural disaster? I was trying to be sympathetic but also trying to let her know that at eighty-one, she and her husband Dooky have had a great run—it's okay if she wanted to put it all down.

"What are you going to do?" I asked. She said, "What do you mean what am I going to do? I am going to renovate the restaurant and open it as fast as I can." She had another fifteen-year run after Katrina. She opened the doors of Dooky Chase's in the 1940s, in the middle of an era when white and Black people could not be served together, yet she served everybody. She could have gone to jail for something that we now take for granted. It's no surprise to me that many in the Civil Rights movement held meetings and made plans in her restaurants.

Brave and skilled, she was just one of these magical people, which is why she was in Beyoncé's "Lemonade" video and Disney created a character inspired by her. At heart, though, she was a chef and a master at making gumbo. When President Barack Obama dropped by Dooky Chase's, Ms. Leah gave him a bowl of gumbo, but when she saw him sprinkle hot sauce on it before he had tasted it, she smacked his hand and said, "Don't mess up your gumbo." She liked Obama, although she once said that presidents come and go, but it's the regular, everyday people that really matter. She was an American hero.

At age 96, Leah passed, and New Orleans celebrated her in the only way New Orleans can: with music and food. This book is dedicated to Leah; we are all Leah's kids. We wouldn't be here without her.

ACTIVE TIME: *30 minutes*
START TO FINISH: *1 hour*
SERVES 6 TO 8

- 3 tablespoons vegetable oil
- ½ cup diced celery
- ½ cup diced red onion
- ½ cup diced red peppers
- 4 cloves garlic, minced
- 1 teaspoon kosher salt
- ½ teaspoon freshly ground black pepper
- 4 ounces ground chorizo
- 1 (14-ounce) can crushed tomatoes
- 12 ounces fresh okra, diced small
- 1 tablespoon smoked paprika
- 1 tablespoon filé powder
- 1 teaspoon cayenne pepper
- 2 cups fish stock
- 2 cups chicken stock
- 2 tablespoons apple cider vinegar
- 1 pound large shrimp, peeled and deveined
- 8 ounces smoked andouille sausage, sliced ¼ inch thick
- 6 cups cooked rice, for serving
- Chopped scallions, for serving
- Chopped fresh parsley, for serving

Heat the vegetable oil in a large saucepan or Dutch oven set over medium-high heat. When the oil shimmers, add the celery, onion, peppers, garlic, salt, and pepper and cook, stirring frequently, until the onion is translucent, 3 to 4 minutes. Add the chorizo and cook for 4 to 5 minutes, stirring frequently. Add the tomatoes, okra, paprika, filé powder, and cayenne and continue cooking for 4 to 5 minutes, stirring frequently. Add the stocks and vinegar and bring to a simmer. Decrease the heat to low, cover, and cook for 20 to 25 minutes, stirring occasionally. The filé powder, which is made by grinding sassafras leaves, will thicken the stew.

Add the shrimp and andouille and stir to combine. Continue to cook for 4 to 5 minutes, until the shrimp are just cooked through. Serve the gumbo over rice, topped with scallions and parsley.

"I'm a direct reflection of the Great Migration."

MASHAMA BAILEY

Executive chef and partner at The Grey in Savannah, Georgia

Chair of the Edna Lewis Foundation, which honors and extends Chef Lewis' legacy of Southern cookery and storytelling

Born in the Bronx, New York

Food memory: Reconnected with her maternal grandmother's seasonal American South cooking while studying in France

To see Mashama Bailey peer through the service window into the bustling dining room of her iconic Savannah restaurant The Grey, it seems like she's been standing at the pass in chef's whites her whole life. But it took a while to get here. The Grey is one of 30 World's Best Restaurants according to *Food & Wine* and *Travel + Leisure*. In 2019 Bailey won a coveted Best Chef Southeast James Beard Award, and the path she took as a New York-born girl growing up between Queens and Savannah has been beautifully rendered in an episode of *Chef's Table* on Netflix. But her road to cooking professionally started in the unemployment line.

Bailey wavered through high school and Sullivan County Community College. She'd grown up nibbling on beef patties from the Jamaican spot and eating lo mein from her favorite Chinese takeout restaurant. But community college "was the first time that I was eating yuca and callaloo and the food people were taught to cook in their homes." She liked good food, but wasn't interested in making a career of it. She graduated with a BA in psychology from Brooklyn College. Her mother, Catherine, whose family is from Waynesboro, Georgia, and her father, David, a Vietnam veteran from Queens, had careers in social work. After an attempt at physical therapy, she followed suit.

It wasn't meant to be. After returning from north Florida, where she'd worked with homeless populations, she led an after-school program at a family shelter. "I ended up getting fired. I just wasn't that great of a leader," she recalls. Around that time a friend needed catering help, and she enrolled in culinary school.

Bailey was engaged but more interested in everyone else's food culture than her own. "I don't remember seeing my culture represented unless you were talking about Southern ingredients." She didn't see Black food culture articulated in cookbooks, dining culture, the media or the classroom. She rattles off noted American food writers, including James Beard, who left Black people out of the conversation. "He talks about all these different cultures of food, but he never really addresses Black food."

She noticed there weren't many Black restaurateurs, particularly in fine dining. "Being represented in the restaurants was important to me because it meant that no one was really eating our food. I never thought of Black cooking as cooking that could sustain a fine dining restaurant. I never thought about it because I didn't see it."

Until France, that is. She earned an externship in Burgundy at the Chateau de Fey cooking school. She learned that all the great men French chefs she'd heard of at culinary school cited their mothers and grandmothers as their teachers, and she saw a parallel. "There was a line between how my grandmother cooked and how these grandmothers in France cooked," Bailey says. "That's when I realized...that my family had something to say in the culinary world."

Returning to New York, she took a job at Prune, the East Village restaurant by Gabrielle Hamilton. Bailey says Prune "was the beginning of me having the courage to experiment." Meanwhile, she was living with her grandmother in Queens and doing most of the cooking at home. "I was still doing this professional white way of cooking....you know, trying to master the lamb chop." None of it impressed her grandmother, who'd often just ask for a good pot of beans.

When Bailey moved to Savannah to open The Grey, she thought about her childhood summer vacations in Georgia, and about her mother's and grandmother's way of cooking. But she struggled with her first menu—"nothing had connection, there was no common thread." She tried to link her family's seasonal cooking, her time in France and later Italy, her training in New York. What does one eat in Savannah in May? In January? Had she forgotten? Did she ever know?

"I'm a direct reflection of the Great Migration. But things start to get watered down when you start to mix cultures," Bailey says. "You're longing to know what your great-grandparents did because that's the only connection you have to who you are in this country," as a Black person. "And then you're kind of not really telling the full story," Bailey says of a generations-long history.

"I'm always trying to figure out the time and place of where we are," Bailey says. "What people are eating now, how that's connected back to The Grey. Where are we, when you walk into this place, do you know where you are? Do you know that you're in Savannah, Georgia?"

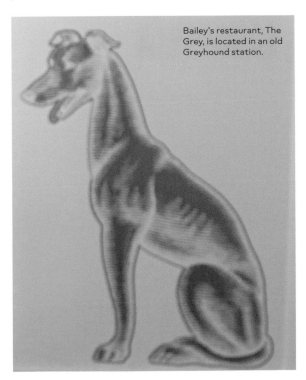

Bailey's restaurant, The Grey, is located in an old Greyhound station.

CHILLED CORN AND TOMATO SOUP

Mashama is such good people. At Harlem EatUp!, she took care of the cooks and was kind to everyone eating. Mashama is a visionary chef with true leadership ability and is so kind. Young cooks would be lucky to have her as a mentor.

In 2014, Mashama, a Bronx native, opened a Southern-style restaurant in the historic district of Savannah. Called The Grey, it's located inside an old renovated Greyhound bus station. The cuisine is inspired by the port city history of Savannah, which includes African and European cultures, Mashama's French culinary education, and the seasonal cooking of her mother and grandmother. The restaurant and Mashama have been racking up accolades. *Time* called The Grey one of the best restaurants in the world, and in 2019 Mashama won the coveted James Beard award for Best Chef in the Southeast. This recipe's rethinking of tomato soup is a nod to what Mashama is known for—reinventing traditional recipes.

ACTIVE TIME: *35 minutes*
START TO FINISH: *About 1 hour, plus time for pickling and soaking*
SERVES 4

1 ear corn

4 cloves garlic, smashed and peeled

1 red onion, quartered

1 cup extra virgin olive oil

⅓ cup leftover cornbread crumbs

1 pound fresh tomatoes, coarsely chopped

1 cup tomato juice

1 cucumber, coarsely chopped

½ teaspoon ground cumin

½ teaspoon Aleppo pepper

Juice of 1 lemon

2 tablespoons sherry vinegar

1 medium jalapeño chile, finely chopped

Kosher salt and freshly ground black pepper

Pickled Green Tomatoes (recipe follows), for serving

Island XO Sauce (recipe follows), for serving

Preheat the oven to 400°F.

Place the corn, 2 cloves of the garlic, and half of the red onion on a small baking sheet or baking dish, add 2 tablespoons of the olive oil, and toss to coat. Roast in the oven for 10 minutes.

Add the cornbread crumbs to one end of the baking sheet and roast for another 10 minutes. Scrape the corn from the cob.

Transfer half of the corn, the raw and roasted garlic, and the raw and roasted onion to a food processor. Add the remaining olive oil, the tomatoes, tomato juice, and two-thirds of the cucumber. Process to puree to consistency desired.

Transfer to a large bowl. Add the cornbread crumbs, remaining corn, and remaining cucumber, along with the cumin, Aleppo pepper, lemon juice, vinegar, and jalapeño and stir to combine. Taste and season with salt and pepper to taste. Chill for several hours. Serve topped with pickled green tomatoes and Island XO sauce.

(Continued)

PICKLED GREEN TOMATOES

ACTIVE TIME: 15 minutes

START TO FINISH: 20 minutes

MAKES 1 PINT

1 large (8-ounce) green tomato, cut into ¼-inch dice

1 clove garlic, smashed and peeled

½ teaspoon red pepper flakes

½ teaspoon dill seed

½ cup white vinegar

½ cup water

1 tablespoon kosher salt

1 teaspoon sugar

Combine the tomato, garlic, pepper flakes, and dill in a pint glass jar with a lid and set aside.

Combine the vinegar, water, salt, and sugar in a small saucepan. Set over high heat and bring to a boil, 5 to 6 minutes. Pour the liquid over the tomatoes to cover completely. Cover with lid and refrigerate overnight before serving. Store in the refrigerator for up to 2 weeks.

ISLAND XO SAUCE

ACTIVE TIME: 20 minutes

START TO FINISH: 9 hours

MAKES ABOUT 2 CUPS

1¼ ounces salt cod

2 tablespoons vegetable oil

¼ cup garlic puree

2 tablespoons ginger puree

½ cup red pepper flakes

2 medium shallots, thinly sliced

5 tablespoons soy sauce

1 small bunch scallions, chopped

Place the salt cod in a bowl, cover with cold water, and refrigerate for 8 hours, changing the water every 2 hours. Remove the fish from the water, rinse thoroughly, and pat dry. Coarsely chop.

Bring the oil, garlic, ginger, and red pepper flakes to a bare simmer in a small saucepan set over medium heat. Decrease the heat to low and continue to cook at a bare simmer for 30 minutes, until thickened.

Add the cod and shallots and continue to cook on low for another 30 minutes, until darkened in color. Remove from the heat, add the soy sauce and scallions, and whisk to combine. Store, refrigerated, for up to 1 month.

FISH CAKES
≪with≫ BIRMINGHAM GREENS SALAD

The green salad in this recipe calls for two types of greens, turnip and mustard. A mess of greens, whether they be turnip, collard, or mustard, have been staples in the homes of African Americans for hundreds of years. Collard leaves are large; mustards have a slightly peppery taste; and turnips are a little bitter. Mashama is one of the most important chefs in the country. This is a dish similar to the one she made for Harlem EatUp!, where her incredible salad was the star of the show. Later that night, she was the star of the dance floor too.

ACTIVE TIME: *1 hour*
START TO FINISH: *About 3 hours*
SERVES 4

TOMATO SAUCE

3 tablespoons extra virgin olive oil

1 small onion, finely diced

2 cloves garlic, minced

½ teaspoon kosher salt, plus more to taste

1 (15-ounce) can crushed tomatoes

FISH CAKES

1 medium (6-ounce) potato, peeled and cut in half

2 tablespoons vegetable oil

½ cup finely diced onion

2 cloves garlic, minced

½ teaspoon kosher salt

½ teaspoon curry powder

12 ounces salt cod, soaked (see XO Island Sauce, page 228), drained, and coarsely chopped

2 teaspoons Worcestershire sauce

Grated zest and juice of 1 lemon

2 large egg yolks

½ cup mayonnaise

BIRMINGHAM GREENS SALAD

¼ cup extra virgin olive oil

2 tablespoons apple cider vinegar

2 teaspoons minced shallot

2 teaspoons sorghum

1 teaspoon Dijon mustard

½ teaspoon kosher salt

Pinch freshly ground black pepper

2 cups tender young mustard greens, washed and spun dry

2 cups tender young turnip greens, washed and spun dry

3 tablespoons coarsely chopped pecans

Make the tomato sauce: Heat the olive oil in a small saucepan set over medium heat. When the oil shimmers, add the onion, garlic, and salt. Cook until the onions are translucent, 4 to 5 minutes. Add the tomatoes, decrease the heat to low, and cover. Cook for 30 to 40 minutes, until the sauce has slightly reduced and no longer has a raw flavor. Taste and season with additional salt as needed. Set aside and keep warm.

Make the fish cakes: Place the potato in a small saucepan, cover with cold water, and bring to a boil over high heat. Boil until tender, about 20 minutes. Drain and pass the potato through a ricer or fine mesh strainer. Set aside.

Heat 1 tablespoon of the vegetable oil in a medium sauté pan set over medium-high heat. When the oil shimmers, add the onion, garlic, salt, and curry powder. Cook until the onion is translucent, 4 to 5 minutes. Add the salt cod and continue to cook until the liquid has dissipated, 2 to 3 minutes.

Transfer the mixture to a medium mixing bowl and add the potato, Worcestershire, lemon zest and juice, egg yolks, and mayonnaise and stir to combine. Refrigerate mixture for 1 hour.

Shape the cod mixture into four patties. Heat the remaining 1 tablespoon vegetable oil in a medium skillet set over medium-high heat. When the oil shimmers, gently add the cod cakes and cook for 4 to 5 minutes on each side, until golden brown and cooked through. Set aside and keep warm until ready to serve.

Make the salad: Combine the olive oil, vinegar, shallot, sorghum, mustard, salt, and pepper in a small glass jar with a lid, cover, and shake to combine.

Place the greens and pecans in a medium bowl, pour over the vinaigrette, and toss to combine.

To serve: Spoon the tomato sauce over the fish cakes and serve with a side of the greens salad.

PEPPER BROTH ⟨with⟩ BEEF HEART

Offal is enjoyed in many cultures throughout the world, from bone marrow and gizzards to sweet-breads and tongue. I've seen beef heart appear on fine dining menus often and it's not hard to fig-ure out why it's popular. It's got a chew to it and tastes quite gamey. Here, the heart is marinated in a sweet sauce, seared, and added to a full and delicious broth. Mashama started her culinary ca-reer at Prune in New York City, where seeing organ meats on the menu was common, so a modern twist on cooking these meats is a great homage to her.

Chef's note: Always sear hard but undercook the heart.

ACTIVE TIME: *20 minutes*
START TO FINISH: *About 2 hours*
SERVES 6 TO 8

BROTH

5 pounds beef bones

2 medium onions, peeled and quartered

Canola oil

1 white fish carcass, just bones

4 ounces fresh ginger, peeled, rinsed, and cut into several pieces

2 pods star anise

Kosher salt

HEART

1 tablespoon extra virgin olive oil

4 (3-ounce) pieces beef heart, trimmed

3 tablespoons soy sauce

2 tablespoons rice wine vinegar

2 teaspoons honey

1 teaspoon brown sugar

4 radishes, quartered

½ teaspoon kosher salt

1 tablespoon chopped fresh cilantro

Make the broth: Place the beef bones in a large stock-pot, cover with water, and bring to a boil over high heat. Boil for 15 to 20 minutes, skimming off the scum as it appears. Transfer the bones to a strainer and rinse with water. Clean the pot and return the bones to the pot.

While the bones are boiling, heat a grill or grill pan to high. Lightly brush the onion quarters with canola oil and grill until charred on most sides, about 30 minutes. Add the onions to the pot with the clean bones when-ever they are ready.

Add the ginger, star anise, and 3 quarts cold water to the bones in the pot. Set over high heat and bring to a simmer, about 30 minutes. Decrease the heat to main-tain a simmer and cook for 1 hour, or until the broth is fragrant and has reduced slightly.

Strain the broth in a fine mesh strainer and discard the solids. Taste the broth and add salt as desired, then set aside and keep warm.

Cook the heart: Heat the olive oil in a medium sauté pan set over high heat. When the oil shimmers and just before it smokes, add the beef heart and sear on each side for 20 seconds.

Remove the heart to a cutting board and very thinly slice on the bias. Transfer the beef to a heatproof bowl, cover, and set aside.

Add the soy sauce, vinegar, honey, and brown sugar to the pan and simmer for 3 minutes, or until slightly reduced. Pour the mixture over the beef, cover, and set aside to marinate for 10 minutes.

Add the heart to the broth and taste and adjust sea-soning as desired. Toss the radishes with the salt. Gar-nish each bowl with radishes and cilantro. Serve hot.

"The deep structure will always be African."

MICHAEL TWITTY

Author, culinary historian, historic interpreter in Washington, DC

Born in Washington, DC

Won the James Beard Award for Writing, and Book of the Year for The Cooking Gene

Known for: Cooking the food of his African ancestors in period costume using the tools and techniques that would have been available to them

Michael Twitty is feeling pretty gratified. Since publication of *The Cooking Gene*, his acclaimed memoir-meets-cultural history that pushes America to engage with its Black culinary roots, he's observed a number of shifts in how people interact with him. In particular, he's seen an awareness develop among white people.

"I like that white people—especially white Southerners—are finally beginning to understand how African they are," he says. He's referencing not just the familial connections, but the cultural ones too. "People put us in an African bubble like we don't move, like we don't grow, like we don't expand. Excuse me. Imagine if they did that to English people. There'd be no tikka masala, there'd be no cloths and patterns they stole from India that they made into paisley and gingham. We can go on."

Twitty interrogates his lineage through the foods he grew up eating. Standards like collard greens, barbecue, mac and cheese, yes, but also beef stroganoff and samosas—hallmarks of his mother's world travels, which she adapted. The stroganoff, for example had rice instead of noodles. "We Blacktified it. We did more garlic. We did paprika." In his book, Twitty equally considers family lore, the dinner plate, and DNA reports from genealogical websites as anchor to the past and rocket into the future. He operates from a historically grounded baseline: While many cultures naturally blur the details of their past over time, African Americans are distinct in the US because they were denied the roadmap of their ancestral languages and traditions, even the basic benefit of familial connections. Such restrictions, codified into the earliest stages of this country and still resonant today, have given African American food a deeper meaning for those seeking links to an often-nebulous past. Africans and their descendants were the go-to cultivators, cooks, and servers of American food for centuries; there are, as with any craft, vestiges of identity in the output.

Twitty emphasizes that the story of Africans and their descendants in the United States is not just for Black people, that in fact, it's this bifurcated education that has deepened false narratives. "This is white people's history," he goes on, underscoring the genetic links. "This is the side of their family tree they never heard about because they were never meant to hear about it. Their ability to learn about it gives me a great thrill...it's the moving beyond the sentimentality for the Black maid, okay?"

As much time as Twitty spends looking back—he lectures and cooks period-specific food for visitors at Colonial Williamsburg in Virginia, dressed as an enslaved person would have been—he is passionate about the evolving nature of cuisine. "We've always borrowed from each other, Twitty says, remembering a nut roll cake by Miss Mattie, a distant cousin on his mother's side. For years Twitty thought the filo-layered pecan dessert was practically a family heirloom. Then he saw a similar recipe in an old Hungarian cookbook. Turns out Miss Mattie's family lived next door to a Hungarian family in Pittsburgh. He now believes his relatives were gifted the cake on occasion and Miss Mattie developed her own creolized recipe. Twitty yearns for more of this mixing with credit given where it's due. Food evolves, he says. "Let's trace it forward."

OUT OF THE MOUNTAIN OF DESPAIR, A STONE OF HOPE

The Martin Luther King Jr. Memorial in Washington, DC

GRILLED SHORT RIBS IN PIRI PIRI MARINADE

If you throw a party and Michael Twitty's at the table—you're going to have a good time. He's smart, fun, and engaging. He's like the piri piri (which means "pepper pepper") in this marinade—unexpected, exciting. Not only is he the coolest guy at the table by far, but when it comes to thinking about what we consider inedible food, he explains how those odds and ends should be given a second look and tells everybody how delicious they can be. His book, *The Cooking Gene*, is a game changer in the industry.

Short ribs are far from "inedible," but the spiciness of this piri piri marinade always makes me think of Michael. Serve them with plantain and corn mash (page 237) or over any of the grain salads (pages 58, 255).

ACTIVE TIME: *10 minutes*

START TO FINISH: *30 minutes, plus 4 to 12 hours to marinate*

SERVES 4 TO 6

1½ to 2 pounds boneless short ribs

Piri Piri Marinade (page 287)

¼ cup plus 2 tablespoons vegetable oil

2 tablespoons sherry vinegar

2 tablespoons honey

Kosher salt and freshly cracked black pepper

Cover the short ribs with half of the marinade, seal in a freezer bag, and marinate in the refrigerator for 4 to 12 hours.

While the short ribs are marinating, make the sauce: Combine the remaining marinade with 2 tablespoons of the oil, the sherry vinegar, and honey. Season to taste with salt and pepper and set aside.

Remove the short ribs from the marinade and allow to sit at room temperature for at least 1 hour before grilling.

Preheat a grill or griddle pan to medium-high and make sure the grates are cleaned and lightly oiled. Coat the short ribs with the remaining ¼ cup oil and season generously with salt and pepper.

Grill the ribs, turning, until charred on all sides and an instant-read thermometer inserted into the thickest part of the meat reads 130°F for medium-rare, 10 to 12 minutes per side. Move the short ribs to a cutting board and allow to rest for at least 10 minutes.

Slice the meat against the grain into 1-inch-thick slices and serve topped with the marinade sauce.

BEAN FRITTERS

Black-eyed peas, which are central to this recipe, are not peas at all, but beans. Being a culinary historian, Michael has written a lot about what his ancestors ate. For instance, he's written that black-eyed peas probably came over from West Africa in the 1700s with the Atlantic slave trade. Did you know they've been a staple in Senegambia for millennia? According to Michael, the bean "grows well in hot, drought-conducive conditions and is a symbol of resilience, mercy, and kindness..." Hmm, sounds like our people. Serve the fritters with the Carrot Double Dip from page 98.

ACTIVE TIME: 30 minutes

START TO FINISH: 45 minutes, plus up to 12 hours soaking time

SERVES 4

1 pound (2 cups) dried black-eyed peas

½ cup fresh flat-leaf parsley, roughly chopped

½ cup fresh cilantro, roughly chopped

¼ cup fresh mint, chopped

¼ cup sliced scallions

1 teaspoon ground coriander

½ teaspoon ground cumin

½ teaspoon ground allspice

½ teaspoon red pepper flakes

¼ teaspoon grated nutmeg

1 teaspoon baking powder

1 tablespoon kosher salt

Sunflower or other vegetable oil, for frying

Soak the beans in cold water for up to 12 hours.

Drain the beans and pulse in a food processor until coarsely chopped. Add the parsley, cilantro, mint, scallions, coriander, cumin, allspice, pepper flakes, nutmeg, baking powder, and salt and pulse to combine into a coarse puree. Chill the fritter batter for at least 20 minutes.

Heat 1 inch of oil in a medium saucepan over medium-high heat to 350°F. Working in batches of about 10 to 12 fritters, drop tablespoons of the batter into the hot oil and cook until golden brown, rotating to cook evenly on both sides, about 4 minutes. Remove the fritters from the oil and allow to drain on paper towels. Repeat the frying until all the batter is used up.

MANGÚ ⟨with⟩ EGGPLANT ESCABECHE

It's funny how mashed potatoes have been brought into fine dining, but mangú and fufu have not. Guess what's coming next. I look at that as a huge missed opportunity—they are really the same dish depending where you are in the world. Fufu is from West Africa and mangú you find in the Dominican Republic and Puerto Rico.

What makes this dish delicious is the comfort of the mash paired with the acid of the eggplant escabeche. Serve as a main dish, or as a side with the Grilled Short Ribs in Piri Piri Marinade (page 287) or Braised Goat with Locust Bean and Chili Oil (page 214).

ACTIVE TIME: *30 minutes*
START TO FINISH: *1 hour*
SERVES 4 TO 6

1 pound baby eggplants, halved lengthwise

6 tablespoons vegetable oil

Kosher salt and freshly ground black pepper

4 yellow plantains (1¼ to 1½ pounds)

2 cups vegetable or chicken stock

1½ cups unsweetened coconut milk

1 cup fresh corn kernels (from 1 ear)

1 bunch scallions, trimmed of root end and sliced

1 small onion, sliced

2 medium bell peppers (any mix of red/orange/yellow), stemmed, seeded, and sliced

6 cloves garlic, minced

2 tablespoons sherry vinegar

2 tablespoons chopped fresh parsley

Toss the eggplant with 4 tablespoons of the oil and lay the pieces in an even layer on a baking sheet. Season with salt and pepper and roast in the oven until the eggplant is tender and golden brown around the edges, 18 to 20 minutes.

Remove the skin from the plantains by making a slit down the length and peeling the skin off as you would a banana. Slice the plantain into 2-inch pieces and place in a medium saucepan. Add the stock and season with a pinch of salt. Over medium heat, bring the plantains and stock to a simmer and cook until the plantains are tender and a knife inserted goes right through, 15 to 18 minutes. At this point, most of the liquid will be absorbed by the plantains. Turn the heat to low and mash the plantain pieces into a slightly chunky puree using a fork or a potato masher. Stir in the coconut milk, corn kernels, and sliced scallions. Season with salt to taste and set aside.

In a medium sauté pan, heat the remaining 2 tablespoons oil over high heat. Add the sliced onion and bell pepper and sauté quickly on high until the vegetables are slightly charred and just softened, 8 to 10 minutes. Reduce the heat to low, add the garlic, and sauté until fragrant, about 1 minute. Add the vinegar and the roasted eggplant pieces. Stir to coat the roasted vegetable in the aromatics and sauce. Remove from the heat and stir in the chopped parsley. Season to taste with salt. Serve the warm plantain mash topped with the eggplant escabeche as a main dish or side.

"Food brings people together. That's my thing."

RODNEY SCOTT

Pitmaster and partner of Rodney Scott's Whole Hog BBQ in Charleston, South Carolina

A leading voice in the tradition of whole-hog barbecue

Born in Philadelphia, Pennsylvania

Influenced by: The practice of pit cookery by Black families in the South Carolina Midlands region

Rodney Scott likes to tell a particular story about his experience with the tradition of whole hog roasting. It's an oft-heard tale for those familiar with the preeminent pitmaster who's cultivated a passionate fan base and prompted renewed appreciation for tending wood-smoked pork. But that's because the story works so well. It goes like this: on the night of his high school graduation in the "very tiny town" of Hemingway, South Carolina, Scott was geared up to party with friends. But his father swiftly reminded Scott that he needed to return home by midnight. There was work to do. "We cook the hogs all night because the average hog that we use is a 12-hour cook time," Scott says. "And we had to have it ready by lunch the next day. I had to fire the hogs and throw wood in the barrel on graduation night."

Firing hogs and throwing wood in the barrel were typical chores for Scott by the time he was a teenager, and they continue to be the foundation of his thriving restaurants. These days, people travel far distances and queue up to taste his pulled pork dressed in a vinegar-based sauce. The James Beard Foundation honored him with a Best Chef award, making him only the second pitmaster in history to receive such recognition.

After a brief period in Philadelphia, Scott's parents returned to his father's hometown in 1972 to open a gas station with a small general store. At Scott's Bar-B-Q, his dad, Roosevelt "Rosie" Scott, would roast a whole hog each week, selling sandwiches and meat platters, increasing production with demand as word got out. Smoking hogs was common in the agricultural region after harvest season and for special occasions and holidays. But it soon became clear that folks didn't mind if someone else did the heavy lifting—cut the wood, load coals, and get up close and personal with half a day's smoke and fire.

A few years after graduation, Scott determined that expanding the food business could be a successful venture. He tweaked his parents' shop relying on business advice from established restaurateurs. He raised prices to reflect the dexterity and care that comes with such a risky cooking process and improved the store's curb appeal to attract newcomers. Scott eventually launched his own brand in Charleston separate from that of his parents. More recently, he opened a second location in Birmingham, Alabama.

Growing up, Scott's mother Ella taught him a wealth of other cooking techniques. Sunday afternoon dinners might feature cabbage rice, pork chops, sweet peas, and candied yams. The banana pudding on Scott's restaurant menu is named for her and topped off with Nilla wafers, just like she used to do. The core of Scott's business is bookended by the expertise his parents passed on to him. He hasn't forgotten that, even as he's looked farther afield. "To come from a 40-year comfort zone of doing the same thing around the same people every day to come into an area as big as Charleston...You have to follow your dreams."

Rodney Scott's Whole Hog BBQ in Charleston

RODNEY'S RIBS ⟨*with*⟩ BAKED COWPEAS

If you've been to Charleston, you've likely heard about Rodney Scott, the James Beard Award–winning chef and barbecue pitmaster. We were lucky enough to have Rodney cook with us in Harlem during the spring of 2018 for Harlem EatUp! where he set up on the corner of 126th and Lenox with a large Jamaican barrel grill, a table, a sink, and a fire extinguisher. Rodney went to town. He cooked ribs from 8 a.m. to 1 p.m. People could smell the pork and his famous sauce wafting through the Harlem streets. Being a Southerner to his core, Rodney would rip off a piece of rib meat and hand it to on-lookers to taste. When we think about BBQ, most of us only think about eating it. Observing Rodney, we see the labor, the tradition, and the community that are an essential part of it.

ACTIVE TIME: *25 minutes*
START TO FINISH: *2 to 3 hours*
SERVES 8 TO 10

RUB AND RIBS

¼ cup packed brown sugar

¼ cup kosher salt

Generous ¼ cup paprika

2 tablespoons onion powder

2 tablespoons garlic powder

1 tablespoon cayenne pepper

4 racks spare ribs

MOP SAUCE

4 cups white vinegar

½ cup chili powder

4½ tablespoons granulated sugar

4½ tablespoons paprika

2 tablespoons freshly ground black pepper

1 tablespoon cayenne pepper

1 tablespoon red pepper flakes

2 lemons

Baked Cowpeas (recipe follows), for serving

Make the rub: Combine the paprika, brown sugar, salt, onion powder, garlic powder, and cayenne in a small bowl.

Sprinkle each rack on both sides with the rub, saving 1 tablespoon for the cowpeas, and set aside at room temperature for 1 hour.

Make the mop sauce: Combine the vinegar, chili powder, granulated sugar, paprika, black pepper, cayenne, and pepper flakes in a 2-quart container. Cut the lemons in half and squeeze the juice into a container. Drop the lemon halves into the sauce and stir to combine. Set aside.

Heat a smoker or grill to 250°F.

Place the ribs on the grill, meat side down and cook over indirect heat for 2 to 3 hours, until tender but not falling off the bone, flipping halfway through cooking. During the last 45 minutes of cooking, mop with sauce every 15 minutes.

Serve hot with the cowpeas.

(Continued)

BAKED COWPEAS

ACTIVE TIME: *10 minutes*
START TO FINISH: *35 minutes*
**SERVES 6 TO 8 AS A SIDE*

4 cups cooked cowpeas
or black-eyed peas,
with liquid

½ cup chopped meat
from Rodney's Ribs
(above)

3 tablespoons cider
vinegar

3 tablespoons ketchup

1 tablespoon rib rub
(above)

Preheat the oven to 375°F.

Combine the peas, rib meat, vinegar, and ketchup
and rub in a medium mixing bowl. Transfer to a 2-quart
casserole dish and bake until heated through and bubbly around the edges, about 25 minutes.

RODNEY'S HUSHPUPPIES
⟪with⟫ PEANUT SUCCOTASH

During the Harlem visit, Rodney's sous chef cooked the crispiest hushpuppies served with honey butter while Rodney sipped bourbon and made his St. Louis pork ribs, with the secret Rodney Sauce and baked beans. The twist here is the peanuts in the succotash, which add a fun and crunchy texture,

ACTIVE TIME: 35 minutes
START TO FINISH: 35 minutes
MAKES 16 TO 18 HUSHPUPPIES

Vegetable oil, for frying

1 cup all-purpose flour

1 cup cornmeal

2½ tablespoons sugar

¾ teaspoon baking soda

¾ teaspoon kosher salt

1 ⅔ cups buttermilk

1 large egg, beaten

1 tablespoon vegetable oil

2 tablespoons finely diced onion

Honey Butter (recipe follows), for serving

Succotash (recipe follows), for serving

Heat 1½ inches vegetable oil in a large, heavy pot or Dutch oven set over medium heat and bring to 350°F to 375°F. Place a paper towel–lined cooling rack in a half-sheet pan and set aside.

Place the flour, cornmeal, sugar, baking soda, and salt in a medium mixing bowl and whisk to combine.

Combine the buttermilk, egg, and oil in a small mixing bowl and whisk to combine.

Add the wet mixture to the dry mixture and use a spatula to combine. Fold in the onion.

In batches of four or five hushpuppies, dip a 2-ounce ice cream scoop into the hot oil, then into the batter and carefully scoop batter into the oil. Fry for 4 to 5 minutes, until golden brown and cooked through. Transfer to prepared cooling rack to drain.

Cool the hush puppies slightly before serving with the honey butter and succotash.

(Continued)

HONEY BUTTER

MAKES 1 CUP

1 cup (2 sticks) unsalted butter, softened

½ teaspoon kosher salt

2 tablespoons honey

Stir together the butter, honey and salt in a bowl.

PEANUT SUCCOTASH

ACTIVE TIME: 45 minutes
START TO FINISH: 1 hour
SERVES 6 TO 8 AS A SIDE

2 tablespoons extra virgin olive oil

¼ cup roasted salted peanuts

2 medium red onions, chopped

1 large clove garlic, minced

2 medium tomatoes, chopped

2½ cups fresh corn kernels (from 2½ ears)

2½ cups fresh lima beans

1 poblano chile, seeded and chopped

2 tablespoons unsalted butter

Juice of 1 lime

3 tablespoons thinly sliced fresh basil

2 tablespoons chopped fresh parsley

2 tablespoons chopped fresh cilantro

Kosher salt and freshly ground pepper

Heat the olive oil in a large skillet over medium heat. Add the peanuts, onions, and garlic and cook until the onions are translucent, about 5 minutes.

Add the tomatoes, corn, lima beans, poblano, and butter to the skillet and simmer for about 15 minutes, until the corn and lima beans are tender.

Add the lime juice, parsley, basil, cilantro, and salt and pepper to taste. Serve warm or at room temperature.

KELEWELE CRUSTED CATFISH ⟨with⟩ YUCCA FRIES AND GARDEN EGG CHOW CHOW

Most people know Carla as the fantastic host of the TV show *The Chew*, but I knew her well before that. She has the greatest spirit and energy and has a passion for people and food. Once, we did an event when Carla donated the use of her kitchen to a young start-up. The cameras weren't there but Carla was in the kitchen, teaching and bringing positive energy to everyone around her. She's always willing to share her time, that's just who Chef Carla is. Kelewele is a snack of spiced fried plantains from Ghana, and we're doing a riff on that here. This recipe takes inspiration from the African Diaspora and from the American South. It's fun, spicy, and delicious.

ACTIVE TIME: *45 minutes*
START TO FINISH: *1 hour 45 minutes*
SERVES 4

1 large green plantain

2 tablespoons unsalted butter, melted

2 tablespoons extra virgin olive oil

4 (4- to 6-ounce) catfish fillets

1 large egg white, lightly beaten

1 tablespoon Kelewele Spice Blend (page 274)

2 pounds yucca, peeled and cut into ¼- by 4-inch sticks

Peanut oil, for frying

1 cup Garden Egg Chow Chow (recipe follows)

Peel the plantain and thinly slice on a mandoline. Place the melted butter and olive oil in a medium bowl and whisk to combine. Add the plantain slices and toss to coat well.

Brush the catfish fillets on one side with the egg white, then lay plantain slices on top, slightly overlapping, until the side is covered. Press down on the plantain to adhere to the fish. Sprinkle with the spice blend. Refrigerate while preparing the remainder of the recipe.

Bring a large pot of water to a boil over high heat. Add the yucca and blanch until almost tender, 6 to 8 minutes. Transfer the yucca to a paper towel–lined cooling rack set in a baking sheet to drain.

Preheat the oven to warm setting. Place a cooling rack in a baking sheet and set in the oven.

Heat 2 tablespoons peanut oil in a Dutch oven or deep, heavy sauté pan set over medium-high heat. When the oil shimmers, add the fish, plantain side down, and cook until plantains are golden brown and crispy, 3 to 4 minutes. Flip and continue cooking until the fish is just cooked through, about 3 minutes, depending on the thickness of the fillet. Transfer the fish to the rack in the oven to keep warm.

Add enough oil to the pan to make it 1 inch deep. Bring the oil to 350°F.

Working in batches, gently add the blanched yucca fries to the oil and fry until golden and cooked through, about 5 minutes. Using a slotted spoon, transfer to a paper towel–lined plate to drain.

Serve the fish with chow chow and a side of yucca fries.

GARDEN EGG CHOW CHOW

ACTIVE TIME: *25 minutes*
START TO FINISH: *1½ hours*
MAKES ABOUT 2½ CUPS

2 cups West African eggplant (garden egg), chopped

1 cup chopped yellow onion

1 cup shredded green cabbage

1 red bell pepper, stemmed, seeded, and chopped

1 green Scotch bonnet (or habanero) chile, stemmed and seeded

2 teaspoons kosher salt

¾ cup apple cider vinegar

½ cup water

½ cup sugar

1 teaspoon mustard seed

1 teaspoon coriander seed

½ teaspoon grain of paradise

¼ teaspoon ground turmeric

In batches, process the eggplant, onion, cabbage, bell pepper, and chile in a food processor, pulsing for 4 to 5 seconds at a time, until roughly chopped. Transfer the vegetables to a large colander and sprinkle with the salt. Toss to combine and set aside to drain for 30 minutes.

Rinse the chopped vegetables under cold water and drain well. Transfer to a medium saucepan and add the vinegar, water, sugar, mustard seed, coriander, grain of paradise, and turmeric. Stir to combine and place over medium heat. Bring to a simmer, reduce the heat to low, and cook until the liquid thickens slightly, taking on a syrupy consistency, about 30 minutes. Transfer the mixture to a large, clean glass jar, cover, and refrigerate for up to 2 weeks.

MONTEGO BAY RUM CAKE

Herb was a sous chef for Patrick Clark, the renowned Washington, DC, chef, for many years before opening Bambou, an upscale Caribbean-style restaurant in New York's East Village in 1996. It was one of the first higher-end Black-owned restaurants in the city. When I think about where Rooster is today, it's because of restaurants like Bambou. As a young chef, I was inspired by these highly aspirational restaurants and saw what was possible. This rum cake takes a cue from Herb's Jamaican heritage.

ACTIVE TIME: 20 minutes
START TO FINISH: 1 hour
SERVES 10 TO 12

4 large eggs

½ cup granulated sugar

1 cup cake flour, plus extra for coating pan

1 teaspoon baking powder

¼ teaspoon kosher salt

¼ cup clarified butter, melted, plus extra for coating pan

¾ cup (12 tablespoons) dark rum

1 teaspoon vanilla extract

1 cup whipping cream

1 tablespoon brown sugar

Preheat the oven to 350°F. Coat an 8-inch round cake pan with butter. Line the bottom of the pan with parchment paper and coat it with butter. Sprinkle with flour and shake until coated evenly over the butter. Discard the excess.

Whisk the eggs in a stand mixer with the whisk attachment for 2 minutes, or until the eggs lighten in color. With the mixer still running, gradually add the granulated sugar over 1 minute and continue to whisk for 15 to 20 minutes, until the batter is pale yellow in color, fluffy, and a ribbon of batter falls off of the whisk and doesn't disappear immediately into the remaining batter.

While the eggs and sugar are whisking, sift together the flour, baking powder, and salt and set aside. Combine the butter, 2 tablespoons of the rum, and the vanilla extract in a small bowl and set aside.

Remove the bowl from the mixer. Add one-fourth of the flour mixture to the batter in the mixer bowl and gently fold until combined. Add the remaining flour mixture and fold in just enough to incorporate. Fold in the butter mixture until no streaks of liquid can be seen.

Scrape the batter into the prepared cake pan. Place on the middle rack of the oven and bake for 25 to 30 minutes, until a toothpick inserted in the cake comes out clean.

Cool in the pan on a wire rack for 10 minutes. Poke holes all over the top of the cake. Pour 9 tablespoons (½ cup plus 1 tablespoon) of the rum all over the top of the cake. Once the cake has soaked up all of the rum, carefully remove the cake from the pan and leave to cool completely.

Combine the cream, brown sugar, and remaining 1 tablespoon rum in a stand mixer and whisk until stiff peaks form.

Spread the whipped cream over the top of the cake and serve.

BOSTON BAY JERK CHICKEN
≪with≫ ROTI

At a very young age, Jerome's cooking talents were inspired by his Filipinx and Caribbean heritage. Jerome is the inaugural executive chef of Sweet Home Café, the restaurant inside the Smithsonian's National Museum of African American History and Culture in DC. He's a young chef, but has already been featured in the *New York Times*, *Time* magazine, and *Bon Appétit*. He did Harlem EatUp! for us in 2018. It was great to cook with him, and I know we will do it again. The dish honors Jerome's Jamaican background. Jerk is the food to get in Boston Bay, Jamaica.

Serve the chicken with Roti (page 51) and Plantain Chips (page 27).

ACTIVE TIME: *30 minutes*
START TO FINISH: *9 hours*
SERVES 4 TO 6

1 medium onion, coarsely chopped

3 scallions, coarsely chopped

2 Scotch bonnet chiles, stemmed and halved

2 cloves garlic, peeled

1 tablespoon five-spice powder

1 tablespoon ground allspice

1 tablespoon coarsely

ground black pepper

1 teaspoon fresh thyme leaves

1 teaspoon freshly grated nutmeg

1 teaspoon kosher salt, plus extra for chicken

½ cup soy sauce

2 tablespoons vegetable oil

2 whole chickens

Combine the onion, scallions, chiles, garlic, five-spice powder, allspice, black pepper, thyme, nutmeg, and salt in a food processor and process until the mixture is a coarse paste.

With the machine running, add the soy sauce and oil in a steady stream. Pour the marinade into a large, shallow dish and set aside.

Using kitchen shears or a knife, cut down one side and then the other of each chicken's backbone and remove. Cut down the center of the breast bone. Place each of the four halves in the dish with the marinade and turn to coat. Cover and refrigerate for 8 hours.

Heat a grill to high. Grill the chicken on both sides until grill marks appear. Then, either continue to cook on the grill completely or transfer the chicken to a 375°F oven and bake for 30 to 35 minutes, until the chicken reaches an internal temperature of 165°F.

COLLARD GREEN AND FRESH CHEESE SALAD

Marvin is a dear, dear friend of mine. He's done every trade in the cooking business. He's owned his own restaurant, he has cooked on a boat, and as a caterer. He was there at Cafe Beulah, off Park Avenue. He's worked all over the world, and he's been at it for forty years. Marvin represents the bridge, and I'm not talking about the Queensboro Bridge. He's the connection between the old school and the new. Before Instagram and social media, before you could look things up on the Internet, Marvin was in the kitchen learning all the skills. He didn't know it then, but that was a very significant time—when Black chefs were trying to make a name for themselves. Marvin's an especially significant example of how Black cooks can succeed when the opportunities often aren't there, and we have to get in where we can fit in. Marvin did all of that. He kept the lights on for all of us.

This is a traditional collard green salad. This dish is delicious. Marvin has Southern ties—he spent a big portion of his life in South Carolina—and the collards give a nod to that. He's also big into cooking healthy food, which is why this salad is the perfect fit.

ACTIVE TIME: 50 minutes
START TO FINISH: 2½ hours
SERVES 6 TO 8

PICKLED PEACHES

4 peaches, peeled, pitted, and cut into ¼-inch slice

1 jalapeño chile, sliced in half lengthwise

2 cups water

¾ cup white wine vinegar

¾ cup sugar

1 teaspoon yellow mustard seed

2 cloves garlic, smashed and peeled

1 star anise

1 bay leaf

FRESH CHEESE

1 cup whole buttermilk

½ cup whole milk

½ teaspoon kosher salt

2 teaspoons chopped chives

COCONUT VINAIGRETTE

4 tablespoons extra virgin olive oil

2 jalapeño chiles, chopped

2 cloves garlic, minced

½ cup coconut flakes

½ cup unsweetened coconut milk

Juice of 1 lemon

2 large egg yolks

1 teaspoon sesame oil

1 teaspoon Dijon mustard

4 dashes Worcestershire sauce

1 tablespoon chopped fresh parsley

SALAD

2 cups packed finely collard greens ribbons

1 cup packed finely sliced napa cabbage

1 radicchio head, finely sliced

1 grapefruit, peeled and segmented

Pickle the peaches: Place the peaches and jalapeño in a 1-quart canning jar.

Combine the water, vinegar, sugar, mustard seed, garlic, star anise, and bay leaf in a small saucepan. Set over medium-high heat and bring just to a boil, 5 to 7 minutes. Using a funnel, pour the hot liquid over the peaches. Put the lid on the jar and refrigerate until ready to use.

Make the cheese: Line a colander or a fine mesh sieve with cheesecloth and set aside.

Combine the buttermilk, milk, and salt in a small saucepan set over medium-high heat and bring just to a boil. Decrease the heat to maintain a bare simmer and cook for 15 minutes. Remove from heat and set aside to cool for 15 minutes.

Transfer the buttermilk mixture to the lined colander and place the colander in a bowl. Cover with a clean dish towel and refrigerate for 1 hour to allow all the liquid to drain and the cheese to cool. Transfer to an airtight container, add the chives, and gently toss to combine. Cover and store in the refrigerator for up to 1 week.

Make the vinaigrette: Heat 1 tablespoon of the olive oil in a small sauté pan set over medium heat. Once the oil shimmers, add the jalapeño and garlic and cook, stirring frequently, for 3 to 4 minutes, until the garlic is fragrant and the jalapeño begins to soften. Add the coconut flakes and continue cooking until lightly browned, 2 to 3 minutes. Set aside to cool slightly.

Combine the remaining 3 tablespoons olive oil, the coconut milk, lemon juice, egg yolks, sesame oil, mustard, and Worcestershire in a blender or small food processor and process until combined and an emulsion is formed. Transfer to a bowl, add the sautéed jalapeño mixture and the parsley, and whisk to combine. Set aside until ready to use.

Assemble and serve the salad: Combine the collard greens, cabbage, and radicchio in a large serving bowl, add the vinaigrette, and toss well. Add the cheese, peaches, and grapefruit and gently toss. Serve immediately.

CALLALOO AND BITTER GREENS SALAD
⟪with⟫ SMOKED FISH AND EGUSI SEEDS

Michael lives in Lagos, where he's a great chef. When I think about modern Nigerian African food, he's at the forefront. I follow him because I always learn what's next in African cuisine. Michael and Kwame Onwuachi (page 212) came up together. Michael trained at Eleven Madison Park. Equally talented, these chefs turn to Africa the way we used to turn to France. Watch out. That's what's coming.

Egusi seeds come from the egusi melon, and are found in Nigerian cooking, where the seeds are usually chopped up and folded into bitter greens. You can buy these seeds at your local West African store. In this dish, the smokiness of the fish pairs wonderfully with the callaloo.

ACTIVE TIME: *45 minutes*

START TO FINISH: *2 to 3 hours*

SERVES 4

1 cup water

½ cup apple cider vinegar

¼ cup sugar

1 tablespoon kosher salt, plus more to taste

1 cup multicolored baby bell peppers, cut into thin ¼-inch slices

½ cup egusi seeds

1 tablespoon extra virgin olive oil

½ teaspoon cayenne pepper

2 cups young callaloo greens, leaves and tender stems (or baby spinach leaves)

4 cups torn bitter greens mix (pick a nice variety, e.g., sorrel, chicory, escarole, dandelion greens, frisée, etc.)

½ cup **Red Palm Oil Vinaigrette** (page 287)

1 cup smoked white fish flakes (like trout), picked of any bones

Combine the water, vinegar, sugar, and salt in a pot. Heat until it just begins to simmer and the sugar has dissolved. Remove from the heat. Place the sliced baby bell peppers in a bowl and then pour the heated pickling liquid over. Allow to sit for at least 30 minutes to pickle.

Toss the egusi seeds with the olive oil in a heavy bottom skillet and season with the cayenne and salt to taste. Toast over low heat until the seeds are golden brown and slightly puffed, 8 to 10 minutes.

To compose the salad, toss the greens in a large bowl. Pour half of the dressing into the bowl and toss again. Divide the greens among four plates, top each with a portion of the smoked trout and some pickled peppers. Sprinkle the toasted egusi seeds over the top. Serve immediately.

GINGER AND HIBISCUS FLOWER GRANITA

Hibiscus flowers take me to the islands of Trinidad or to West Africa. The dried flower can be used to make sorbets or teas. This granita is a wonderfully refreshing summertime treat or after-dinner palate cleanser. Michael is an amazing chef who worked at Eleven Madison Park with Kwame before moving back to Lagos. He is such an important link to West Africa for upcoming Black chefs. This is a light and refreshing dessert, perfect for a hot day either in the States or in Lagos.

ACTIVE TIME: *15 minutes*
START TO FINISH: *2½ hours*
MAKES ABOUT 2½ CUPS (4 TO 6 SERVINGS)

2 cups water

1 cup dried hibiscus leaves

Grated zest of 1 lime

1 tablespoon fresh lime juice

2-inch piece fresh ginger, peeled and grated

¾ cup sugar

Freshly ground black pepper

In a small saucepan, combine the water and dried hibiscus leaves. Place over high heat and bring to a boil. Remove from the heat, cover, and set aside to steep for 10 minutes.

Remove the hibiscus leaves using a slotted spoon and discard. Add the lime zest, lime juice, grated ginger, and sugar to the pan. Return to medium heat and stir until the sugar dissolves. Remove from the heat and set aside to cool to room temperature, then strain through a fine mesh strainer.

Pour into a 9-inch square baking pan and place in the freezer. As the mixture begins to freeze around the edges, about 20 minutes, drag a fork across the surface and stir the edges into the center. Repeat this process every 20 minutes, until the mixture is the texture of shaved ice, 1 to 2 hours.

To serve, scoop the granita into a glass bowl or ramekin and lightly sprinkle with freshly cracked black pepper.

TARO AND MILLET CROQUETTES

You'll find the taro root in West Africa, the Caribbean, and Hawaii. It's one of those comforting foods that I think is just delicious, and it also happens to be my wife's favorite vegetable. It's sort of nubby in its flavor and makes a superb croquette. The taro root goes by many names around the world: dasheen, yautia, and kalo. In Kenya, natives call it nduma, and it is boiled and eaten with fresh veggies.

ACTIVE TIME: *45 minutes*
START TO FINISH: *1 hour 15 minutes*
MAKES 20 CROQUETTES

Kosher salt

8 ounces millet

1 pound (2 to 3 medium) taro root (or Japanese white sweet potatoes), peeled and shredded (on the large side of a box grater or medium julienne if using a mandoline)

1 cup thinly sliced scallions, light and white green parts only

½ cup fresh cilantro leaves and tender stems, chopped

2 cloves garlic, grated

1 teaspoon grated fresh ginger

1 tablespoon dried shrimp (optional)

2 tablespoons corn flour

½ teaspoon ground turmeric

¼ teaspoon cayenne pepper

2 large eggs, lightly beaten

Freshly ground black pepper

Vegetable oil, for frying

Lime wedges, for serving

Benne Seed Dressing (page 284) or Peanut Sauce (page 244), for serving

Bring a large stockpot of salted water to a boil. Add the millet and cook for 18 to 20 minutes, until it is just tender but still has some bite. Drain off any remaining liquid in a sieve, fluff, and set aside to cool.

In a large mixing bowl, combine the cooked millet, shredded taro, scallions, cilantro, garlic, ginger, and dried shrimp, if using. In a separate bowl, combine the corn flour, turmeric, cayenne, and eggs. Pour the egg mixture into the millet mixture and mix well to incorporate ingredients. Season the batter generously with salt and pepper.

Heat 2 inches vegetable oil in a deep saucepan over medium-high heat to 350°F.

Using a 2-ounce scoop or your hands, form golf ball–sized portions of batter, compacted to ensure they do not separate. Working in batches, gently slide the croquettes into the hot oil and fry until golden brown on all sides and cooked through, 3 to 4 minutes. Transfer to a cooling rack set in a baking sheet to drain and season lightly with salt.

Serve the croquettes hot or at room temperature with lime wedges for squeezing, and benne seed dressing or peanut sauce for dipping.

SHORT RIBS
«with» GET UP SAUCE AND GREEN BEANS

When I came to New York, Patrick Clark was one of the most talked-about Black chefs in the country, and I had an opportunity to work with him many times before he passed in 1998. One of the highlights during my career was working with his son Preston. Today, Preston's a chef who has been cooking for over twenty years, and when I look at him, I am reminded of what we can learn and achieve if we only have a strong example set for us. Patrick came from the generation where most Black chefs could only graduate to be sous chefs, but he pushed through that invisible ceiling and became an executive chef at Tavern on the Green. And Preston was witness to that. Because of his father's example, he knew that was a goal he could reach if he worked hard enough. Patrick's achievements had a real impact on a lot of Black people who work tirelessly in restaurant kitchens. It was like he opened a door for the rest of us.

ACTIVE TIME: *35 minutes*
START TO FINISH: *3 hours 45 minutes*
SERVES 6 TO 8

5 pounds short ribs	4 sprigs fresh thyme
1 tablespoon kosher salt	3 bay leaves
1½ teaspoons freshly ground black pepper	½ cup pomegranate molasses
3 tablespoons vegetable oil	½ cup red wine
1 large onion, sliced	1 quart beef stock
2 medium carrots, sliced	3 cups Get Up Sauce (page 282)
2 stalks celery, sliced	1½ pounds green beans, blanched
3 cloves garlic, sliced	½ cup chopped roasted peanuts, for garnish

Season the ribs on all sides with the salt and pepper. Heat the oil in an 8- to 10-quart roasting pan or Dutch oven set over high heat. When the oil shimmers, add the ribs and brown on all sides, 10 to 15 minutes. Remove the ribs from the pan.

Preheat the oven to 325°F.

Add the onion, carrots, celery, garlic, thyme, and bay leaves to the pot and cook, stirring occasionally, until the onion is translucent, about 5 minutes. Add the pomegranate molasses and wine and deglaze the pan. Cook, stirring occasionally, until the liquid is reduced to a syrupy consistency, about 5 minutes.

Add the beef stock and bring to a boil. Add the short ribs, cover the pot, and transfer to the oven to braise until the rib meat is tender and just falling away from the bone, about 3 hours.

Remove the short ribs from the pot. Add 2 cups of the get up sauce to the pot and stir to combine. Return the ribs to the pot and cook until the sauce is heated through.

Place the green beans in a large mixing bowl, add the remaining 1 cup of the get up sauce, and toss to combine. Garnish the ribs and beans with the peanuts and serve immediately.

FARRO IN JOLLOF SAUCE

A Senegal native, Pierre is a chef and a restaurateur, but he's also a teacher. He constantly introduces people to ingredients that are native to West Africa and shows us how we can use them here in America. Farro is just one of the many African super grains he showcases at his restaurants.

ACTIVE TIME: 50 minutes
START TO FINISH: 1½ hours, plus overnight soak
SERVES 4 TO 6

1 cup farro

Kosher salt

1 large red onion, peeled

1 red bell pepper, stemmed, seeded, and coarsely chopped

3 ripe plum tomatoes, halved

6 cloves garlic, peeled

1 Scotch bonnet (or habanero) chile, stemmed

2 tablespoons vegetable oil

1 teaspoon fresh thyme leaves

2 tablespoons unsalted butter

2 tablespoons chopped fresh parsley

2 tablespoons sliced scallions

Freshly ground black pepper

Place the farro in a large bowl, cover with water by at least 3 inches, and set aside at room temperature to soak overnight. Drain.

Bring 5 cups water to a boil in a medium saucepan set over high heat. Add the farro and 1 teaspoon salt. Stir to combine, decrease the heat to maintain a simmer, and cook just until the farro begins to become tender, 30 to 45 minutes. Strain and reserve ¾ cup of the cooking liquid. Set aside.

Cut the onion in half. Quarter one half and dice the remaining half. Place the quartered onion half, bell pepper, tomatoes, garlic, chile, and ½ cup water in a blender or a food processor and puree until finely chopped.

Heat the vegetable oil in a large sauté pan set over medium-high heat. Once the oil shimmers, add the diced onion, and 1½ teaspoons salt and cook until translucent, 2 to 3 minutes.

Add the puree to the sauté pan and continue to cook until the liquid has evaporated and the sauce deepens in color, about 15 minutes. Add the farro and the thyme and stir to combine.

Reduce the heat to low and, starting with ¼ cup, pour in the reserved cooking liquid. Stir the farro mixture as you would a risotto until the liquid is almost completely absorbed. Stir another ¼ cup and repeat the process of stirring and adding liquid until all the reserved cooking liquid has been used up and the farro is tender with some liquid remaining in the pan, about 20 minutes.

Remove the farro from the heat and add the butter, stirring to coat. Add the parsley and scallions and stir to combine. Taste and season with additional salt and black pepper.

FONIO STUFFED COLLARDS
《with》 PEPPER SAMBAL AND SAUCE MOYO

Fonio is one of these ingredients that we're just starting to see at the supermarkets, but it's the kind of grain Pierre has long been introducing to his diners. Fonio is an ancient grain that has been grown and eaten for thousands of years in West Africa. The grains are so tiny that cooked fonio is like a fine couscous. The dawadawa powder, made from fermented locust beans, adds an umami flavor.

ACTIVE TIME: *1½ hours*
START TO FINISH: *1¾ hours*
MAKES ABOUT 20 ROLLS

FONIO STUFFING

2 cups water

½ cup fonio

1 tablespoon red palm oil, plus more for brushing

1 small red onion, diced

3 cloves garlic, minced

1 tablespoon chopped fresh thyme

1 teaspoon dawadawa powder

1 teaspoon dried shrimp powder (optional)

2 tablespoons chopped fresh mint leaves

2 tablespoons chopped fresh cilantro

Grated zest of 1 lime

2 tablespoons fresh lime juice

Kosher salt and freshly ground black pepper

Roasted Red Pepper Sambal (page 288)

¾ cup chicken stock

1 small bunch collard greens, about 20 leaves

Sauce Moyo (page 289), for serving

Make the stuffing: Place the fonio in a small bowl and cover with cool water. Swirl around and allow any chaff to float to the top. Drain and repeat once or twice, until the water is clear.

Bring the water to a boil in a small saucepan set over medium-high heat. Add the fonio and stir. Decrease the heat to maintain a simmer, cover, and cook, stirring frequently, for 4 to 5 minutes, until the water is absorbed and the grains are tender. Transfer the fonio to a parchment-lined baking sheet and spread the grains to cool.

Heat the palm oil in a small sauté pan set over medium heat. When the oil shimmers, add the onion and sauté until softened, about 2 minutes. Add the garlic, thyme, and the dawadawa powder and sauté until fragrant, about 1 minute. Add the dried shrimp powder if using. Stir to combine and remove from the heat. Stir in the mint, cilantro, lime zest, and juice.

Transfer the fonio to a large mixing bowl, add the onion mixture, and stir to combine. Taste and adjust the seasoning with salt and pepper as needed.

Place the sambal and the chicken stock in a medium bowl and whisk to combine. Set aside.

Bring a pot of generously salted water to a boil and prepare an ice bath. Shave down the middle vein of each collard leaf to a similar height as the leaf so that the leaf is pliable and can bend without breaking. Trim the stalk close to the leaf leaving a ½-inch piece. Blanch each leaf for 30 seconds in the boiling water, removing once the leaf turns dark green. Shock immediately in the ice bath and repeat the process until all the leaves have been blanched.

To stuff the collards, spread a leaf on a board or work surface with the vein side down. Brush the leaf lightly with red palm oil and sprinkle with salt and pepper. Patch any tears or rips with pieces from the extra leaves. Place 2 tablespoons of the fonio stuffing in the center of the leaf and press down on the filling to flatten the top. Roll the leaf tightly around the filling, starting from the stem end and folding in the left and right sides of the leaf to enclose the filling completely. You should end up with approximately a 1½-inch-thick roll depending on the size of the leaf. Repeat the stuffing and rolling process until all the collard leaves have been used up.

Preheat the oven to 350°F. Spread half of the sambal mixture over the bottom of a 2-quart casserole or baking dish and lay the collard rolls side by side over the sauce; it's okay to stack some rolls over the top of the bottom layer if they don't all fit in a single layer.

Cover the collard rolls with the remaining sambal sauce and cover the dish with foil. Bake until the rolls are heated through and sauce is bubbling, about 45 minutes.

Uncover the dish and allow to cool for at least 10 minutes. Serve the stewed collard rolls hot topped with sauce moyo.

SPICED BUTTER-POACHED SHRIMP AND POTATOES

Sometimes I ask myself why we cook, and why we're so serious about it, then I look at Jaqueta and think—that's why. She's the heartbeat of the Rooster's kitchen—fierce, curious about food, tough. Born and raised in Harlem, she was already talented when she came to us. Her ambition is there, and her presence in the kitchen makes everything we cook more delicious. She is a great role model in the kitchen, coming up strong. Techniques used here—such as poaching in butter—are like learning a new language and watching Jay master new techniques has been incredible to watch.

Here, you're using fermented products to bring out the taste of foods with African origins. The aged butter in this dish, that's really where the flavor is going to come from. A good aged butter is often clarified and if you don't put your fingers into it, it'll keep for months. The longer it sits, the better it gets.

ACTIVE TIME: *15 minutes*
START TO FINISH: *2 weeks*
SERVES 4 TO 6

Aged Butter (recipe follows)

1 pound fingerling potatoes, cut in half lengthwise

⅓ cup white wine

1 lemon, cut in half

2 teaspoons sambal oelek

2 teaspoons oyster sauce

4 drops fish sauce

1 pound (21 to 25) shrimp, shell on

2 teaspoons fresh chopped dill

2 teaspoons fresh chopped cilantro

Combine the aged butter and potatoes in a medium, high-sided sauté pan set over medium-high heat and bring to a simmer. Decrease the heat to maintain a simmer and cook for 10 minutes, until the potatoes are just tender.

Add the white wine, juice from half the lemon, the sambal, oyster sauce, and fish sauce and stir to combine. Fold in the shrimp and poach for 3 minutes, until the shrimp are just cooked through. Squeeze the remaining lemon over all, sprinkle with dill and cilantro, and toss to combine. Serve immediately.

AGED BUTTER

ACTIVE TIME: *25 minutes*
START TO FINISH: *2 weeks*
MAKES 2 CUPS

1 pound (4 sticks) unsalted butter

1 teaspoon miso

1 teaspoon shrimp powder

2 cloves garlic, peeled

1 teaspoon ground turmeric

1 teaspoon ground coriander

Place the butter, miso, shrimp powder, garlic, turmeric, and coriander in a small saucepan set over medium heat and bring to a simmer. Reduce the heat to low and simmer for 20 minutes. Strain out the garlic pieces and refrigerate for at least 2 weeks.

TEFF AND BROWN BUTTER BISCUITS
⟪with⟫ SHAVED COUNTRY HAM

Roblé found the sweet spot between cooking and entertainment: as a chef with a catering company, he's all in on social media, he cooks with tons of celebrities, and he's built a great Instagram presence—@chefroble. He has found his niche and he's thriving. His professional journey shows that there's a different path and that you can succeed in the cooking sphere outside of being a traditional restaurant chef. His energy is amazing. He inspires a lot of young people to get into the industry. Maybe they come in through the restaurant door, maybe they come in through the catering door, but they all come in after seeing Roblé in action.

Roblé has roots in Somalia, East Africa—this recipe is where Ethiopia meets the South. Biscuits have long been a Southern tradition, and teff, originally from Ethiopia, is one of the oldest grains in the world. Here we bring the ancient grain together with the Southern skills of making something out of nothing.

ACTIVE TIME: 40 minutes
START TO FINISH: 3 hours
MAKES 12 TO 14 BISCUITS

1 cup (2 sticks) unsalted butter

2¼ cups teff flour

2 cups cake flour, plus more for rolling

1 tablespoon baking powder

1½ teaspoons baking soda

1½ tablespoons kosher salt

1½ teaspoons sugar

2¼ cups cold buttermilk

½ cup Sorghum Butter (page 278)

12 to 24 thin slices country ham

Melt 1 stick of the butter in a light-colored, medium saucepan set over medium-high heat. Once the butter has completely melted and begins to take on color, swirl the pan as it cooks to ensure even coloring. The butter will begin to take on a light brown color, at this point begin to stir, scraping up the milk solids sticking to the bottom of the pan. Continue cooking until the butter becomes a deep brown color, 5 to 6 minutes. It should smell nutty and toasted. Once the butter has reached the correct color, immediately pour it into another heat-proof container, scraping out all the browned milk solids. Place the container in the refrigerator until solidified, 30 to 40 minutes.

Cut both the remaining 1 stick butter and the browned butter into ½-inch cubes. Chill all of the butter in the freezer until frozen, at least 2 hours.

Preheat the oven to 375°F. Line a baking sheet with parchment.

Place the teff flour, cake flour, baking powder, baking soda, salt, and sugar in a medium mixing bowl and whisk to combine. Transfer half of this dry mixture to the bowl of a food processor, add all the frozen butter, and pulse until the butter is cut into smaller pieces but are still visible. Transfer to the bowl with remaining dry ingredients and stir to combine.

Form a well in the center of the dry mixture and pour in the buttermilk. Using a rubber spatula, stir to combine and form a dough. Turn the dough out onto a well-floured surface and press together just enough to form a slightly uniform dough. Do not knead or overwork.

Roll out the dough to an even ¾-inch thickness. Use a 3-inch round biscuit cutter to cut out rounds. Place the rounds on the prepared baking sheet, leaving no space in between the biscuits. Press the biscuit scraps back together and cut out rounds one more time to make a total of twelve to fourteen biscuits. Discard remaining scraps.

Brush the biscuit tops with some of the sorghum butter and bake for 8 minutes. Rotate the pan, decrease the temperature to 350°F, and bake for another 8 min-

utes, until the biscuits are cooked through and a toothpick inserted into a center comes out clean. Remove from the oven and allow to cool on the pan for 10 to 15 minutes.

To serve, slice each warm biscuit in half. Slather with sorghum butter, add country ham slices, top with the other half of the biscuit, and serve immediately.

SEA MOSS DELIGHT SMOOTHIE

Vegan chef Lauren is someone we could all learn from. Now based in Miami, she made waves as a private chef for Venus and Serena Williams and many other celebrities and when then-First Lady Michelle Obama invited Lauren to be a chef for Let's Move, the childhood obesity prevention campaign. Lauren's tenacity inspires me. As a teen growing up in DC, a stab wound nearly killed her, but she was fortunate to find the personal strength and mentorship that enabled the life she has now. Sea moss is a popular ingredient that's widely distributed in health food stores today, but I remember walking along the parks in Harlem or Brooklyn and the Rastafarians or other Caribbean street vendors would have it—it's long been a part of those cultures' diets. This refreshing smoothie will get you right.

ACTIVE TIME: *10 minutes*

START TO FINISH: *10 minutes, plus overnight soak*

SERVES 4

3 ounces (about 1 cup) Irish sea moss	Juice of 2 grapefruits
2 Granny Smith apples	2 tablespoons sliced almonds
½-inch piece fresh ginger	4 fresh dates, seeds removed
½ medium cucumber	Pinch of cayenne pepper

Place the sea moss in a bowl, cover with water, and soak for 15 minutes. Drain and cover with water again. Soak overnight at room temperature.

Drain the sea moss, cut into small pieces, and set aside.

Juice the apples, ginger, and cucumber and combine with the grapefruit juice.

Add the juice to a high-speed blender along with the sea moss, almonds, dates, and cayenne and process until smooth. Pour into glasses and serve immediately.

Chapter 5

ORIGIN

A pantry of ingredients, techniques, and recipes relating to the African diaspora.

SPICES, SPICE BLENDS, AND POWDERS
Crayfish Powder
Kelewele Spice Blend
Berbere Seasoning
Berbere Spice Brown Butter
Kibbeh
Sorghum Butter
Chermoula Spice Blend
Dukkah Spice Blend
Yaji (Suya Spice) Blend
Ras el Hanout Spice Blend
Za'atar Spice Blend
Harissa Spice Blend
Durban Curry Masala
Grain of Paradise
Cardamom
Sumac

WET PANTRY: MARINADES, DRESSINGS, VINAIGRETTES, SAUCES, CONDIMENTS, AND PASTES
Awaze
Caramelized Honey Vinaigrette
Get Up Sauce
Benne Seed Dressing
Harissa Charred Tomato Vinaigrette
Locust Bean and Chili Oil
Piri Piri Marinade
Red Palm Oil Vinaigrette
Roasted Red Pepper Sambal
Sauce Moyo
Yaji (Suya Spice) Aioli
Shito

FLOURS, GRAINS, AND STAPLES
Millet
Coconut
Coffee
Broken Rice
Couscous
Chickpea Flour
Teff
Bulgur
Fufu

NUTS, NUT VARIATIONS, AND SEEDS
Tigernuts
Groundnut
Egusi Seeds
Benne Seeds

MORE
Ayib
Basic Tigernut Pie Crust
Fermented Shrimp Paste
Toasted Pecan and Date Molasses Butter
Shiro
Okra
Chow Chow
Argan Oil
Ghee
Cocoa Beans
Vanilla Beans
Sorrel
Tapioca
Bissap
Banana Leaves
Plantains

These days it's easier than ever to stock your kitchen with pantry staples from around the world. It's my hope that you want to. Can you imagine a time in the United States when having soy sauce or Sriracha in the refrigerator was only common if you were from certain cultures? Today, I don't know many people who don't have both.

Finding items that are new to you might mean shopping online. But more than likely, you have a market, bodega, or retailer in your community whose aisles you've never walked down. Is there a street vendor you've never tried? Are there whole neighborhoods you just drive past or walk by? Is there a vendor at the farmers' market you never talk to?

We're at the end of the book now, so you know my next question for you: Why is that? What are the assumptions that make some people think the carniceria doesn't carry great meat? What are the dismissals that presume the whole fish on ice at the Asian market is somehow less desirable than the pre-cut filet in the shape of a perfect rectangle? I can assure you, you're missing out. You might learn that the Egyptian woman running the strip-mall market across from the taqueria has the best baklava and labneh options for miles. You might learn that the Indian grocer has a vibrant stock of fresh curry leaves.

African ingredients, or ingredients that are commonly used in African and African diaspora cooking, are all around you. Plantains are usually right next to the bananas in the produce section. You can often buy them green to enjoy immediately for crunchier, savory uses. Many stores stock them as the skins turn black, or you can ripen them on the counter at home so they'll be perfect for sweeter servings.

If you're into hummus, then you're only a step away from shiro, a stew we eat in Ethiopia that calls for chickpea flour. Miso is everywhere (as it should be!) but you can get umami from shrimp paste, too, which is common to recipes from Senegal. Tigernuts are tubers that have grown in West Africa for thousands of years and you can find them whole or ground—in milk form they're often used as a lactose replacement.

Here's the thing. Where we shop and what we buy *matters*. And that behavior is connected to how we dine. Chefs and restaurants, and the writers who tell their stories, can inspire us with what to eat and what those foods mean. But you taking the next step of buying those ingredients for your home preparation conveys to the economic market that this food matters to you and that you want to see more of it.

If you head to a store that's new to you, remember: These folks have been here. Often for generations. In my personal experience, I've always felt welcome whether it's a tiny stall or a huge market. But I always act like a guest in a loved one's home. These folks carved out their own havens because they had to, needed to. Just like the authorship of Black creators has been systemically erased in fine dining and cookbook publishing, there's a reason so many culture's ingredients end up shoved into one "ethnic food" aisle at the mass grocer. The indie market isn't trying to recreate the vibe of that big chain up the road. Be like my friends and colleagues in this book—adapt!

I promise you, the outcome will be delicious. And your cooking across all disciplines will be better for the African-inspired bounty within your reach.

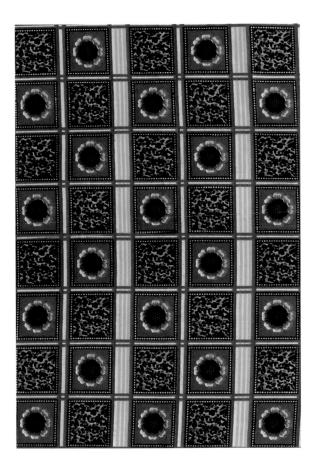

CRAYFISH POWDER

Crayfish powder is a seasoning used in West African cooking, particularly in dishes from Ghana, Nigeria, and Senegal. It is made by grinding dried crayfish into flakes, and has a distinctive umami-rich flavor. Add it to any seafood broth and you'll get an intense boost in flavor. I use it when I want to add depth to my cooking.

KELEWELE SPICE BLEND

Not to be confused with the spiced plantain snack sold by Ghanaian street vendors, kelewele spice blend is a warm and slightly spicy mix that is perfect on anything, but especially good on fish and seafood.

ACTIVE TIME: 5 minutes
START TO FINISH: 5 minutes
MAKES 6 TABLESPOONS

1 tablespoon kosher salt   paprika

1 tablespoon ground ginger

1½ teaspoons freshly grated nutmeg

1 tablespoon ground turmeric

1½ teaspoons cayenne pepper

1 tablespoon smoked

Place the salt, ginger, turmeric, paprika, nutmeg, and cayenne pepper in a small, lidded glass jar and shake to combine. Store in a cool dry place for up to 1 month.

PIMENTÓN DE LA VERA
DENOMINACIÓN DE ORIGEN PROTEGIDA
LA DALIA

MARCA
REGISTRADA

Alimentos
de Extremadura

SMOKED PAPRIKA
Dulce - Sweet - Doux

Peso neto. Net Weight - Poid Net 70 g / 2.469 oz

Kelewele Spice Blend

Berbere Seasoning

BERBERE SEASONING

Berbere is a complex spice mix containing ground chiles, garlic, coriander, and more—some versions include 20 spices, and one of my favorite blends also includes fenugreek, cardamom, allspice, paprika, ginger, cinnamon, and nutmeg.

In Ethiopia, berbere is almost a currency. It's what people make at home, but it's also something they trade with at the market. We put it on everything. I'm so happy to see berbere gaining in popularity with chefs and others outside the Ethiopian community. Sprinkle berbere on grilled carrots or roasted chicken or a piece of lamb.

BERBERE SPICE BROWN BUTTER

Another great way to use berbere is to add it to butter. You brown the butter, which gives you one level of flavor, then you add spices to it to make kibbeh, and finally add berbere on top of that. Put it on anything poached or grilled and get ready to smack your lips.

ACTIVE TIME: 10 minutes
START TO FINISH: 10 minutes
MAKES ABOUT 1½ CUPS

Kibbeh (recipe follows)   1 tablespoon berbere
                             seasoning

Melt the niter kibbeh in a small saucepan set over medium-low heat. Add the berbere spice and stir to combine.

Store refrigerated in an airtight container for up to 3 weeks.

NITER KIBBEH

Niter kibbeh is a staple of Ethiopian and Eritrean cooking. A seasoned clarified butter, niter kibbeh is similar to Indian ghee but infused with spices before the dairy solids are removed. That aromatic flavor is imparted to whatever is cooked with it—seared fish or meat, or stirred into legumes or a stew like doro wat. It can take high heat without burning and ferments well. The longer it sits, the better it tastes.

ACTIVE TIME: 15 minutes
START TO FINISH: About 1 hour
MAKES ABOUT 1½ CUPS

1 pound (4 sticks) unsalted butter	1 teaspoon fenugreek seeds
1 small red onion, coarsely chopped	1 teaspoon ground cumin
3-inch piece fresh ginger, peeled and coarsely chopped	1 teaspoon dried oregano
3 cloves garlic, minced	½ teaspoon ground turmeric
1 cinnamon stick	4 sprigs fresh thyme
4 cardamom pods	

Melt the butter in a medium saucepan over low heat, stirring occasionally. As foam rises to the top, skim and discard it. Continue cooking, without letting the butter brown, until no more foam appears. Add the onion, ginger, garlic, cinnamon stick, cardamom, fenugreek, cumin, oregano, turmeric, and thyme and continue cooking for 15 minutes, stirring occasionally, until the onion is lightly browned and aromatic.

Remove from the heat and set aside to infuse for 30 minutes.

Strain through a fine mesh strainer lined with a cheesecloth. Store refrigerated in an airtight container for up to 3 weeks.

SORGHUM BUTTER

ACTIVE TIME: 10 minutes
MAKES ABOUT ½ CUP

½ cup (1 stick) butter, softened to room temperature

2 tablespoons sorghum

Mix the butter and sorghum together. Store refrigerated in an airtight container for up to 3 weeks.

CHERMOULA SPICE BLEND

A bright combination of spices that, in North Africa, is used primarily as a seasoning on fish. It is also a delicious addition to any type of meat or vegetable.

ACTIVE TIME: 15 minutes
START TO FINISH: 20 minutes
MAKES ABOUT ½ CUP

2 tablespoons cumin seeds

2 tablespoons coriander seeds

4 teaspoons fennel seeds

4 teaspoons grated lemon zest

2 teaspoons whole black peppercorns

2 teaspoons red pepper flakes

2 teaspoons ground

cardamom

1½ teaspoons ground ginger

1½ teaspoons freshly grated nutmeg

1 teaspoon ground allspice

1 teaspoon ground cinnamon

1 teaspoon ground turmeric

½ teaspoon garlic powder

Toast the cumin seeds, coriander seeds, fennel seeds, lemon zest, black peppercorns and red pepper flakes into a dry sauté pan set over medium heat until just beginning to brown and become fragrant, 4 to 5 minutes. Allow to cool slightly.

Transfer to a spice grinder and coarsely grind.

Transfer this mixture to a small mixing bowl and add the cardamom, ginger, nutmeg, allspice, cinnamon, turmeric, and garlic powder and whisk to combine. Store in an airtight container in a cool dry place for up to 1 month.

DUKKAH SPICE BLEND

Dukkah is a traditional Egyptian spice blend created by combining toasted spices, seeds, and nuts. Dukkah is addictive. Like many spice blends, the "recipe" for dukkah varies from household to household, depending on region and flavor preferences. It is best made fresh and can be used for just about anything—from a crunchy topping on fish or vegetables, to combining with olive oil and brushing on crusty bread—but you can get this at any Middle Eastern store, ready to go. Use it in place of breadcrumbs for a gluten-free crunch. Or just lick it off the back of your hand. It's that good. If you're interested in another take on dukkah, try the blend on page 116.

ACTIVE TIME: *10 minutes*
START TO FINISH: *10 minutes*
MAKES ABOUT 1 CUP

⅓ cup sesame seeds

2½ tablespoons coriander seeds

1 tablespoon cumin seeds

⅓ cup hazelnuts, chopped

1 teaspoon kosher salt

½ teaspoon ground black pepper

Toast the sesame seeds, coriander seeds, cumin seeds, and hazelnuts in a small frying pan over low heat for 1 to 2 minutes, until browned. Let cool, then pulse in a small food processor until coarsely ground. Transfer to a bowl and add salt and pepper. Refrigerate or freeze in an airtight container for up to 3 months.

YAJI (SUYA SPICE) BLEND

This bold, peppery spice blend works on everything, from burgers to fish and vegetables. It's found throughout West Africa and used in the preparation of seasoned, grilled skewers of meat called suya. The spice blend is available online or in local West African markets—or make your own, as here. I used to live in the West African community in Harlem, on 118th Street, and found this spice blend in my local markets.

ACTIVE TIME: *10 minutes*
START TO FINISH: *15 minutes*
MAKES ABOUT ¾ CUP

½ cup roasted peanuts

2 tablespoons ground ginger

1 teaspoon kosher salt

1 teaspoon paprika

1 teaspoon garlic powder

1 teaspoon onion powder

1 teaspoon cayenne pepper

Place the peanuts in the bowl of a small food processor and pulse until finely chopped. Be careful not to puree into peanut butter. Add the ginger, salt, paprika, garlic powder, onion powder, and cayenne and continue to pulse until well combined and the mixture is almost powder-like. Refrigerate or freeze in an airtight container for up to 3 months.

RAS EL HANOUT SPICE BLEND

Ras el hanout means "top of the shop" in Arabic. The top spice blender—the head of the shop—would make this in traditional markets, almost like the top butcher having a special cut. No two versions of this Moroccan spice blend are the same, but most recipes include cardamom, nutmeg, anise, mace, cinnamon, ginger, various peppers, and turmeric.

ZA'ATAR SPICE BLEND

Variations of this spice blend are common in all the countries of North Africa and the Middle East. Typically, za'atar is a blend of dried thyme, oregano, marjoram, sumac, toasted sesame seeds, and salt.

HARISSA SPICE BLEND

Harissa is a hot chile paste that is commonly found in North African cooking, mainly Moroccan, Algerian, and Tunisian cuisines. It is made from a blend of cayenne, chiles de arbol, and other spices.

DURBAN CURRY MASALA

Durban curry masala is a spice blend from the city of Durban, in the South African province of KwaZulu-Natal. Most of South Africa's Indian population is concentrated in Durban. Durban curry is a very hot and spicy blend of curry powder characterized by its red color.

GRAINS OF PARADISE

Grains of paradise seeds originate in West Africa and look similar to black peppercorns. They provide a deep, warm flavor similar to that of cardamom and coriander with a hint of citrus. The spice is a member of the ginger and turmeric family and is used ground or whole.

CARDAMOM

Cardamom is a spice native to India that is now used in cuisines the world over to season dishes ranging from sweet to savory. It has an intense, earthy, almost minty flavor, and is said to have a myriad of anti-inflammatory and digestive health benefits.

SUMAC

Sumac is a spice made by grinding the dried berries of the sumac plant into a deep red powder. It has an acidic flavor that adds tartness to dishes without citrus, and is used widely in Middle Eastern cuisine. It's a great addition to marinades and spice rubs, as well as grilled meats and vegetables.

AWAZE

Awaze is sometimes a marinade, sometimes a vinaigrette, sometimes a hot sauce. But it's always incredible. The berbere is the base. It's good on vegetables; it's terrific on lamb. I crave it on my burgers.

ACTIVE TIME: *5 minutes*
START TO FINISH: *5 minutes*
MAKES ABOUT 1½ CUPS

½ cup berbere seasoning

½ cup Berbere Spice Brown Butter (page 277), melted and cooled slightly

¼ cup rum

2 tablespoons red wine

½ teaspoon kosher salt

Place the berbere spice, berbere butter, rum, red wine, and salt in a pint jar with a lid. Close the container and shake to combine.

Store in the refrigerator for up to 3 months. When using awaze, also squeeze the juice of 1 lime onto the dish.

CARAMELIZED HONEY VINAIGRETTE

Ethiopia produces about a quarter of all the honey on the continent of Africa. Honey is widely used in Ethiopian cooking and in the production of the fermented beverage tej. This vinaigrette builds on the complex sweetness of honey by caramelizing it before emulsifying it with oil, mustard, and lemon juice.

ACTIVE TIME: *15 minutes*
START TO FINISH: *15 minutes*
MAKES ½ CUP

¼ cup honey

2 tablespoons fresh lemon juice

2 teaspoons whole grain mustard

¼ cup extra virgin olive oil

Kosher salt and freshly ground black pepper

Cook the honey in a small saucepan set over medium heat, swirling continually until the honey caramelizes and turns a deep golden-brown color, 4 to 5 minutes. Transfer the honey to a small mixing bowl and allow to cool slightly.

Add the lemon juice and mustard and whisk to combine. Pour in the olive oil in a thin stream, whisking constantly, until the mixture emulsifies. Taste and season with salt and pepper as desired.

GET UP SAUCE

This incredibly flavorful sauce uses chocolate from Ghana. It's spicy, hot, and perfect for ribs, chicken, and beef. Check it out on barbecued beef. Or toss it with grilled chicken or dress it on roasted vegetables. So delicious.

ACTIVE TIME: *45 minutes*
START TO FINISH: *2 hours 15 minutes*
MAKES ABOUT 2 QUARTS

1 poblano chile

5 dried ancho chiles

1 pound tomatillos

1 pound tomatoes

1 medium yellow onion, sliced

¾ cup cloves garlic, sliced

¾ cup cloves

1 teaspoon kosher salt, plus more to taste

1 teaspoon whole black peppercorns

6 whole cloves

1 tablespoon cumin seeds

1 tablespoon dried oregano

½ teaspoon whole allspice

1½ ounces sliced almonds (about ½ cup)

⅓ cup sesame seeds

1 teaspoon ground cinnamon

2 ounces raisins (about ½ cup)

2 ounces cubed baguette (about 1 cup)

1 ripe plantain, peeled and sliced

3 cups beef or chicken stock, plus additional if needed

¼ cup lard

3 ounces dark Ghanaian chocolate, finely chopped

Preheat the oven to 400°F.

Arrange the poblano peppers, ancho chiles, tomatillos, and tomatoes separately on a baking sheet. Roast for 5 to 6 minutes, until the anchos are fragrant.

Remove the anchos and set aside until cool enough to handle. Remove the stems and seeds, place the chiles in a bowl, and cover with boiling water. Set aside for 20 minutes.

Meanwhile, roast the remaining vegetables until they are slightly blackened and are soft and collapsed, about 30 minutes longer. Set aside until cool enough to handle, then remove the stem and seeds from the poblano.

Make the chile puree: Remove the ancho chiles from the water and transfer to a blender. Add the poblano and just enough of the ancho soaking liquid (about ½ cup) to make a puree. Puree until smooth. Set the chile puree aside.

Make the tomato puree: Transfer the roasted tomatillos and tomatoes to the blender and puree.

Cook the onion, garlic, and salt in a dry sauté pan set over medium heat, stirring continually, until the onions are slightly browned, about 10 minutes. Add the onion mixture to the blender.

Toast the peppercorns, cloves, cumin, oregano, and allspice in the sauté pan over medium-high heat until fragrant, about 5 minutes. Transfer to the blender and puree with tomatoes and onion mixture. Set the tomato puree aside.

Make the plantain puree: Toast the almonds, sesame seeds, cinnamon, raisins, and baguette in the sauté pan over medium heat until the almonds and sesame seeds are toasted, about 5 minutes. Transfer to the blender.

Return the sauté pan to the heat and increase to medium-high. Add the plantain and cook about 3 minutes on each side, until well charred. Transfer the plantain to the blender. Add the stock and puree until smooth.

Heat the lard in a large (4- to 6-quart) saucepan over medium heat. When the oil shimmers, add the chile puree and cook, stirring frequently, until reduced slightly, about 15 minutes.

Add the tomato puree and continue to cook, stirring frequently, about 20 minutes. Decrease the heat to low, add the plantain puree, and cook, stirring occasionally, for another 30 minutes, adding additional stock if sauce is too thick.

Add the chocolate and cook, stirring frequently, until the chocolate has melted and flavors are melded. Taste and season with additional salt as needed.

BENNE SEED DRESSING

Benne seeds, used throughout West Africa, are delicious in vinaigrettes, salads, and sauces and, being derived from the same plant, they make a great substitute for sesame seeds. One of the many foods that European and white American traders imported from Africa during the enslavement period. Benne followed the rice growers, which is how it became common to the Low Country.

You can make your own benne seed paste by lightly toasting benne seeds, allowing to cool completely, and then pounding them into a paste using a mortar and pestle. The paste will keep, topped with some sesame seed or a neutral oil in an airtight container, for up to 1 month in the refrigerator.

ACTIVE TIME: *15 minutes*
START TO FINISH: *15 minutes*
MAKES ABOUT 1 CUP

1 tablespoon sorghum syrup or wildflower honey

2 cloves garlic, grated

Grated zest of 1 lemon

¼ cup fresh lemon juice

2 tablespoons water

2 tablespoons benne seed paste (or tahini)

¼ cup sesame seed oil

Kosher salt and cracked black pepper

2 tablespoons toasted benne seeds (or sesame seeds)

In a blender, combine the sorghum syrup, garlic, lemon zest, juice, and water. In a mixing bowl, combine the benne seed paste and oil. With the blender going, add the oil mixture in a thin stream and blend until vinaigrette comes together and emulsifies. Season with salt and cracked black pepper and stir in the benne seeds.

HARISSA CHARRED TOMATO VINAIGRETTE

Rub harissa on heirloom tomatoes before charring them on a hot grill to make this vinaigrette that is reminiscent of Northern Africa with flavors of cumin, fiery peppers, and garlic. It's perfect for spooning over steak, fish, or vegetables. Charring produces that wonderful blistered texture that makes everything you plan to cook taste better. It's a perfect hot weather thing to do, bringing back for many the memory of backyard barbecues.

ACTIVE TIME: 20 minutes
START TO FINISH: 20 minutes
MAKES ABOUT 2 CUPS

2 large heirloom tomatoes

2 tablespoons harissa

2 tablespoons sherry vinegar

½ teaspoon kosher salt

¼ teaspoon freshly ground black pepper

¼ cup extra virgin olive oil

½ small red onion, sliced

Heat a charcoal grill to high heat, or a gas grill or griddle pan on high.

Rub the tomatoes all over with the harissa.

Once the grill is sufficiently heated, grill the tomatoes, turning frequently, until nicely charred and blistered all around, 10 to 15 minutes. When cool enough to handle, roughly chop and reserve any juices for the vinaigrette.

Combine the chopped tomatoes and any tomato juice with the sherry vinegar, salt, and pepper. Whisk in the olive oil. Add the sliced red onion, taste, and adjust seasoning as desired. Refrigerate in an airtight container for up to 4 days.

LOCUST BEAN AND CHILI OIL

Fermented locust bean, known as iru in Yoruba, is a seasoning or condiment used in soups and stews to add umami flavor. You can find dried locust beans online or in local West African markets. Here, we mix locust beans with benne seeds, chiles, peanuts, and ginger to make an intensely flavorful and crunchy oil that carries a bit of heat.

ACTIVE TIME: *20 minutes*
START TO FINISH: *1½ hours*
MAKES ABOUT 2 CUPS

2 tablespoons fermented locust beans

½ cup diced red onion

1-inch piece fresh ginger, peeled and finely chopped

3 cloves garlic, minced

1 cup extra virgin olive oil

2 tablespoons red palm oil

¼ cup raw peanuts

¼ cup benne seeds (or sesame seeds)

4 dried bird's-eye chiles, stemmed

1 dried chipotle chile, stemmed and torn into small pieces

1 tablespoon ground cayenne pepper

1 teaspoon kosher salt

Place the locust beans in a small bowl and cover with warm water. Set aside until softened, about 10 minutes. Transfer to a fine mesh strainer and rinse under cool water until the water runs clear, 15 to 20 seconds.

Combine the locust beans, onion, ginger, garlic, olive oil, and palm oil in a medium saucepan. Set over medium-low heat and bring to a gentle simmer. Cook, stirring frequently, for 15 to 20 minutes, until the onion is translucent and the garlic and ginger are softened. Do not allow the mixture to brown.

Meanwhile, place the peanuts, benne seeds, and dried chiles in the bowl of a small food processor and pulse until finely chopped. Transfer to a 1-quart glass jar and add the cayenne and salt.

Carefully add the warm oil to the jar, place a lid on top, seal, and shake to combine. Set aside at room temperature for at least 1 hour to infuse before using. The chile oil will keep refrigerated in an airtight container for up to 3 months.

PIRI PIRI MARINADE

Piri piri is a pepper that is commonly found in hot sauces or marinades. I love marinating chicken and fish with piri piri. You can use it as a sauce or dry rub. It's found in Portuguese-speaking Africa and some places in South Africa.

ACTIVE TIME: *10 minutes*
START TO FINISH: *10 minutes*
MAKES ABOUT ½ CUP

2 small shallots, peeled	2 tablespoons fresh lemon juice
1-inch piece fresh ginger, peeled	2 tablespoons canola oil
4 cloves garlic, peeled	2 teaspoons paprika
1 Scotch bonnet chile, stemmed	1 teaspoon kosher salt

Combine the shallots, ginger, garlic, and chile in a food processor and pulse to a coarse puree. (Alternatively, pound into a coarse paste using a mortar and pestle.) Stir in the lemon juice, oil, and paprika and season with salt. Refrigerate in an airtight container for up to 1 month.

RED PALM OIL VINAIGRETTE

Red palm oil is a staple of West African cooking. Its floral, earthy taste derived from the bright red fruit of the oil palm tree binds many dishes together and is wholly separate from environmental issues about *refined* palm oil which appears in many beauty products in Western countries. The cultivation of the oil palm tree and its resulting red palm oil exists in harmony with the land and its ecosystems, as it has for generations.

ACTIVE TIME: *15 minutes*
START TO FINISH: *15 minutes*
MAKES ABOUT 1 CUP

1 tablespoon grated lime zest	¼ cup red palm oil, melted and cooled slightly
¼ cup fresh lime juice	2 tablespoons canola oil
2 tablespoons grated peeled fresh ginger	1 shallot, thinly sliced
2 cloves garlic, grated	Freshly ground black pepper
1 tablespoon honey	
¼ teaspoon kosher salt	

Place the lime zest, lime juice, ginger, garlic, honey, and salt in a small mixing bowl and whisk to combine. Drizzle the palm oil and canola oil in a thin stream into the bowl, whisking continually until the mixture emulsifies.

Add the shallot and whisk to combine. Taste and season with freshly ground black pepper to taste.

ROASTED RED PEPPER SAMBAL

Sambal is a chile sauce or paste. Often described as "Indonesian relish," sambal's etymology can be traced to Java, long before trade between Malaysia and Indonesia eventually took sambal to South Africa.

ACTIVE TIME: *30 minutes*
START TO FINISH: *1 hour*
MAKES 1 CUP

2 red bell peppers

3 tablespoons extra virgin olive oil

1 small red onion, quartered

2 plum tomatoes, halved and seeded

1 habanero chile, stemmed

4 cloves garlic, minced

1 tablespoon minced fresh ginger

¼ cup finely chopped lemongrass (about 2 stalks)

1 teaspoon ground cumin

1 teaspoon paprika

1 tablespoon tamarind paste

Kosher salt and freshly ground black pepper

Preheat the oven to high broil setting.

Toss the red peppers with 1 tablespoon of the olive oil and place on a baking sheet. Roast in the oven, rotating frequently, until the peppers are just softened, blistered, and blackened in spots, about 15 minutes. Remove the peppers from the oven and let cool slightly. When cool enough to handle, remove the seeds and stem and roughly chop.

Place the peppers, onion, tomatoes, and habanero chile in a food processor and pulse into a coarsely chopped puree. Set aside.

Heat the remaining 2 tablespoons oil in a medium saucepan set over medium-low heat. When the oil shimmers, add the garlic, ginger, and lemongrass and sauté until fragrant, about 2 minutes. Add the cumin and paprika and continue to cook for about 30 seconds. Add the pepper puree and bring up to a simmer. Allow the sauce to simmer on low until the liquid is slightly reduced, about 15 minutes. Add the tamarind paste and mash to combine.

Taste and season with salt and black pepper as desired and let cool. The sauce will keep for up to 1 month in an airtight container.

SAUCE MOYO

You put a little bit of this on top of fish, chicken, or vegetables to make it delicious. It's a hot condiment due to the Scotch bonnet.

ACTIVE TIME: *15 minutes*
START TO FINISH: *35 minutes*
MAKES 2½ CUPS

1 Scotch bonnet (or habanero) chile, stemmed and halved

1 small red onion, thinly sliced

1 cup cherry tomatoes, halved

1 mango, pitted, peeled, and diced

1 teaspoon ground Selim pepper

1 tablespoon grapeseed oil or other neutral oil

Juice of 1 lime

Kosher salt

Combine the chile, onion, cherry tomatoes, mango, Selim, oil, and lime juice together in a medium bowl. Toss together to incorporate ingredients and season with salt. Cover and refrigerate for at least 20 minutes before serving. Store in an airtight container in the refrigerator for up to 2 weeks.

YAJI (SUYA SPICE) AIOLI

Think about this as a mayo with tons of flavor that's great on seafood and grilled vegetables. It's a condiment where two worlds come together in a mixture of West African spices and the European technique of aioli. You can find a condiment like this in the 18th arrondissement of Paris in Little Africa or in Harlem, spread on a baguette. It's delicious to eat just a warm baguette with this spread on top. The aioli is made by putting two yolks in a bowl, then whisking in the spices and oil.

ACTIVE TIME: *10 minutes*
START TO FINISH: *10 minutes*
MAKES 1 CUP

2 large egg yolks

1 tablespoon fresh lemon juice

¾ cup peanut oil

1 clove garlic, grated

1 tablespoon Yaji (Suya Spice) Blend (page 279)

1 small shallot, minced

2 tablespoons finely chopped chives

Kosher salt

Place the yolks in a bowl, pour in the lemon juice, and whisk together. Beginning with a few drops at a time, pour the peanut oil, in a thin stream, into the yolk mixture, whisking constantly, until all the oil is incorporated and the mixture is emulsified, 3 to 4 minutes. Whisk in the garlic, yaji blend, shallot, and chives. Taste and season with salt as desired. Refrigerate in an airtight container for up to 3 days.

SHITO

This is a versatile, spicy chili sauce from Ghana. It's used with fish, meat, white rice, and vegetables, both as a marinade and as a dressing or topping.

ACTIVE TIME: *35 minutes*
START TO FINISH: *1 hour 20 minutes*
**MAKES ABOUT 2½ CUPS*

2 medium red onions, diced

1¼ cups peanut oil

2 cloves garlic, minced

1½ ounces (about 4) green Scotch bonnet chiles, stemmed and finely chopped

1½-inch piece fresh ginger, peeled and grated

2 teaspoons finely chopped fresh thyme leaves

2 tablespoons tomato paste

1 cup crushed tomatoes

½ cup chili powder

2 tablespoons dried shrimp powder

2 tablespoons crayfish powder

½ teaspoon sea salt

½ teaspoon freshly ground black pepper

Cook the onions in the oil in a medium saucepan set over medium heat, stirring frequently, until translucent, 4 to 5 minutes. Add the garlic, chiles, and ginger and continue cooking for 2 to 3 minutes, until the chiles begin to wilt. Add the thyme, tomato paste, crushed tomatoes, 1 cup water, and chili powder. Decrease the heat to medium-low and continue to cook, stirring frequently, for 25 minutes, until aromatic.

Add the shrimp powder, crayfish powder, salt, and pepper and cook, stirring frequently, until the mixture turns darker, almost black in color, and the oil separates, about 15 minutes.

Taste and adjust the seasoning as desired. Cool completely. Place in a clean glass jar, seal, and store in the refrigerator for up to 1 month.

TAHINI

Tahini is a wonderful, versatile condiment made from toasted sesame seeds that are hulled and ground into a paste, and used in the cooking of North Africa, the Middle East, and the Mediterranean. It's commonly used as an ingredient in hummus and baba ghanoush, and can also be used on its own as a dip.

TAMARIND PASTE

Tamarind paste is made from the fruit of the tamarind tree. Dark reddish-brown in color, and with a flavor that is complex, sticky-sweet, and tart all at once, it is prevalent in Mexican, Caribbean, Latin, and South and South East Asian cuisines.

MILLET

This ancient grain has been used in Africa since for-ever. If you go to places like Senegal in West Africa, millet is the main staple and a part of everyday life and as common as white flour here in the United States. It's gluten free, delicious, comforting, and versatile—smooth like oatmeal, crunchy like gra-nola, and fluffy like rice. It's also packed with pro-tein and high in fiber.

COCONUT

In Africa, all parts of the coconut are used: Coconut water is available at roadside carts, flakes are used as a topping, and the oil is used for cooking and a beauty product. Africans use coconut the way Ital-ians use olives.

COFFEE

Coffee's birthplace is Ethiopia, and we are finally starting to acknowledge its origins in Africa—not in Italy or France. Grown all over Africa, coffee is one of the continent's most important products and showcases the great brands coming from Af-rica.

BROKEN RICE

West African broken rice is exactly that: rice that was broken during the harvesting process. Here in America, South Carolina's Low Country was fa-mous for its harvesting of rice, but sometimes the rice broke, and couldn't be shipped or exported. Resourceful Gullah Geechee cooks helped make the creamy "broken rice," or "middlins," a staple in Southern cooking. Broken rice is celebrated by a wide array of chefs and continues to be in high demand. It is even repackaged as "rice grits," hailed for its velvety and smooth texture. Think of it as kin to risotto.

COUSCOUS

Couscous is a North African staple food made from coarsely ground semolina that is formed into tiny pellets

CHICKPEA FLOUR

Chickpea flour, or gram, garbanzo bean, or besan flour, is a naturally gluten-free flour made from ground raw chickpeas that is widely used in many cuisines around the world, including in North Africa.

TEFF

Teff is an ancient grain widely used in Ethiopia and Eritrea, perhaps best known for its use in the flatbread injera (page 79).

BULGUR

Bulgur is made from partially-cooked cracked wheat berries. It is known for its light, somewhat nutty flavor and its presence in North African and Middle Eastern food

FUFU

Fufu is a staple of West and Central African cuisine, made by pounding boiled starches such as cassava, yam, or green plantain. Fufu commonly accompanies soups and stews.

TIGERNUTS

Tigernuts, also known as chufa, aren't really nuts. They're tubers that grow in the soil like sweet potatoes. This fiber-rich superfood has been around for a long time.

GROUNDNUT

Groundnut refers to the family of legumes that are native to both Africa and the Americas, one of which is the peanut. While the peanut can be eaten raw, other varieties of groundnuts should be boiled before eating. Despite its name, the groundnut is not a nut, but a legume that flowers above the ground and fruits below it. History has noted uses of groundnuts from India to West Africa to the Americas dating back hundreds of years to the Incas.

EGUSI SEEDS

Egusi seeds come from the egusi, a gourd that's popular in West Africa. Ground into small bits or flour it can be used to thicken soups and stews, but the seeds also make a great snack. Egusi soup, often stewed with meat and bitter leaf, is popular throughout the region, enjoyed with fufu.

BENNE SEEDS

Benne, a flowering plant that is derived from the same plant as sesame seeds, has one of the highest oil contents of any seed. Benne seed is one of the oldest oilseed crops known, domesticated well over 3,000 years ago. It has many other species, most being wild and native to sub-Saharan Africa.

Benne Seeds

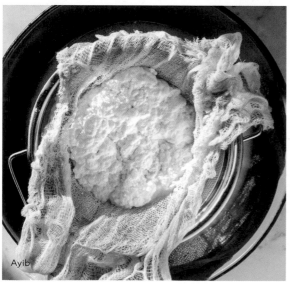
Ayib

AYIB

This is Ethiopia's fresh cheese. The mere thought of making cheese causes some of us to break out in a cold sweat, but ayib is easy to make. It's very often made with a few simple ingredients you maybe already have, buttermilk or whole milk or yogurt. You can make everything, start to finish, in an afternoon. That makes it less intimidating and more amazing.

ACTIVE TIME: 5 minutes
START TO FINISH: 3 hours 20 minutes
MAKES ABOUT 2 CUPS

2 quarts whole milk   **½ teaspoon kosher salt**
½ cup fresh lemon juice

Line a colander or a fine mesh sieve with a layer of cheesecloth. Set aside.

Place the milk in a medium saucepan, set over medium-low heat, and bring to a slight simmer, or 200°F to 205°F. Remove the pot from the heat and slowly stir in the lemon juice. Continue slowly stirring until curds begin to form, 1 to 2 minutes.

Spoon the curds into the prepared colander. Gently rinse under cold running water until the water runs clear. Place the sieve in a bowl and cover with a clean dish towel. Refrigerate for 3 hours to allow the liquid to drain. Transfer the ayib to an airtight container, add salt, and gently toss to combine. Store in the refrigerator for up to 1 week.

BASIC TIGERNUT PIE CRUST

You can bring flavor into anything, even a pie crust. A key ingredient can and should have great taste. You always need a basic pie dough on hand, so you can fill it with different delicious items, whether it's peaches or apples, or whether you feel like a cherry tart or a bird pie. This is something that you need to have in your refrigerator, because you never know what might suddenly become available. I grew up with a lot of berries and often made a pie as a dessert.

For a not-so-basic version of this crust, substitute 2 tablespoons Berbere Spice Brown Butter for 2 tablespoons of the regular butter and add ½ teaspoon ground cardamom, ¼ teaspoon ground cloves, and ¼ teaspoon ground cinnamon.

ACTIVE TIME: *15 minutes*
START TO FINISH: *1 hour*
MAKES 1 (9½-INCH) PIE CRUST OR TART SHELL

1½ cups tigernut flour, plus extra for rolling

2 tablespoons powdered sugar

1 teaspoon kosher salt

½ cup (1 stick) unsalted butter, cubed and chilled

2 large egg yolks

Place the tigernut flour, powdered sugar, and salt in a large mixing bowl and whisk to combine. Work in the butter using a pastry blender, a fork, or your fingers until the mixture resembles coarse crumbs. Add the egg yolks and mix until combined and the dough comes together. Gather the dough into a ball and flatten into a disk. Wrap in plastic and refrigerate for at least 30 minutes.

Preheat the oven to 375°F.

Roll out the dough on a floured countertop to a 10½-inch round. Using the rolling pin as an aid, transfer the dough to a 9½-inch pie or tart pan and fit in. Seal any cracks in the dough. Trim the overhang to ¼ inch and press into the sides of the pan.

Line the pie or tart shell with a piece of parchment and fill with pie weights or dried beans. Bake until the sides are set, about 20 minutes. Remove the weights and foil. Bake the crust until the sides are golden and the bottom is set, pressing with the back of a spoon if the crust bubbles, about 10 minutes longer. Allow the crust to cool completely before filling.

FERMENTED SHRIMP PASTE

People use shrimp paste in Southeast Asian and West African cooking. When you enter a fish market in the Philippines or Senegal, that smell you're smelling is shrimp paste. It's strong, but it's also delicious—and you don't need a lot of it. Think of shrimp paste the way you would miso. You can add it to soups, you can toss it with vegetables, and you can use it as a substitute for fish sauce.

TOASTED PECAN AND DATE MOLASSES BUTTER

Toasting pecans brings out their nutty flavor, and the molasses adds a sweet taste that goes well with the richness of butter. You can use this with desserts or as a topping for brussels sprouts and other vegetables.

ACTIVE TIME: 5 minutes
START TO FINISH: 15 minutes
MAKES ABOUT 1 CUP

½ cup coarsely chopped raw pecans

2 tablespoons date molasses

1 cup (2 sticks) unsalted butter, room temperature

2 teaspoons sea salt

Preheat the oven to 350°F.

Spread the pecans in an even layer on a baking sheet. Toast in the oven until the pecans are fragrant, 5 to 6 minutes, rotating the nuts halfway through. Set aside and let cool completely.

Place the butter, molasses, and salt in the bowl of a stand mixer with the paddle attachment and combine on medium speed for 4 to 5 minutes, stopping to scrape down the sides of the bowl several times.

Add the pecans and continue to mix until incorporated. Refrigerate in an airtight container for up to a month.

SHIRO

In Ethiopia, everybody eats shiro. It's a stew made with chickpea flour and a blend of seasonings like garlic, ginger, tomato, and berbere. It says something that in a country where people are very tied to their religion—Ethiopia has over 220 fasting days—shiro has become the meal that often breaks their fast. It's affordable, filling, and delicious, and people of all religions can eat it.

ACTIVE TIME: *15 minutes*
START TO FINISH: *About 30 minutes*
MAKES ABOUT 2 CUPS

1 medium onion, finely chopped	2 tablespoons berbere seasoning
¼ cup grapeseed, canola, or other neutral oil	1 cup water
1 medium tomato, finely chopped	1 tablespoon Berbere Spice Brown Butter (page 277)
3 cloves garlic, minced	1 teaspoon kosher salt, plus more to taste
¼ cup chickpea flour	

Cook the onions in a dry, medium saucepan set over medium-high heat, stirring frequently, until just begin to lightly brown, 3 to 4 minutes. Add the oil, tomato, and garlic and cook, stirring continually for another 3 to 4 minutes, until the garlic is fragrant.

Gradually whisk in the chickpea flour and berbere spice and cook for another 4 to 5 minutes, until the mixture darkens a bit in color. Gradually whisk in the water until it is all incorporated.

Add the berbere butter and salt and whisk until the butter is melted. Taste and add more salt if desired. Serve immediately with injera.

OKRA

Okra, which comes from Africa and was imported by European traders along with other goods to feed the enslaved, is a staple in the American South. (Global trade over the centuries has made okra a favorite in many cultures, like in India.) Eat it dredged and fried, stirred into soups or stews, or sautéed over a bed of rice.

CHOW CHOW

Chow chow is a pickled relish with regional inflections throughout the United States. In the South, it's primarily pickled cabbage and an assortment of vegetables. Hot, sweet, and tangy—people scoop it on top of bowls of beans or add it to hot dogs and sandwiches. Give it a try. It's one of those condiments that makes your mouth pucker.

ARGAN OIL

Argan oil is produced from the kernels of the argan tree. In Morocco, it's drizzled on bread or couscous or pasta. It has an almond flavor and is great to cook with. I'd recommend mixing it with olive oil to stretch it further.

GHEE

Ghee is unsalted butter from which the milk solids have been removed, leaving behind a lactose-free, pure fat with a high smoking point. Ghee, or clarified butter, is called kibbeh in Ethiopia. Typically, we add spices to it. Before refrigeration, people would often bury the butter to keep it cool.

COCOA BEANS

Beans from the cocoa tree are called cocoa beans or cacao beans. Cocoa butter and cocoa solids are extracted from them for the base for making chocolate. The word cocoa comes from the Spanish *cacao* and the Nahuatl *cacahuatl*. Nearly 70 percent of the world crop today is grown in West Africa.

VANILLA BEANS

The vanilla bean is not a bean, but the fruit of an orchid. Mexico was once the main producer of vanilla, but since the mid-19th century, Madagascar has come to produce the majority of the crop. While vanilla extract can be a great, more affordable option, use the beans themselves when you really want to highlight the vanilla flavor in a dish.

SORREL

Sorrel is the flower of the hibiscus plant. Throughout West Africa and the Caribbean, people make a colorful drink out of the dried flower. You boil the leaves, add ginger and sugar, then steep and strain. You can flavor it with cardamom and nutmeg.

TAPIOCA

Tapioca is a gluten-free starch made from the roots of the cassava or yuca plant. A staple food and an essential ingredient in cooking all over the world, it can be used as a flour or a thickening agent. It's also often formed into pearls and used in desserts.

BISSAP

Bissap is a refreshing drink made by infusing the sepals of the hibiscus flower in hot water, turning it red. The drink is called sorrel in the Caribbean region and goes by various names in Africa. In Spanish-speaking cultures it is called jamaica (pronounced ha-my-ka). In Africa, Nigerians call it zobo, Ghanaians call it sobolo, while Senegalese, Congolese, Malians, and Burkinabes call it bissap and it is actually the national drink in Senegal.

ACTIVE TIME: *5 minutes*
START TO FINISH: *30 minutes*
MAKES 2 QUARTS

2 quarts water	**ginger, peeled and sliced**
2 cups dried sorrel (hibiscus) petals	**½ cup sugar**
1-inch piece fresh	

Bring the water just to a boil in a large pot set over high heat. Add the hibiscus and ginger and boil for 1 minute. Remove from the heat, cover, and allow to steep for 15 minutes.

Strain through a fine mesh strainer into a large, heatproof container. Add the sugar and stir until dissolved. Add 1 cup ice and refrigerate until chilled completely.

Serve over ice.

BANANA LEAVES

Banana leaves are versatile, waterproof, and sturdy, and are a part of many cultures in tropical areas of the world. They can be used for cooking, but are also used to wrap and serve food

PLANTAINS

Plantains are a major food staple in West and Central Africa, the Caribbean islands, Central America, and parts of South America. Delightfully versatile, plantains can be enjoyed in all their stages. When the skins are green, the plantain is starchy, so make tostones or fritters. When the skin is yellow, or even better, black, the starch has converted to sugar. Mash it, roast it, or fry sweet slices as maduros or dodo, as it is called in Nigeria.

INGREDIENT RESOURCES

Online and brick and mortar stores
specializing in African and Caribbean foods

KALUSTYAN'S
123 Lexington Avenue
New York, NY 10016
(212) 685-3451
foodsofnations.com

ROYAL AFRICAN AND CARIBBEAN FOODS INC.
2957 Webster Ave
Bronx, NY 10458
(718) 620-8000
royacshop.com

AFRICAN GROCERY AND MEAT MARKET
6243 Little River Turnpike
Alexandria, VA 22312
(703) 914-2525

AFRIK INTERNATIONAL FOOD MARKET
6689 Old Landover Rd
Hyattsville, MD 20785
(301) 322-3080

WORLD SPICE MERCHANTS
1509 Western Avenue
Seattle, WA 98101
(206) 682-7274
worldspice.com

AUZOUD, LLC
Seattle, WA
hello@auzoud.com
(503) 999.1377
www.auzoud.com

URBAN FARMER
120 E. 161st Street
Westfield, IN 46074
(317) 600-2807
Ufseeds.com

SOLA'S AFRICAN MARKET
8720 Sepulveda Blvd
North Hills, CA 91343
(818) 920-6561

WAZOBIA AFRICAN MARKET
16203 Westheimer Road.
Suite 160
Houston, TX 77082
832-230-3893
wazobia.market

ANSON MILLS
1922 C Gervais Street
Columbia, SC 29201
(803) 467-4122
ansonmills.com

GEECHIE BOY MILL
2995 Highway 174
Edisto Island, SC 29438
(843) 631-0077
geechieboymill.com

ZAMOURI SPICES
1250 N. Winchester Blvd. Suite I
Olathe, KS 66061
(913) 829-5988
zamourispices.com

HAPPY AFRICAN TROPICAL FOODS
P.O. Box 5175
Alpharetta, GA 30023
(770) 740-9515
happyafricantropicalfoods.com

BUFORD HIGHWAY FARMERS MARKET
5600 Buford Hwy NE
Doraville, GA 30340
(770) 455-0770

CAYCE FOODS INTERNATIONAL
1680 Roswell St
Smyrna, GA 30080
(770) 432-6967
www.caycefoods.com

MAKOLA AFRICAN SUPERMARKET
1019 W Wilson Ave #1017
Chicago, IL 60640
(773) 654-1971

YADO AFRICAN & CARIBBEAN MARKET
1651 E 87th St
Chicago, IL 60617
(872) 802-4724
yado-african-caribbean-market.
business.site/

ADDA BLOOMS
addablooms.com/shop

FEATURED CHEFS AND EXPERTS

To keep up to date with these chefs and experts,
follow them on Instagram where noted below.

Eric Adjepong,
chef, Washington, DC—
@chefericadjepong

Roblé Ali,
New York, NY—@chefroble

Nyesha Arrington,
chef, Los Angeles, CA—
@nyeshajoyce

Mashama Bailey,
chef, Savannah, GA—
@mashamabailey

Tavel Bristol-Joseph,
chef, Austin, TX—@tavel19

Edward Brumfield,
chef, New York, NY—
@bk.chef.ed

Leah Chase,
chef, New Orleans, LA
(Rest in Peace)—
@dookychaserestaurant

Adrienne Cheatham,
chef, New York, NY—
@chefadriennecheatham

Patrick Clark,
chef, Washington DC
(Rest in Peace)

Nina Compton,
chef, New Orleans, LA—
@ninacompton

Devita Davison,
activist, Detroit, MI—
@devita_davison

Cheryl Day,
chef, Savannah, GA—
@cherylday

BJ Dennis,
chef, Charleston, SC—
@chefbjdennis

Michael Adé Elégbèdé,
Lagos, Nigeria—
@michael__elegbede

Osayi Endolyn,
writer, New York, NY—
@osayiendolyn

Tristen Epps,
chef, New York, NY—
@eppsandflows

Eden Fesehaye,
home cook, New York, NY—
@massawanyc

Tiana Gee,
chef, New York, NY—
@cheftianagee

Eric Gestel,
chef, New York, NY—
@egestel68

Patricia Gonzalez,
chef, New York, NY—
@iampatriciagnz

Gregory Gourdet,
chef, Portland, OR—@gg30000

Jerome Grant,
chef, Washington DC—
@chefjeromegrant

Carla Hall,
chef and television host,
New York, NY—@carlahall

Jessica B. Harris,
historian, Brooklyn, NY—
@africooks

Kingsley John,
chef, New York, NY

JJ Johnson,
chef, New York, NY—@chefjj

Tiffany Jones,
chef, New York, NY

Edouardo Jordan,
chef, Seattle, WA—
@edouardojordan

Yewande Komolafe,
cook and author, New York,
NY—@yewande_komolafe

André Hueston Mack,
winemaker, New York, NY—
@andrehmack

Adrian Miller,
author, Denver, CO—
@soulfoodscholar

Therese Nelson,
writer and chef, New York, NY—
@blackculinary

Kwame Onwuachi,
chef, Washington, DC—
@chefkwameonwuachi

Fred Opie,
historian, Boston, MA—@fdopie

Donna Pierce,
journalist, Chicago, IL—
@DonnaBPierce on Twitter

**Matthew Raiford
and Jovan Sage,**
chef-farmer and herb alchemist,
Brunswick, GA—
@chefarmermatthew and
@sageslarder

Darrell Raymond,
chef, New York, NY

Jonny Rhodes,
chef, Houston, TX—
@restaurant_indigohtx

Mariya Russell,
chef, Chicago, IL—
@mariyaleniserussell

Maya Haile Samuelsson,
model, New York, NY—
@mayahaile

Stephen Satterfield,
magazine publisher
and podcast host,
San Francisco, CA—
@isawstephen

Rodney Scott,
chef and pitmaster,
Charleston, SC—
@pitmasterrodneyscott

Almira Session,
chef, New York, NY—
@chef_annieas14

Shakirah Simley,
political aide/activist,
San Francisco, CA—
@shak_simley

Alexander Smalls,
restaurateur, New York, NY—
@asmalls777

Joe Stinchcomb,
bartender, Oxford, MO—
@unclemom31

Pierre Thiam,
New York, NY—
@chefpierrethiam

Toni Tipton-Martin,
author, Baltimore, MD—
@tonitiptonmartin

Jaqueta Tucker,
chef, New York, NY—@_chefjay_

Michael Twitty,
author, Washington, DC—
@thecookinggene

Lauren von der Pool,
Los Angeles, CA—
@queenofgreen

Chris Williams,
chef, Houston, TX—
@chef_chriswilliams

Herb Wilson,
chef, Miami, FL—
@ChefHerbWilson on Twitter

Melba Wilson,
chef, New York, NY—
@melbasharlem

Marvin Woods,
chef, Atlanta, GA—
@chefmarvinwoods

Alberta Wright,
restaurateur, New York, NY
(Rest in Peace)

David Zilber,
chef,
Copenhagen, Denmark—
@david_zilber

MORE CHEFS TO WATCH

There are so many more brilliant Black chefs to follow.
Please see below for more names featured in *Toques in Black,* my colleague
Alan Battman's book, and beyond. This is by no means an exhaustive list.

Hilary Ambrose
Jameeale Arzeno
Kevin Ashade
Jamie Barnes
Scott Alves Barton
Earlest Bell
Jennifer Hill Booker
Michael Bowling
Kimberly Brock Brown
Marc Anthony Bynum
Bernard Carmouche
Erika Dupree Cline
Vicky Colas
Marcellus Coleman
Gregory Collier
Newton Cootes
Jessica Craig
Ian Davis
Samantha Davis
Timothy Dean
Tiffany Derry
Ron Duprat
Jermain Edwards
Christopher Faulkner
Janielle Ford
Brian Fowler, Jr.
Cassondra G. Armstrong
Charles Gabriel
Justin Gaines
Nicole Gajadhar
Michael Garrett

Kenny Gilbert
Lexis Gonzalez
Jackie Gordon
Lisa Graves
Jeff Henderson
Cleophus Hethington
Kennardo Holder
Tanya Holland
Chef Irie
Michael Jenkins
Brad Johnson
Kirk Johnson
Amaris Jones
Jesse Jones
Lance Knowling
Kemis Lawrence
Kevin Lewis
Cynthia Long
Brother Luck
Jamaine Lynes
Mawa McQueen
Dolester Miles
Kevin Mitchell
Celestia Mobley
Raymond Mohan
Duane Nutter
Anwuli Obidi
Dadisi Olutosin
Morou Ouattara
Greg Payne
Lasheeda Perry

Joe Randall
Darnell Reed
Resha
Levi Richard
Radisha Rowe
Dejuan Roy
Yves Samake
Danielle Saunders
Christopher Scott
Tom Scott
Shacafrica Simmons
Roderick "Pete" Smith
Anthony Smith
Denise Smith
Walter Smith
Nigel Spence
Digby Stridiron
Kermit Sullivan
Haile Thomas
Geoffrey Tulloch
Jamie Turner
Brandon Walker
William Walker
Nick Wallace
Leon West
Tre Wilcox
Greg Williams
Iesha Williams
Randy Stricklin Witherspoon
Leticia Skai Young

MEDIA AND OTHER RESOURCES

Here are several of my favorite sources to learn more about Black excellence in the food world and beyond, including projects from those featured in the pages of this book.
This is just a taste of some incredible books, magazines, podcasts, and organizations to learn from. Dive in.

BOOKS

Black, White, and The Grey: The Story of an Unexpected Friendship and a Landmark Restaurant by Mashama Bailey and John O. Morisano

Pearl's Kitchen: An Extraordinary Cookbook by Pearl Bailey

The Ideal Bartender by Tom Bullock

And Still I Cook by Leah Chase

Down Home Healthy: Family Recipes of Black American Chefs by Leah Chase

The Dooky Chase Cookbook by Leah Chase

Franchise: The Golden Arches in Black America by Marcia Chatelain

The Back in the Day Bakery Made with Love: More Than 100 Recipes and Make-It-Yourself Projects to Create and Share by Cheryl and Griffith Day

The Back in the Day Bakery Cookbook: More than 100 Recipes from the Best Little Bakery in the South by Cheryl and Griffith Day

Cooking with My Mother by Elsy Dinvil

Spice Up: Simple Dishes with a Haitian Twist by Elsy Dinvil

The New Way to Cake by Benjamin Ebuehi

Black Girl Baking: Wholesome Recipes Inspired by a Soulful Upbringing by Jerrelle Guy

Carla Hall's Soul Food: Everyday and Celebration by Carla Hall

Carla's Comfort Foods: Favorite Dishes from Around the World by Carla Hall

Cooking with Love: Comfort Food that Hugs You by Carla Hall

The Africa Cookbook: Tastes of a Continent by Jessica B. Harris

Beyond Gumbo: Creole Fusion Food from the Atlantic Rim by Jessica B. Harris

High on the Hog: A Culinary Journey from Africa to America by Jessica B. Harris

Iron Pots and Wooden Spoons: Africa's Gifts to New World Cooking by Jessica B. Harris

A Kwanzaa Keepsake: Celebrating the Holiday with New Traditions and Feasts by Jessica B. Harris

My Soul Looks Back by Jessica B. Harris

Rum Drinks: 50 Caribbean Cocktails, from Cuba Libre to Rum Daisy by Jessica B. Harris

Sky Juice and Flying Fish: Traditional Caribbean Cooking by Jessica B. Harris

The Welcome Table: African-American Heritage Cooking by Jessica B. Harris

In Bibi's Kitchen by Hawa Hassan

Brown Sugar Kitchen: New-Style, Down-Home Recipes from Sweet West Oakland by Tanya Holland

New Soul Cooking: Updating a Cuisine Rich in Flavor and Tradition by Tanya Holland

Soulful Sweets to Sing About by Patti LaBelle

Recipes to Sing About by Patti LaBelle

Patti LaBelle's Lite Cuisine by Patti LaBelle

Recipes for the Good Life by Patti LaBelle

In Pursuit of Flavor by Edna Lewis

The Edna Lewis Cookbook by Edna Lewis

The Gift of Southern Cooking by Edna Lewis

The Taste of Country Cooking by Edna Lewis

Sweet Home Cafe Cookbook: A Celebration of African American Cooking by Albert Lukas and Jessica B. Harris, with contributions by Jerome Grant

Son of a Southern Chef by Lazarus Lynch

99 Bottles: A Black Sheep's Guide to Life-Changing Wines by André Hueston Mack and Rob Deborde

The President's Kitchen Cabinet: The Story of the African Americans Who Have Fed Our First Families, from the Washingtons to the Obamas by Adrian Miller

Soul Food: The Surprising Story of an American Cuisine, One Plate at a Time by Adrian Miller

Cooking Solo by Klancy Miller

Tiki: Modern Tropical Cocktails by Shannon Mustipher

Notes from a Young Black Chef: A Memoir by Kwame Onwuachi

Hog and Hominy: Soul Food from Africa to America by Frederick Douglass Opie

Southern Food and Civil Rights: Feeding the Revolution by Frederick Douglass Opie

Zora Neale Hurston on Florida Food: Recipes, Remedies, & Simple Pleasures by Frederick Douglass Opie

Soul: A Chef's Culinary Evolution in 150 Recipes by Todd Richards

Between Heaven and Harlem: Afro-Asian-American Cooking for Big Nights, Weeknights, and Every Day by Alexander Smalls, JJ Johnson, and Veronica Chambers

Grace the Table: Stories and Recipes from My Southern Revival by Alexander Smalls

Meals, Music, and Muses: Recipes from My African American Kitchen by Alexander Smalls and Veronica Chambers

Vibration Cooking: or, The Travel Notes of a Geechee Girl by Vertamae Smart-Grosvenor

Overground Railroad: The Green Book and the Roots of Black Travel in America by Candacy Taylor

The Up South Cookbook: Chasing Dixie in a Brooklyn Kitchen by Nicole Taylor

Afro-Vegan: Farm-Fresh African, Caribbean, and Southern Flavors Remixed by Bryant Terry

The Inspired Vegan: Seasonal Ingredients, Creative Recipes, Mouthwatering Menus by Bryant Terry

Vegan Soul Kitchen: Fresh, Healthy, and Creative African-American Cuisine by Bryant Terry

Vegetable Kingdom: The Abundant World of Vegan Recipes by Bryant Terry

Senegal: Modern Senegalese Recipes from the Source to the Bowl by Pierre Thiam

The Fonio Cookbook: An Ancient Grain Rediscovered by Pierre Thiam and Adam Bartos

A Taste of Heritage: The New African American Cuisine by Toni Tipton-Martin and Joe Randall

The Jemima Code: Two Centuries of African American Cookbooks by Toni Tipton-Martin

Jubilee: Recipes from Two Centuries of African American Cooking: A Cookbook by Toni Tipton-Martin

Cooking with Patrick Clark: A Tribute to the Man and His Cuisine by Charlie Trotter

The Cooking Gene: A Journey Through African American Culinary History in the Old South by Michael Twitty

Eat Yourself Sexy! The Goddess Edition: A Beginner's Beauty Guide to Glowing Skin, Healthy Hair, Weight Loss and Total Well-Being by Lauren von der Pool

Melba's American Comfort: 100 Recipes from My Heart to Your Kitchen by Melba Wilson

New Low-Country Cooking: 125 Recipes for Coastal Southern Cooking with Innovative Style by Marvin Woods

The Noma Guide to Fermentation by Rene Redzepi and David Zilber

CULINARY MEDIA

Black Culinary History—blackculinaryhistory.com

Black Food Folks—@blackfoodfolks on Instagram

For the Culture—fortheculturefoodmag.com

SoulPhoodie—soulphoodie.com

Whetstone Media—whetstonemedia.co

PODCASTS

1619, hosted by Nikole Hannah-Jones

About Race, hosted by Reni Eddo-Lodge

Afros + Knives, hosted by Tiffani Rozier

Black Food Tales, hosted by Lisimba Pink

Code Switch, hosted by Shereen Marisol Meraji, Gene Demby, and Karen Grigsby Bates

Food Heaven, hosted by Wendy Lopez and Jessica Jones

A Hungry Society, hosted by Korsha Wilson

Intersectionality Matters!, hosted by Kimberlé Crenshaw

Jemele Hill Is Unbothered, hosted by Toure

Momentum, hosted by Chevon and Hiba

Point of Origin, hosted by Stephen Satterfield

Still Processing, hosted by Jenna Wortham and Wesley Morris

The Stoop, hosted by Hana Baba and Leila Day

Tanya's Table, hosted by Tanya Holland

Uncivil, hosted by Chenjerai Kumanyika and Jack Hitt

CULINARY ORGANIZATIONS

The Black Culinary Alliance—bcaglobal.org and @bcaglobal

Black Urban Growers—blackurbangrowers.org

Black Farmers Fund—blackfarmerfund.org

Careers through Culinary Arts Program (C-CAP)—ccapinc.org and @ccapinc

Equity at the Table—equityatthetable.com and @equityatthetable

National Black Farmers Association—nationalblackfarmersassociation.org

National Black Food and Justice Alliance—blackfoodjustice.org and @blackfoodjustice

The Okra Project—theokraproject.com and @theokraproject

ORGANIZATIONS FOR SOCIAL CHANGE

American Civil Liberties Union—aclu.org

Audre Lorde Project—alp.org

Black Lives Matter—blacklivesmatter.org

Center for Antiracist Research at Boston University—bu.edu/antiracism-center

Colorlines—colorlines.com

Color of Change—colorofchange.org

The Conscious Kid—theconsciouskid.org

Equal Justice Initiative—eji.org

The Gathering for Justice—gatheringforjustice.org

The Leadership Conference on Civil & Human Rights—civilrights.org

NAACP Legal Defense Fund—naacpldf.org

National Urban League—nul.org

Showing Up for Racial Justice—showingupforracialjustice.org

Southern Poverty Law Center—splcenter.org

ACKNOWLEDGMENTS

This book would not have been possible without the incredible writing from Osayi Endolyn, who interviewed each of the featured chefs and experts in this book and carefully constructed their stories. Beyond those features, her thinking and writing were integral to the development of this project, and I am grateful to have been the recipient of her valuable insights as she helped it come together. Thanks also to Tatsha Robertson and April Mosolino for their writing contributions. I would like to thank Yewande Komolafe and Tamie Cook for their insightful and delicious recipe development. My deepest gratitude to Angie Mosier for her profound and vibrant photography, and to Linda Haile and Yohannes Syoum for letting us capture many of these images in their beautiful Harlem brownstone.

Thank you to all of the chefs, writers, and other creators and experts who generously gave their time to share their work with us for this book. It is an honor to be entrusted with your stories. And to every person who is helping to make this moment of change become a movement: thank you.

A very special thank you to my business partner and CEO of our restaurant group, Derek Evans, and to my literary agent, Jay Mandel, for helping to assemble the team that brought this book together. I would like to thank our project manager, Leslie Stoker, and Jason Tuckman from my team who guided this book to life.

To my editor at Voracious, Michael Szczerban, thank you for your insight and tireless effort from the inception of *The Rise* to its finish line. And thank you to the fantastic team at Little, Brown: especially editorial assistant Thea Diklich-Newell, assistant director of publicity Juliana Horbachevsky, production editor Michael Noon, associate director of marketing Kimberly Sheu, and production director Nyamekye Waliyaya. Thanks to Lucy Kim for the gorgeous jacket and to Shubhani Sarkar for the beautiful design of these pages.

Thank you to my amazing culinary team, which I am grateful to surround myself with each day: Culinary Director James Bowen and especially the crew at Red Rooster Harlem where we made most of these recipes—Chef Edward Brumfield, Tiana Gee, Tiffany Jones, Almira Session, and Jaqueta Tucker. And to all of our company staff and advisors who helped bring the book to fruition, including Angela Bankhead, Courtney Bolden, Jenn Burka, Joanna Campbell, Chloe Mata Crane, Dylan Farrell, Nina Shamloo, and Kaitlyn Vincent. Thank you to Eden Fesehaye, whose work on my earlier book, *The Soul of a New Cuisine*, helped shape the ideas for this book

Finally, thank you to my wife, Maya, and son, Zion. My love for you both is why I cook and tell these stories.

INDEX

ABOUT THE AUTHORS

Marcus Samuelsson is the acclaimed chef behind many restaurants worldwide, including Red Rooster Harlem, Marcus Restaurant + Terrace in Montreal, and Marcus B&P in Newark. Samuelsson was the youngest person to receive a three-star review from the *New York Times* and was the guest chef for the Obama Administration's first state dinner. He has won multiple James Beard Foundation awards including Best Chef: New York City and Outstanding Personality for *No Passport Required*, his television series with VOX/Eater. Samuelsson was crowned champion of *Top Chef Masters* and *Chopped All Stars*, he was the winning mentor on *The Taste*, and he is an executive producer of Viceland's *HUSTLE*. He currently serves as Executive Chef in Residence of Buzzfeed Tasty's newly launched talent program.

Samuelsson is the author of multiple books including the *New York Times*–bestselling memoir *Yes, Chef* and *The Soul of a New Cuisine: A Discovery of the Foods and Flavors of Africa*. Recipes from his latest book, *The Red Rooster Cookbook: The Story of Food and Hustle in Harlem*, are also featured in his bestselling Audible original, *Our Harlem: Seven Days of Cooking, Music and Soul at the Red Rooster.* He also hosts the podcast *This Moment* with Jason Diakité. A committed philanthropist, Samuelsson is co-chair of Careers through Culinary Arts Program (C-CAP), an enrichment program for underserved youth. He also co-produces the annual weeklong festival Harlem EatUp!, which celebrates the food, art, and culture of Harlem. He is the recipient of the 2019 Vilcek Foundation Prize in Culinary Arts, awarded to immigrants who have made lasting contributions to American Society.

Follow him on Instagram, Facebook, and Twitter at @MarcusCooks.

Osayi Endolyn is a James Beard Award–winning writer with work in *Time*, the *Washington Post*, the *Los Angeles Times*, the *Wall Street Journal*, *Eater*, *Food & Wine*, *Condé Nast Traveler*, and the *Oxford American*. She appears in *Chef's Table* and *Ugly Delicious* on Netflix, and has been featured on NPR's *1A*, *Splendid Table*, *Special Sauce with Ed Levine*, and the *Sporkful* podcast, for which she won a Webby. She is a recipient of the UC Berkeley–11th Hour Food & Farming Journalism Fellowship, and *Southern Living* named her one of thirty women moving Southern food forward. In addition to other book collaborations, Endolyn is working on a narrative about the history of systemic racism in American restaurant and dining culture.

Follow her @osayiendolyn on Twitter and Instagram.